COMPROMISE

NOMOS

LIX

NOMOS

Harvard University Press
I *Authority* 1958, reissued in 1982 by Greenwood Press

The Liberal Arts Press
II *Community* 1959
III *Responsibility* 1960

Atherton Press
IV *Liberty* 1962
V *The Public Interest* 1962
VI *Justice* 1963, reissued in 1974
VII *Rational Decision* 1964
VIII *Revolution* 1966
IX *Equality* 1967
X *Representation* 1968
XI *Voluntary Associations* 1969
XII *Political and Legal Obligation* 1970
XIII *Privacy* 1971

Aldine-Atherton Press
XIV *Coercion* 1972

Lieber-Atherton Press
XV *The Limits of Law* 1974
XVI *Participation in Politics* 1975

New York University Press
XVII *Human Nature in Politics* 1977
XVIII *Due Process* 1977
XIX *Anarchism* 1978
XX *Constitutionalism* 1979
XXI *Compromise in Ethics, Law, and Politics* 1979
XXII *Property* 1980
XXIII *Human Rights* 1981

NOMOS LIX
Yearbook of the American Society for Political and Legal Philosophy

COMPROMISE

Edited by

Jack Knight

NEW YORK UNIVERSITY PRESS • *New York*

NEW YORK UNIVERSITY PRESS
New York
www.nyupress.org

References to Internet websites (URLs) were accurate at the time of writing.
Neither the author nor New York University Press is responsible for URLs that may
have expired or changed since the manuscript was prepared.

Library of Congress Cataloging-in-Publication Data
Names: Knight, Jack, 1952– editor.
Title: Compromise / edited by Jack Knight.
Description: New York : New York University Press, 2018. |
Series: Nomos ; LIX | Includes bibliographical references and index.
Identifiers: LCCN 2017038143 | ISBN 9781479836369 (cl : alk. paper)
Subjects: LCSH: Political ethics. | Compromise (Ethics)
Classification: LCC JA79 .C648 2018 | DDC 172–dc23
LC record available at https://lccn.loc.gov/2017038143

New York University Press books are printed on acid-free paper, and their binding
materials are chosen for strength and durability. We strive to use environmentally
responsible suppliers and materials to the greatest extent possible in publishing
our books.

Manufactured in the United States of America

10 9 8 7 6 5 4 3 2 1

Also available as an ebook

CONTENTS

PREFACE

JACK KNIGHT

This volume of NOMOS—the 59th in the series—emerged from papers and commentaries given at the annual meeting of the American Society for Political and Legal Philosophy in Chicago, Illinois on February 27–28, 2014, held in conjunction with the annual meeting of the American Philosophical Association. Our topic, "Compromise," was selected by the Society's membership.

The conference consisted of three panels: (1) "Compromise and Negotiation," (2) "The Problem of Clean Hands: Legislative Compromise and Obstructivism," and (3) "Democratic Conflict and the Political Morality of Compromise." The volume includes revised versions of the principal papers delivered at that conference by Eric Beerbohm, Amy Cohen, and Michele Moody-Adams. It also includes essays that developed out of the original commentaries on those papers by Simon May, Melissa Schwartzberg, Anton Ford, David Dyzenhaus, Amy Sepinwall, and Andrew Sabl. After the conference we asked Alexander Kirshner to contribute an additional paper to the volume. We are grateful to all of these authors for their insightful contributions.

Thanks are also due to the editors and production team at New York University Press, and particularly to Caelyn Cobb and Alexia Traganas. On behalf of the Society we wish to express our gratitude for the Press's ongoing support for the series and the tradition of interdisciplinary scholarship that it represents.

Finally, thanks to Samuel Bagg and Isak Travnik of Duke University for providing expert assistance during the editorial and production phases of this volume.

CONTRIBUTORS

ERIC BEERBOHM
Professor of Government, Harvard University

AMY J. COHEN
Professor of Law, Ohio State University

DAVID DYZENHAUS
University Professor, University of Toronto

ANTON FORD
Assistant Professor of Philosophy, University of Chicago

ALEXANDER S. KIRSHNER
Assistant Professor of Political Science, Duke University

SIMON CĂBULEA MAY
Assistant Professor of Philosophy, Florida State University

MICHELE M. MOODY-ADAMS
Joseph Straus Professor of Political Philosophy and Legal Theory, Columbia University

ANDREW SABL
Visiting Professor of Political Science, Yale University

MELISSA SCHWARTZBERG
Professor of Politics, New York University

AMY J. SEPINWALL
Assistant Professor of Legal Studies and Business Ethics, University of Pennsylvania

xi

1

THE PROBLEM OF CLEAN HANDS

NEGOTIATED COMPROMISE IN LAWMAKING

ERIC BEERBOHM

The problem of dirty hands isn't *ours*. It gets its grip from the point of view of the official who acts in our name. Suppose a coalition of lawmakers votes for an unjust bill. In their floor speeches, they stress that they are public servants, acting on behalf of their constituency. But don't lose any sleep over this vote. The textbook model of dirty hands denies that you bear any responsibility. It doesn't matter whether you advocated for the bill, or that you voted for a candidate who was committed to enacting this policy. You and I are morally insulated from the actions of our lawmakers. Performing unjust actions in our name but without commensurate blame is part of their job description. To refrain would reveal a grating self-preoccupation. They are doing us a favor, shielding us from the blame and resentment of our fellow citizens who have been wronged. From the perspective of the democratic citizen, there doesn't look to be any moral problem here, but a convenient solution. We can aid and abet the passage of an unjust law without any liability. We don't own the logrolling, horse-trading, or the floor votes of our representatives. They do.

In framing the problem this way, I've revealed my hand. Citizens can't escape responsibility by authorizing another agent to do their dirty work. An agency relationship with injustice may well compound their blameworthiness. Nor should elected officials act in ways that are, as Bernard Williams politely puts it, "morally disagreeable."[1] When they "hustle[], lie[] and intrigue[] *for us*," it's implausible to think that they alone can retain responsibility for their public acts.[2] We can co-own responsibility for an unjust law. I will assume that any plausible concept of democracy will acknowledge that moral liability is shared in some way. The premise of insulation is faulty, and it makes the begrudging acceptance of the dirty-handed lawmaker unsound. There isn't a genuine problem here.[3] I'm going to ask you to imagine it away.[4] But dissolving one puzzle can create another.

The problem that emerges is *ours*. It's owned by democratic citizens concerned with complicity in legislated injustice. If we place special weight on the fact that *we* can be used as tools of injustice, this agent-relative concern can seem to threaten a central feature of lawmaking institutions. Call the *practice of compromise* that set of rules that bear upon a process of mutual concessions that aims at joint uptake of a legislative solution. We tend to assume that politics demands some willingness to engage in adjustments and even concessions to other viewpoints within a legislative body. This seems to hold even when lawmakers are in the commanding position to ignore their outvoted colleagues. My argument taps the widespread commitment that a healthy civic life involves some accommodation of the sincerely held views of others. So it's surprising that attempts to motivate compromise have turned to values not fully endogenous to a concept of democracy—fraternity, community, or the commitment to a union. I don't think we need to introduce these values as complements to, or even rivals of, our working idea of democracy—unless we see it as a "crude hydraulic device."[5] The best rationale for treating compromise as a noninstrumental value relies upon a conception of democracy as a complex array of relationships.

If lawmakers aren't our moral middlemen, then, it's tempting to demand that they refuse to go along with any compromise proposal. We might even insist that they opt out entirely—either by engaging in pure bargaining in the process, or by refusing to accept concession in the product. Yet this posture can be unsustainable when adopted by elected representatives, who participate in a complex agency relationship with ordinary citizens. To demand that they act as purists can throw our political system into a perennial state of obstruction. That's the first hazard. But suppose we reject purism, and ask them to serve as simple bargainers. They are to make deals that advance our first-order principles of justice, with no concessions that aren't strictly needed to achieve the compromise. Here the hazard is subtler. We've authorized a series of agency relationships that put legislators—and, by extension, ordinary citizens—into relationships that may not be compatible with our ideal of democracy.

We can steer clear of these two ways of thinking about compromise. A lawmaker who places genuine weight on the accommodation of disagreeing parties need not betray our principles. There's a real sense that compromise can, given certain background conditions, make a piece of legislation more democratic. My argument turns on the view that lawmakers generally have a weightier moral reason to countenance compromise than ordinary citizens. Assigning differential weight can seem puzzling. How can the refusal to participate in compromise be permissible—even laudatory—for you and me, while the same posture can seem morally vain when insisted upon by our elected official? Turning to a simple role-theoretic explanation to deliver a special responsibility looks suspiciously ad hoc. What features of the legislator's role are capable of explaining—let alone generating—a stronger moral reason to compromise than that of citizens? If the lawmaker stands in a rudimentary agency relationship, it is hard to argue that the lawmaker's moral situation is any different from that of her constituents. The agent's powers derive from their relationship to the principal. It's natural to think that the weight of moral reasons holds steady when one agent authorizes another to act. So where does this asymmetrical moral reason come from? Or is it wishful alchemy?

I work out an answer in four parts. Section one sketches the package of constitutive rules that make possible the joint activity of legislative compromise. I challenge proponents of deliberative negotiation for relying upon a picture of compromise that can make sincere participants prey to unscrupulous negotiators. Faced with individuals who are attempting to exploit the practice, we can be permitted to act in ways that are presumptively wrong. Section two begins by casting two characters, the *purist* and the *strategist*. Neither is capable of fully participating in compromise. I then introduce a composite figure, the *practitioner*, who is committed to principled compromise. Section three offers a rationale for the practitioner's willingness to play in this crucial legislative game, offering non-strategic concessions. The value of co-ownership describes a way of relating to each other as co-citizens who share equal authority over lawmaking. If this democratic ideal has force, we can defend the practice of legislative compromise. But there's a remaining worry that any defense of compromise will invite. Section four clarifies how the compromise enabler that I've defended can be defeated under a range of unjust and undemocratic conditions.

I. Legislative Compromise as a Practice

The furniture of legislative compromise is too familiar. It's easy to miss the details of this designed environment. There's a large table for extended face-to-face exchange, scheduled breaks for parties to huddle, and the contrapuntal procession of offer and counter-offer. This stage setting reminds us of two features of this practice that are not obviously compatible. First, negotiation on the way to compromise isn't a fully cooperative activity. It's a competitive exchange of speech acts, some aimed at persuading, others at urging. The "smoke-filled room" has become a metaphor for the crafted ambiguity of the speech acts exchanged in this setting. Parties are careful not to reveal too much of their hand, and they face powerful incentives to misrepresent their positions. Legislative compromise is a partially suspended context, where certain kinds of speech acts needn't be treated as sincere or true within this practice. Here communication is, in Thomas Schelling's words, "neither entirely impossible nor entirely reliable."[6]

At the same time, compromise is joint activity. Within it, rival lawmakers act together against the backdrop of rules.[7] These rules are constitutive of, and logically prior to, actions within the practice. So, as long as my fellow players and I share a commitment to honor the rules of the game, we can be said to be playing baseball together even while competing against each other. Within this practice our actions—even the objects of our environment—take on a different meaning. Canvas bags on the ground become bases. There are a series of actions that I can now perform that were unavailable outside the practice. It is not possible for me to balk on an attempted pitch if I am not a participant.[8] The literature on shared agency has focused on the activities *downstream* from a joint intention, whether together painting a house or entering the battlefield. It describes the conditions for sharing an intention and then considers what this means for agents who co-participate in an activity. Here we are giving equal attention to those actions *upstream* of joint agency—the delicate process by which they are fastened together.

We can sketch the constitutive rules that mark out legislative compromise. Start with the characteristic *aim* of parties to compromise:

> Co-Deliberation with Disagreement: Participants seek a resolution to a collective decision that they can accept, given background moral disagreement.

We still haven't figured out how to live together. Our disagreements at the legislative level implicate unavoidably moral principles. But legislators aren't your ordinary participants to a moral disagreement. So we need a way to capture their authorized position:

> Agency Relationship: Participants are elected legislators who stand in a principal-agent relationship to their constituency.

This leaves open the demands of this paired agency relationship. We are supposing that the principal is a constituency and the agent is their legislator, but we don't yet need to spell out how the agent needs to answer to the principal. Legislative compromise is a joint *activity* with a characteristic *agreement.* So we need to register the transactional character of this activity:

> Shared Commitment: Participants share a commitment to place weight on accommodating the other participant's position in the service of agreement.

Accommodation is the policy of assigning some weight to a consideration, rather than any given accommodation that one makes.[9] Participants can share this commitment to place weight on a consideration without that consideration winning out as the

all-things-considered thing to do. On my account, this commitment to accommodation is what Michael Bratman calls a "shared
policy." To see how this policy of "weighting" works, consider an
admissions committee that agrees to a policy that places some
weight on legacy candidates.[10] If, after a day of deliberating about
files, they end up admitting no legacy candidates, it would be too
quick to conclude that they haven't in fact shared this commitment in their decision-making. A candidate's file can be below
the bar even after applying this shared policy of giving the extra
weight. Thus, parties can participate in this practice without, in
the end, offering any accommodations, if they are assigning the
appropriate weight to this consideration.

By construing the *activity* of compromise as a shared commitment to weight accommodation, we are able to register the moral
significance of parties who "come to the table" and invest in the
relationships that make legislative compromise possible. Contrast
this with approaches that describe a set of necessary and sufficient
conditions. Without a deal, they are unable to notice that the
activity of compromise has taken place. But even if the deal isn't
required, seeking it is a characteristic feature of this practice:

> Co-Acceptance: Barring defeaters, participants offer non-strategic
> concessions that make the package acceptable to the other party.

Non-strategic concessions, I will argue, are the watermark of
negotiation in democratic settings. All compromise—whether haggling with the street vendor or pleading for a higher grade—is
shot through with instrumental concessions. But lawmakers aren't
haggling over prices; they are engaging in a process that ends in
authoritative demands backed by armed men and women. In the
morally momentous setting of enacting coercive law, we place
independent value on broad agreement as to the content of the
law. To preview my position, lawmakers have a defeasible reason
to make concessions that honor the procedural value of deciding
together. The possibility of co-acceptance depends on a "sticki-
ness" built in to this process. Part of agreeing to a concession is
the joint intention to honor this settlement. The time frame will
depend on the mutual expectations of the parties, and may well
be built into the agreement with a sunsetting provision that will

induce future legislatures to revisit the compromise package. So this final rule introduces the iterative character of the legislative setting.

My approach to legislative compromise is sandboxed. While it will share constitutive rules with other forms of compromise, it doesn't treat unity as a dominant theoretical aim. It is mistaken, I think, to aim for the most generic description of compromise available. We should take this less unified route for two related reasons. First, it is easy to see the moral distinctiveness of *legislated* law. That a group of people can gather together, write some words down on sheets of paper, and by their communication alone have changed the law is a brazen thought. Now what constitutes "the law" is furiously contested, and I will attempt to avoid taking a position here. So long as positivists and non-positivists accept that legislatures take actions that change our moral obligations, we can leave open precisely how legislators make the law what it is.[11] Second, the kind of reasoning in legislative compromise is different in kind from pure bargaining models. The prudential reasoning involved in negotiating a record deal is a distant relative of the back-and-forth concessions that make enacting laws possible.

The Practice's Exploits

Describing a practice can throw light on its inherent vulnerabilities. You start to notice its seams and stitching. Or, to mix low- and high-tech metaphors, you begin to see potential exploits lying in plain sight. These tactics are well-known in classic discussions of bargaining, but they haven't been systematically surveyed in settings where the subject of collective decisions is irreducibly moral in character. When we "port" these incentives from the domain of pure bargaining to legislative compromise, we can see how the tactics and strategy of compromisers are intimately related. The process of offer and counter-offer creates incentives to exploit the constitutive rules that we rehearsed earlier. The lesson is that practices don't just create new forms of joint activity; they also make space for ingenious ways to manipulate and coerce others.

Within a negotiation, dirty hands can seem to insinuate itself as a genuine problem. What's the practitioner to do when she goes face-to-face with a ruthless party? To an unscrupulous participant, compromise can open up novel forms of moral abuse. But these potential exploits aren't just for the ill-willed. Even morally motivated parties can feel the temptation to use unsavory tactics to induce a legislative solution that satisfies their moral principles—or at least more closely approximates them. Keyed into these tactics, Bernard Williams held that bargaining politicians should engage in a battery of presumptive wrongs: "lying, or at least concealment and the making of misleading statements; breaking promises; special pleading; temporary coalition with the distasteful; and (at least if in a sufficiently important position) coercion up to blackmail."[12] We know that parties to negotiations face threats, coercion, and bullying. A commitment to the constitutive rules of the practice can put us in a vulnerable position. Aren't we likely to be duped or even coerced into accepting positions that are morally troubling? Let's take up the two of these acts most central to legislative negotiation.

Misrepresentation. If you've ever engaged in price bargaining, you know to treat the initial offer as a conceit. There's an inoffensive sense in which parties *should* ask for more than they think they will or should get. This is permitted in prudential contexts— famously in the used-car sale. But within a legislature it can be troubling. Consider the announcement of opening positions in a two-legislator case. Neither party wants to reveal the extent of concessions she is prepared to make. Each realizes that insisting on a stronger position from the start can leverage her negotiating power. They might even be aware of the power of anchoring effects in framing judgments.[13] This will compound their incentive to advance false positions conversationally. The iterative character of legislative compromise can even make possible double-bluffing. Say a compromising party with a track record for bluffing announces her support for a position, fully expecting that she will be disbelieved in this announcement. Her audience will assume she is falsely announcing his support to bluff them, so they arrive at the (correct) belief that the party supports the position. If her move is successful, her speech act has transmitted accurate information to her audience.[14]

This creates a strong incentive to demand publicly what parties believe to be unjustified. Suppose your political principles justify a single-payer system of healthcare, but oppose a government-run system where healthcare personnel are state employees. Yet you recognize that pre-announcing your support for the "extra-strength" proposal—the one that you believe to be morally objectionable—will increase the chances you will be able to bargain toward the former system. This kind of misrepresentation can mislead parties, but even if they manage to call your bluff, it is objectionable in another way. The public backing of a policy that you believe to be unjust looks like a galling form of hypocrisy.[15] This demand is of a different kind than insisting on an unreasonably high starting price for your vehicle. Of course, bluffing doesn't always involve this kind of facial inconsistency. A strict libertarian can start negotiations by demanding an ultra-minimal state knowing fully well that this offer will be a non-starter. Here the bluff doesn't involve announcing support for a position that one rejects, but rather implying that this is a plausible starting point given the opening positions of the parties at the table.

Notice that bluffing isn't strictly necessary to take advantage of this exploit. Suppose a lawmaker recognizes the advantage of starting with an extreme position, but seeks to avoid public misrepresentation. This may be done for principled reasons: the desire not to defend a position one believes to be incorrect. Or it might be done because the lawmaker doubts she will be an effective bluffer at the table. Our lawmaker isn't a naïve voluntarist about beliefs. She can't change them on the fly. But she can work, in indirect and familiar ways, to nudge her beliefs in a direction favorable to her bargaining position.[16] She might caucus with more extreme members of her party. Perhaps repeated exposure to their reasons will recalibrate her position as she honestly grapples with their views. She might put herself on a strict media diet, closing herself off from moderating positions. If successful, this will push her opening position in a predictable way. The lawmaker may avoid making publicly deceptive statements. But the cost of this kind of tampering with one's own moral convictions may be high.[17]

Threats. Rational bargainers face incentives to make credible threats. These needn't be all-out coercive. You can threaten to walk away if my party makes another demand without offering anything in return. You can warn your rival that when the tables are turned, you will follow their lead and resort to a tactic that you had previously ruled out. The difference between a *threat* and a *warning* is notoriously thorny.[18] A lawmaker may warn parties that she cannot accept an offer in light of fellow party members who are less moderate. "Here's my problem," Representative Barney Frank said to the chairmen of the Banking Committee, "I've got some pretty radical guys on the left on my committee, and they're not going to like this. They're purists, and they don't want any compromise at all."[19] But bargainers have long realized that extreme threats can be the most effective. A negotiator who can credibly threaten to "rock the boat," risking all parties, stands in a strong position. You might insist that I row the boat, or you'll tip it over and drown us both.[20] This can give me a reason to accept your offer, despite its transparent coercion. A demand neatly packaged with a threat can profoundly alter the leverage of the two parties.

To make this credible, parties have an incentive to pre-commit themselves to destructive courses of action. In Schelling's classic example of this rational commitment, "If one driver speeds up so that he cannot stop, and the other realizes it, the latter has to yield."[21] The analogue is the now familiar "legislative triggers." Compromising parties conditionally accept a series of automatic actions that are designed to be mutually unacceptable to all parties. Their aim is to make a more credible compromise co-possible for the parties. The most common objection to this device is that this type of legislation is defeasible—it lacks credible enforcement mechanisms, particularly if it applies to a future session of the legislature. In 1985, the Balanced Budget and Emergency Deficit Control Act contained a trigger that would automatically cut domestic spending across the board. When the triggers activated twice, a later session of Congress blocked the cuts or greatly reduced them. But there are deeper theoretical worries about how triggers and their accompanying supercommittees are structured. Members of committees designed to facilitate compromise have the possibility of recognizing each other as sincere peers on a subset of issues; hence they may need considerable time for deliberation and isolation from external factors. Insofar as triggers are buck-passing devices, they are not successful in transferring moral liability. The members of a legislative body who vote for a trigger bill can be no less responsible than the committee that fails to arrive at a compromise. When we attempt to assess the blameworthiness of those who together pass the trigger and those who fail to disarm it, we can use this conception of distributed liability to make sense of the roles in play—the principal and agent, the co-sponsor and the co-signer—these will help us assess which of the parties are most plausibly seen as holding principal responsibility and secondary responsibility.

To the good faith participant, the most arresting threat is not mutual threats, but moral blackmail.[22] The other party of the practice doesn't just pair their "offer" with a threat, but the threat directly targets your moral standing. They threaten to perform a grave moral wrong if you don't commit a lesser wrong. On their telling, you will be implicated in the greater wrong if you refuse the offer. This kind of blackmail takes place in perfectly ordinary political discourse. We might imagine the blackmailer presenting the argument first-personally:

P1. The national economy would be devastated by a debt default.
P2. I won't raise the debt ceiling unless you accept this concession.
C1. So, you should accept my offer.
C2. Otherwise, you'll be responsible for the default.[23]

Let's run the interpersonal test by varying the speaker/audience. If the argument misfires when a particular speaker is presenting it to a particular group, this reveals it to be fault as a public argument. So an offer by a participant may fail in its justificatory role "on the lips" of that party.[24] There are potentially two compounding wrongs here. First, you *make* the minor premise (P2) true by your announcement of an intention. Second, you have conversationally run the argument. That may be in independent site of wrong. First-personally advancing the argument made plain its unjustifiability. Put in the third person, the minor premise takes on a different valence. If our side is huddled in the corner, and the threat is credible, varying the speaker can make the argument plausible-sounding. The threatened party might insist: "So, *we* should accept their offer." Then they are viewing the makers of the threat from the objective, rather than participant, stance. They *suppose* they will carry out an unjustifiable threat, taking their non-compliance as a feature of the world we need to negotiate around. There may be decisive reasons not to accept this kind of offer, especially if we expect to return to the table soon. The practice of compromise is paradigmatically about offer and counter-offer, so it's especially susceptible to speaker-relativity. What's interesting here is that the party performing the interpersonal delivery of arguments can bear on its justificatory success. This shows that parties attempting to compromise can criticize each other in two basic ways. They can challenge the substance of a position, or they can question whether the *person* mounting the argument is in the position to make it. It is this second-order attention to the speaker's license to advance a claim, given his own record of speech acts extending back to past negotiation, that is most relevant for our purposes.

How to Avoid Duping

If you aim to honor the constitutive rules that make up legislative compromise, what should you do when faced with these known exploits? The weight that you place on the shared commitment to accommodation is authentic. But the practitioner's stance can seem to invite duping and other forms of misdirection. Suppose two lawmakers meet to negotiate the content of a pending statute. You assume that I am negotiating in good faith. You believe that I share the commitment to admitting considerations that facilitate agreement. This includes non-deceptively conveying your concerns, listening to your reasons, and searching for policy proposals that could bridge our disagreements. Over time it dawns on you that I am not engaging in the activity. I may well be buying time—hoping that working days in the legislative session will run out. My noncompliance can deprive you of the ability to act as a compromiser, since actions constituted by practices depend upon participants jointly satisfying them. As a result, you are now denied the possibility of participating in this activity.[25]

We are engaged in different games. It turns out that you *only thought* that I was a party to a candidate compromise.[26] If this description is right, and the practice is unavailable, you might want nothing to do with me, now that you've come to see the depth of my bluffing tactics. If you are a strong purist, you may avoid any kind of working relationship with me. Or you might shift to a strategic stance, willing to search for small gains that might be made against a recalcitrant party like me. I think the core of this diagnosis is appealing. There's a sense in which the practice of compromise is dependent on jointly held attitudes, and absent those attitudes, one can't authentically engage in the activity. A striking limitation of most treatments of compromise is their working assumption of full compliance. They see themselves as writing a rulebook that both parties to a negotiation will honor.

The most difficult problems for the practice of compromise arise under conditions of noncompliance, when the rules are abused, skirted, or selectively honored, and a good faith dealer is unsure how to respond. If a lawmaker is merely using this practice as a way of biding time or finding the weak points in another party's positions, this diagnosis seems to me right. There's a party who isn't playing the game. In our case, you have updated your view of our interactions: whatever we were doing, it wasn't the activity of negotiating to a compromise. The exchanges and good faith gestures made you think I was compromising. But that wasn't the case. For an analogy, suppose you are celebrating your resounding victory against the rival team. But there's a problem. The other team thought the rules of baseball awarded victory to the lowest scoring team. We can agree that your opponents were not playing baseball. But a credible case can be made that you weren't either. I don't want to put too much weight on this particular linguistic intuition. For our purposes here, these kinds of all-or-none judgments of whether a player really is playing a game aren't necessary.

In actual political life, the model is rarely this tidy. A lawmaker may be participating in compromise, offering concessions at the table, *while* engaging in selective truth-telling and implicit threats. A virtue of the practice approach is that it promises to unify our understanding of the *activity* and the *product* of compromise. Thus, your readiness to co-accept a compromise will turn upon how you've been treated in the back and forth of the process. To take a case where the activity of bargaining bears on the acceptability of its outcome, consider this exchange:

SENATOR PAT GEARY: I can get you a gaming license. The price is $250,000, plus a monthly payment of five percent of the gross of all four hotels.

MICHAEL CORLEONE: Now, the price of a gaming license is less than $20,000. Is that right?

SENATOR: That's right.
CORLEONE: So why would I ever consider paying more than that?
SENATOR: Because I intend to squeeze you. I don't like your kind
of people. I don't like to see you come out to this clean country
with your oily hair, dressed up in those silk suits, passing your-
selves off as decent Americans. I'll do business with you, but the
fact is that I despise your masquerade, the dishonest way you
pose yourself. Yourself and your whole fucking family.
CORLEONE: Senator. We're both part of the same hypocrisy . . .
but never think it applies to my family.
SENATOR: Okay. Some people need to play little games. You play
yours. Let's just say that you'll pay me because it's in your interest to pay me. But I want your answer and the money by noon
tomorrow.
CORLEONE: Senator? You can have my answer now, if you like.
My offer is this: nothing.[27]

Prudential reasoning among scoundrels is, we hope, of a different piece than the moral reasoning about collective decisions. But
unscrupulous tactics are not uncommon events within legislatures.
The threat here could not be clearer: "I intend to squeeze you."
And the underlying rationale for the threat is spelled out in xeno-
phobic detail. Senator Geary makes clear his intent to exhort.[28]
When Corleone stresses that they are "part of the same hypocrisy,"
he reminds the senator that they are playing a game. In response,
the senator reframes his threat in the language of a traditional
offer. He's willing to play this "little game," where each party
advances its interests. Corleone walks away, with a simple counter-
offer and the suggestion that the senator personally pay the license
fee. The foul tactic that produced the counter-offer was, of course,
the insult to family. Wrongful tactics can make a deal rejectable,
even if the terms of the deal are acceptable on their face. We can't
look at the text of an agreement alone.
    To see how the interplay of the activity and the product of com-
promises function together, let's walk through the two exploits
from earlier. Misrepresentation can put parties in a stronger position. Take a party's announcements of its opening position. If concessions are measured from the opening baseline set out by each
party, the farther they can place that position, the less of substance

they will need to give up. This seems to give the insincere and hypocritical party undeserved leverage. Seana Shiffrin raises the stakes of this objection:

> Deliberate misrepresentation not only eviscerates the point of compromise, it fuels its cynical opposition. It justifies the suspicion that parties are not negotiating and compromising from genuine positions of conviction but rather that they are advancing false positions to gain leverage and advantage. Misrepresentation undermines the crucial sense of reciprocity—of mutual commitment to good-faith—that is essential to sustaining a culture of well-considered compromise.[29]

We can accept the form of this objection. But when a party to a compromise engages in this species of bluffing, does that relax this kind of condemnation? Suppose you recognize the other party's opening position as a deliberate misrepresentation. You might be inclined to simply leave the table. But this reaction may be too quick. The other party has already violated a rule of the practice, where each side sincerely presents the position that fits with its principles. Your opponents didn't just state the position that follows from their principles. They were engaged in a different price-setting activity: they attempted to credibly assert a more extreme position in an effort to gain leverage.

Faced with deliberative misrepresentation, can you respond in kind? An opening offer can be put in terms that don't assert the correctness of a position. So you might spell out your opening policy position without insisting that it is the policy that you think is all-things-considered justified. Here we can follow David Lewis's picture of conversation as a game with an "evolving scoreboard."[30] What your opponent *says* they are telling you and what they are actually saying are coming apart. You understand the other party's opening offer to be a deliberately overplayed position. Now using similar standards of precision can be acceptable. So when you counter with the claim, "Our opening position is X," and you are careful not to insist on X's following from your political convictions, you may be engaged in a permissible speech act. This will depend on the relevant context. In J. L. Austin's famous example, when you say, "France is hexagonal," you may be saying something true or false. At a cartography conference, you've just made a false claim. When uttered to a tourist who is having trouble identifying France on a map, you've told the truth.[31] When you encounter the misrepresenting legislator, you recognize the context of their assertion and respond with a claim that is not untrue, but also not a full representation of your beliefs about the policy issue. This permission is only available to a negotiator who has faced misrepresentation. Absent the infraction by the other party, the context of your opening offer would be different. In that case, the norms of sincerity and good faith would not allow you to speak in this type of coached and potentially misleading words.

In ordinary legislating, there is considerable range in how each side presents an opening policy position. A common blunder occurs when one party engages in what we might call "pre-compromise." The opening offer isn't a genuine statement of their policy position, nor is it an attempt to misrepresent their position to gain leverage.[32] The pre-compromiser announces a position that includes hypothetical concessions in advance of negotiation. Here is its characteristic form: "While it's not my ideal plan to further reduce the deficit, it's a compromise I'm willing to accept."[33] To be sure, after a compromise has been agreed to, this kind of language seems perfectly apt. A lawmaker will want to publicly clarify the terms that they co-authored and the terms that they merely accepted as accommodations.

Before the negotiation process, pre-compromise makes one vulnerable to duping. A legislator reveals the actual, not hypothetical, give-and-take that pre-compromise precludes. A former legislator puts it this way: "To get to an end point, you have to plant a flag, get reactions, then you have to move, that is, compromise, and you get to a product that is hopefully what you want. If you start here [he gestured to the middle], you're never going to get here [he gestured to a place on the edge]."[34] The pre-compromiser fails to appreciate the relational side of legislative life. Accepting the concession of another party at the negotiation table is importantly different from imagining what they might say. The actual dealing in the former case involves what I will call "co-ownership." One side has either *accepted* or even *offered* a policy that represents a concession. Their acceptance is critical to the liability-sharing process that produces co-owned legislation. When a pre-compromise merely imagines what a reasonable version of the other party might assent to, this kind of shared liability isn't possible, since there is no genuine transaction.

Democratic theorists have taken an alarmingly purist posture toward negotiated compromise.[35] In their account of deliberative negotiation, Jane Mansbridge and Mark Warren condemn threats and misrepresentation. I will argue that they take an overly rigoristic line on both exploits. There are, of course, subtle ways for threats to be implied within the context of negotiation. Consider a violation of the sincerity condition of ordinary speech. The party across the table says: "If I were you, I would accept that compromise." Suppose the context of this remark clarifies that it is a veiled threat. Deliberative theorists treat this as a paradigm of objectionable negotiation. But on my view, this judgment is premature. We'll need further contextual details to draw this conclusion. Who offered what? And what was threatened? In a competitive electoral system where representatives can be held accountable for their voting record, it can be perfectly acceptable to threaten to "target" a representative if they don't accept a particular concession.

The worry is that deliberative negotiation makes the practice of negotiation impossible. Mansbridge and Warren hold that "not revealing one's reservation price . . . border[s] on the unethical."[36] Let's assume, plausibly, that we generally shouldn't engage in activities that are borderline unethical. Without the ability to hold this information tight, it is hardly clear that lawmakers can be parties to negotiation as commonly understood. In legislative compromise, the "reservation price" is shorthand for the enablers and defeaters that parties bring to the table. At what point would they be willing to offer a concession in return for a counter-concession? What kind of concession would be enough for them to accept the package as a whole? Even the judgment of how much an apparent concession *really* is a concession is a piece of information that parties will want to keep close in hand. But on my reading, protecting information of this kind isn't available to defenders of deliberative negotiation. We don't normally think that we need to convey the particular position where a party will co-accept a compromise. I take this to be a low-level feature of negotiation as we know the practice. To demand this kind of pre-announcement invites the same duping as we saw with pre-compromise. Deliberative

democrats express reservations when parties leverage "asymmetric information."[37] But why should this condition undermine the
conditions for deliberative negotiation? In any legislature, information will be unevenly distributed.[38] Some lawmakers will choose
to put themselves in epistemic bubbles, where they will have little
exposure to the opposing social-scientific literature. If, in a compromise setting, my preferred concession seems significant to
another party because of their ignorance, why should I have to
inform them otherwise? This kind of prohibition relies upon an
unnecessary rigorism. After all, even Kant distinguished between
lying to the murderer and merely failing to inform.[39]

I have attempted to show how revisionary of ordinary legislative practice deliberative approaches can be.[40] We know that the
practice of negotiating toward a compromise can be exploited by
bluffing and threats. But it can be undermined just as surely by
stringent rules that require real-time disclosure of one's mental
contents. I've claimed that this demand for self-revelation by parties is not obviously compatible with legislative compromise as a
sustainable practice. What we need to find is a place for strategic
speech within legislative settings. To see how essential this feature
of speech is within the legislative markup of a bill, consider a paradigm use of implicature. We are participating in the practice of
compromise. In our exchange of demands, we are willing to implicate more than what we can make explicit with our words. If we
have to reveal much of our agenda as we enter negotiations, making explicit our aims ex ante, the possibility of us making progress
will be greatly diminished. Proponents of deliberative negotiation
neglect the value of avoiding explicit claiming within the practice.
In sketching this permission to conceal intentions and information, I've attempted to steer in between two objectionable conceptions of the negotiating context. It is neither a fully suspended
context, where outright lies are fair game, nor is it continuous with
ordinary interpersonal speech, where concealment and implicature can be worrisome.[41]

Behind the rigorism of deliberative negotiation is a picture of
compromise as an essentially cooperative activity. If you and I are
cooperatively building a Lego set together, failing to disclose to
you how to connect the 4 x 4 brick to the steering wheel would be
unacceptable. When you are stumped and I keep this information

from you, it is no longer plausible to think of our activity as cooperative. A competitive, but still jointly performed, activity is more tolerant of the failure to disclose information. It can allow for some inequalities in bargaining power and it can acknowledge the competitive dimension of the activity. Each side can rightly attempt to "get the better deal" in good faith. There need not be anything off-putting about this aim. We can allow room for the ordinary parts of the practice, jockeying for position, maneuvering to a concession by making a "compromise gesture," and sequencing issues to prime the pump for major issues to be negotiated downstream.[42]

A modest picture of joint action needn't place an all-out ban on deception, coercion, and differences in power. We've seen how negotiation itself depends on the availability of low-grade deception to participants. Arguably, without the bluff participants may perceive themselves in a very different activity, much closer to discursive accounts of democratic decision-making. If this is right, strategists may feel vindicated, since they never conceived of this practice as involving actions jointly doing anything interesting. But I think this conclusion comes too easily. Even when negotiations begin to break down, it's hard to deny that there is genuine shared activity occurring. The spiral of reciprocal expectations may bring the activity down.

My account of the tactics of compromise, then, isn't sanguine. One party's violation of a rule creates a cascade of further rule violations, each of which is a permissible reaction to non-compliance. Facing procedural exploits and grave injustices, Lyndon Johnson's license to deceive, threaten, and act uncivilly may be justified in the partially suspended context of negotiation with unjust and undemocratic parties.[43] The license to act in ways that are normally uncivil does not, I think, solely follow from the fact that his opponents were insensitive to moral considerations. Suppose Johnson's segregationist colleagues were motivated by an intrinsic or extrinsic racism, contorted to fit their moral beliefs. They were morally motivated in this most minimalist sense. It doesn't necessarily follow, as Amy Gutmann and Dennis Thompson suggest, that some amount of civility—they describe magnanimity as a close cousin to civility—is owed on the grounds that one's opponent is not indifferent to moral status.[44]

My practice conception gives us a better explanation of why we depart from the normally required attitudes of members of this practice. Namely, that Johnson was not constitutively able to negotiate a compromise or even practice civility in an authentic way. There remains an attenuated sense in which one can continue to compromise or exhibit civility under conditions as non-ideal as this case. One may be able to go through the motions of a compromiser or deliberator, knowing full well that these actions are not fully possible. At this point one's action would be better described as a form of method acting, serving an expressive function. Like any shared activity, compromise can be gradually and even unintentionally brought down by participants, brick-by-brick. There's nothing dramatic about this collapse—it can creep up upon a legislative body. Lawmakers can find themselves in a situation where this activity is no longer available. Later I will consider how a practice this fragile, yet potentially fecund to democratic life, can be rebuilt.

II. THREE PLAYERS

The Purist

Purist legislators wave a familiar banner: "I won't compromise on issues of moral principle." They take this slogan to rule out two constitutive rules: *Shared Commitment* and *Co-Acceptance*. Purists won't accept a policy that places weight on accommodating the other party's position. For them, it isn't enough to refuse to sign on to a compromise package. They view the activity of legislative compromise as potentially corrupting, since it gives weight to positions that are, by their own lights, unjustifiable.[45] To structure our deliberation in this way is to put our finger on the scale. This isn't just a failure to act according to our principles. It suggests a betrayal of them. Given the weight carried by the notion of "principles," it is striking how little purists say about their form and function. They tend to take the idea as primitive. "When something is a matter of principle for a person," Onora O'Neill and C. A. J. Coady write, "it is fundamental and not up for negotiation."[46] This line builds non-negotiability into the function of principles. While I'll be referring to the all-out purist, the more familiar form of purist in political life is selective. It holds this posture around a particular issue, or for a tract of time.[47] To participate in the practice is to support legislation that fails to satisfy each party's respective moral principles. The intuitive worry is that holding a moral principle involves having a durable commitment to *its* realization. But the compromising party goes along with a paler version within arm's reach. The purist argument relies on two premises:

Complicity Premise: It is impermissible to cooperate with individuals in jointly authoring and assenting to an unjust policy.

Cooperation Premise: The practice of legislative compromise is necessarily a cooperative form of joint action.

Conclusion: So, participating in legislative compromise is impermissible.

Let us assess the ethical premise before taking up the action-theoretic premise. The major premise expresses the agent-relative constraint that you shouldn't personally collaborate in the production of a morally unsatisfactory piece of legislation, even when that statute would reduce the overall amount of injustice in your political institutions. It makes a distinctive position-sensitive demand: that *you* not play a role in accepting an unjust law. This turns upon a legislative version of the distinction between doing and allowing.[48] The purist may well *allow* an institutional injustice in the status quo to remain by refusing to *jointly act* with co-lawmakers in placing weight on concessions to opposing parties. Perhaps she is in the position to block a piece of legislation in committee, as the gatekeeping theory of committee power explains.[49] Her unwillingness to co-accept a deal doesn't flinch, even when a compromise will almost certainly nudge her political institutions closer to realizing her own moral principles.[50]

Purists fix on a curious property of moral compromise—mutually perceived unjustifiability by all signing parties.[51] On the one hand, you risk betraying your principles when you insist upon their complete realization, knowing that they will find no traction in the world. On the other, when you sign on to policies that deviate from your principles, this can seem to reduce them to fungible rules of thumb. Consider this imagined exchange between Hubert

Humphrey and Lyndon Johnson on the 1957 Civil Rights Act. In *All the Way*, Humphrey experiences the force of both of these moral pulls:

> SENATOR HUBERT HUMPHREY: If I am anything like what you say, it's because people know I stand by my principles. I can't sell what I don't believe in! I won't.
> LBJ: This ain't about Principles, it's about Votes. That's the problem with you Liberals—you don't know how to fight! You wanta get something done in the real world, Hubert, you're gonna have to get your hands wet.[52]

The purist isn't fully satisfied by the usual response to this alleged paradox. Individuals who are genuinely committed to a moral principle have reason to care about their realization. If, under conditions of disagreement, compromising on the principle's verdicts can lead to their partial satisfaction, then the purist polity can be charged with a serious misunderstanding. Its members fail to appreciate the practical role of principles, which provide direction-guidance to agents under seriously imperfect conditions.

Are purists committing an easy conceptual mistake? Are they assimilating the value of principles both as *convictions* that structure our evaluative lives and as *regulative devices* that we attempt to put into practice? Are they eliding principles of justice with rules of regulation?[53] When parties to a compromise sign on to a policy framework, it seems clear that they are accepting a policy that does not fully satisfy their moral principles. But to think that they have compromised their principles is to misunderstand the activity they have engaged in: the site of the back and forth of compromise was what rules of regulation to adopt, given the background disagreement about their moral principles. To make matters worse, they can seem to be in the grip of a crude picture of moral reasoning. For them, we can "read off" policy verdicts from our collection of moral principles, with little or no judgment. We then derive verdicts by applying a relevant rule.[54] Maybe they are overly impressed with the tidiness of the algorithmic approach. If we see moral principles as issuing normally conclusive reasons for certain courses of action, this can remove the purist's stinging charge that compromisers are putting a price on their principles.

Setting these conceptual worries aside, I suspect that the purists' principal mistake is deeper and more philosophically interesting. When they inspect the practice of legislative compromise, purists conflate cooperation with shared action.[55] Later I will attempt to pry apart these two concepts. For now, we can note the rational pressure that this puts on the purist to accept the minor premise. To act under the constitutive rules of legislative compromise, on their view, *just is* to become a plural subject with their fellow legislators. The upshot of this strong ontology is that they would be "jointly committed to doing something as a body—in a broad sense of 'do.'"[56] To the purist, political talk of Gangs of Seven legislators then takes on a more ominous meaning. Maybe these really are gangs in the teamlike and colluding sense. This is where the purist draws the line. They might put the worry this way: "Expecting me to participate in this practice is asking too much. It is one thing to hold one's nose when voting for an imperfect law in a floor vote. But there can't be a moral reason to co-produce—and even co-author—a statute that contains significant injustices." This stronger idea of shared agency raises the moral stakes considerably for purists. They are not merely being asked to *allow* the passage of a piece of legislation that is morally disagreeable. They are now asked to become an equal partner at the table. They may perceive this as a direct affront to their integrity, or to the integrity of segments of their constituency.[57]

This way of thinking about compromise—as a robustly cooperative activity—carries with it a notion of shared moral responsibility that repels the purist. To see this, let's begin with the most famous purist in normative ethics. The murderer knocks on your door and politely asks you whether your friend is hiding in the attic. Suppose you deceive this visitor, but despite your effort, this deceptive speech act leads him back to your friend. What is most striking about the Kantian verdict is that you now share full liability for the murder. Once you violated a moral principle prohibiting deception, you come to own all the consequences of your infraction. In Kant's damning verdict, you become the "author"[58]—presumably he means the *co-author*—of your friend's death. The conception

of moral liability here is strict, since unforeseeability can serve as
no excuse. And the internal logic of this view carries over to purist legislators. They view their refusal to take part in the activity of
compromise as a way of cancelling their moral connection to an
objectionable policy. To engage in this practice would open them
up to the charge that they share in responsibility for the accepted
package. Take a minority party that is considering whether to
come to the table. If they participate in this practice, they might
see themselves as cooperators in the full-bodied sense: *equally sharing* in responsibility for the creation and enactment of a law that
violates their moral principles.[59]

The purist's posture contains an enduring intuitive force. Most
of us accept that compromises have defeaters. Some candidate
compromises are so unjust that they should be rejected, even if
they would make the world morally better by one's lights. Counte-
nancing a policy at odds with our moral principles can, in certain
circumstances, betray them. The admirable feature of purists is
their recognition that there are genuinely "rotten" compromises.[60]
The problem with purists is that they treat every consideration as
a defeater, to use Hobbes's metaphor, they play their trump card
"on every occasion."[61]

I will suggest a way to accept the presence of defeaters without
an approach so preoccupied with one's agency. But first, we need
to get to know the purist's alter ego.

The Strategist

Strategists have a way of looking right through the practice of compromise. What they see is a series of causal levers that they can
pull to maximize the advancement of their substantive principles
of justice. As a result, they may find themselves engaged in a give
and take in *Shared Commitment*. But their reasons for placing extra
weight on the positions of disagreeing parties will always be instrumental. If being perceived by others as concessionary will maximize the fulfillment of their first-order moral principles, they will
gladly engage in this tradition. And when they face an up-or-down
vote, they will often find themselves willing to sign on to a policy
proposal that is seriously morally inferior by their own moral principles. If it is done in service of the closest available approximation

of their moral principles, they will participate in *Co-Acceptance*. But their willingness to join will turn on whether their participation is likely to satisfy their own moral commitments, given the institutional obstacles in the background.

The strategist's game plan is deceptively simple: "to plant the flag of his convictions," as Ronald Dworkin pictured it, "over as large a domain of power or rules as possible."[62] We can leave open the temporal "give"—how long a game our strategist plays—and how she runs her risk-rewards analysis when entertaining a concession. There isn't a single strategist but a larger cast of characters that share an instrumental way of conceiving their involvement in compromise and the other legislative activities—whether agenda-setting, representation, or oversight. Let's take our initial model of the strategist to be a fair dealer. She refuses to engage in the ruthless tactics familiar to negotiations. Even without the power to grossly misrepresent her position or threaten her rivals, there remains something ruthless about this political figure. When the numbers are on her side, and the anticipated repercussions will be few, her counter-offer to the party out of power will be: nothing.

My portrait of the strategist has been, I confess, a bit unfair. If anything, the strategist occupies a presumptively justified role in negotiation. In a political society where levels of party polarization have no precedent,[63] the logic of planting the flag as far as possible can be mesmerizing. The strategist isn't concerned with an array of defeaters; she only has one. Her deal-breaker is any proposal that doesn't advance her substantive principles. She is acutely "tolerant of small gains" and more than willing to "settle for less in order to prevent even worse."[64] This kind of unsentimental view of legislative life may well earn her the laudatory title of the "pragmatist."[65] Placed within a system that provides incentives for participation in the practice, at least some of the time, the strategist is perfectly willing to strike a concessionary pose. But notice that her willingness to give anything—no matter how small or low-ranked on her agenda—must be forced out of the strategist's hands. In interactions where the numbers are on her side and the institutional incentives are not present, her demand will be total capitulation.[66]

My hope is that this character is beginning to look less appealing. The strategic position toward flesh-and-blood parties is actuarial. You begin to see the other parties as potential obstacles to the realization of your first-order principles. Those posturing agents across the table aren't interestingly different from impediments in the natural world. This brings into focus what the strategist is missing as a member of a lawmaking body. In short, no value is placed on enacting law together. The strategist, I will argue, doesn't relate to her co-legislators in a way that appreciates their shared moral predicament. They are in the unusual situation of simultaneously being the law's co-producers and its co-subjects, authorized with the terrifying power to alter our moral requirements by simply writing down some words and publishing them.[67] If democracy's value lies in the relationship of shared authority that it makes possible, we can detect an impaired relationship among co-legislators. This move, I think, doesn't require a strong civic analogue to friendship.[68]

If the practice of legislative compromise is necessary for sustaining valuable democratic relationships, we will have in hand a moral reason for legislators to participate in the practice. That "if," of course, is substantial. Why you and I should particularly care about the terms on which our authorized representatives are relating to each other. How do those relationships bear upon how we relate to each other as citizens? The strategist has a ready-made response: Why shouldn't we concern ourselves solely with a legislature's productive output, the substantive acceptability of legislative law? I've only hinted at the countertype to the strategist here, the legislator who interacts with fellow lawmakers on more than purely instrumental terms. Such a concern can seem far removed for the usual values we draw upon in democratic theory. Allow me, then, ask you to suspend judgment until the next section, when we'll cast a final character, designed to avoid the shortcomings of the previous two.

We began by building out the constitutive rules that together make up this fragile practice. I claimed that we could see legislative compromise as a morally distinctive activity, one that resisted attempts to fold it into a generic account of the conditions for compromise. It's useful to see how strategists challenge this claim. They seem content to treat all negotiation—whether private labor disputes or legislative contest over the minimum wage—as much more unified than I'm assuming here. Strategists hold no pretension that legislative compromise is a cooperative practice. They take seriously its competitive character. My worry is that they lose sight of its valuable character as a vehicle for us to make decisions together. Strategists, I will argue, fail to recognize compromises as a joint activity whose worth is not exhausted by its production value. Strategists refuse to participate in the practice of legislative compromise. Their willingness to use negotiation as a piece of social technology falls short of authentic participation. To begin with an analogy, it is subversive of the practice of baseball when a batter pleads with the umpire for "just one more strike." Now imagine a team whose win-lose record is so poor that they have stopped aiming a victory. They show up for games. But their effort is not one of players collectively attempting to win a game. Suppose this becomes clear after repeated interactions. At some point an observer will conclude that it's overwhelmingly likely that this team isn't participating in the practice.[69] So, too, strategists are selective in their policy of assigning weights to the accommodation of other parties' positions. Or when their decision to co-accept the product of a compromise turns on a purely instrumental calculation. But this suggests that their "play" within the practice isn't enough. They utilize the practice without accepting the standing policies that would mark them out as participants. They have found a way to take advantage of the practice without resorting to the familiar series of bluffs and threats. The charge of non-participation is not an indictment of the strategist. Whether lawmakers have moral reason to participate in compromise will turn upon its function in a representative democracy. We'll address this question in the next two sections, where we will search for a figure and an accompanying rationale that avoids instrumentalism.

The Practitioner

In their own signature ways, the purist and strategist lawmakers keep their hands clean. Purists wear this ambition prominently, abandoning negotiation rather than entering a genuine process of give and take and refusing co-acceptance even when they agree that the compromise would improve their moral situation. Participating in a practice entails cooperation, they think, and this tight-knit level of shared agency threatened their integrity. Their concern to avoid collaboration with injustice is all-trumping. Strategists also keep a certain distance from a practice, not by walking away, but by selective participation. After repeated interactions, other parties come to notice the strategist's bargain, and learn to read them in the "spiral of mutual expectations" that marks out negotiation and compromise. What results from this dialectic, I hope, isn't a compromised figure—at least in the pejorative sense. My aim, instead, is to construct a composite character who incorporates attractive properties of our two figures.

Let's call the legislator who attempts to comply with the letter and spirit of the constitutive rules of compromise the *practitioner*. This breaks with purists, who refuse to place any weight on accommodation. They viewed compromise as a kind of "pay-to-play" scheme that unacceptably put them in collaboration with injustice. They refuse to pay that price. Purists violate the letter of the practice, refusing to share in a policy that assigns weights to any substantive position that they rejected. Strategists, in contrast, violate the spirit of the practice by only accepting its norms when it served the purposes of advancing their first-order principles. Practitioners strike a unified pose toward both the means and ends of legislative compromise.[70] To appreciate this unique stance, notice the two silos in which political theorists have discussed compromise. They have considered the limits of negotiation in isolation of their policy substance. Or they have set a threshold for rejecting a compromise—its "rottenness" point—without taking into account the significance of the give and take of negotiations. I'm proposing that these two sites work together in a systemic way.[71] We can see this interplay by mapping the three ways that legislators can relate to each other and the citizens who authorize them. How do these attitudes bear on the means and ends of negotiated compromise?

TABLE 1.1: TWO ACTS, THREE CHARACTERS

	Purist	Strategist	Practitioner
Negotiation Means: Speech Context	Unsuspended	Fully Suspended	Partially Suspended
Negotiation Ends: Legislative Content	Rigorism	Instrumentalism	Non-Instrumentalism

Here we've placed our three characters into two acts: one about process and the other about substance. Purists are so averse to complicity that they are only loosely involved in the process of compromise, listening but never conceding anything to a mistaken peer. They are tempted to only have relationships to colleagues who are in full moral agreement. Purists about the means of negotiation won't bluff, mislead, or even withhold details about their first-best policy. For them, there's nothing distinctive about the speech context of negotiators that permits them to act differently from any other domain of speech. This is consistent with purists about ends. They only sign on to policies that satisfy their principles of justice. There simply aren't permissions to settle for anything less.

In contrast, strategists about means see the practice as a game that allows them to say anything, short of making coercive threats, that will help them achieve their political aims. This doesn't commit them to a self-defeating policy of habitual deceit. Otherwise they wouldn't earn their name. Strategists put the default constraints on deception and false promising on hold, since they take themselves to stand in a fully suspended context. This reflects their view of relationships with their co-legislators as purely instrumental.

In turn, this makes room for a middle stance toward the means and ends of negotiation. For practitioners, negotiations are partially suspended contexts. Certain types of misrepresentation can be permitted and even required of participants. When faced with means-strategists who attempt to dupe them, practitioners acquire further permissions to engage in deception. They don't take the context of negotiation as fixed, since opposing parties to negotiation can, quite literally, change the game they find themselves playing. What motivates practitioners is concern about relating to their fellow lawmakers—and by extension, the whole democratic citizenry—as equally sharing in authority. Consequently, they place independent weight on accommodation when co-parties to a compromise meet certain procedural and substantive conditions. This follows not from a calculation of their long-term political goals, from the value of relating to their co-citizens on justifiable terms. In the next section, I will say more about how the relational good of democracy underwrites my argument.

Let me preview the form of the argument. The practice of compromise, on my view, is a response to the value we place in deciding together, even when serious disagreements remain. Democracy's value can only be captured relationally in the equal sharing in authority over our political institutions. The practice can make disagreeing legislators "co-owners" of a legislature's outputs. I will argue that the available rationales for compromise—solidarity, magnanimity, or commitment to union—are less successful at motivating the practitioner's posture.[72] In the absence of other mechanisms that allow citizens to share responsibility for their political institutions, compromise can play an essential part in a democratic system. Let me mention three limits of this abductive argument. First, it brings on board a particular idea of democracy for free. Second, the argument is only as good as the list of explanations you start with. This invites the charge that your favored explanation is merely "the best of a bad lot."[73] To avoid this known bug in abductive reasoning, we'll canvass leading defenses of non-instrumental reasons to compromise as offering an alternative explanation. Third, the argument doesn't yield a conclusive verdict. Even if you accept its soundness and validity, it only makes compromise an essential practice when there is no alternative mechanism capable of playing this role. I think these limits end up working in the argument's favor, but let's first step back and see the fruits of our extended dialectic.

III. CO-OWNERSHIP AS A DEMOCRATIC VALUE

Think of a piece of democratic pageantry. The parties to a compromise lavish praise on a brokered piece of legislation. They insist that the process made the proposal a *better law*. To the cynic, the parties have become so acclimated to bluffing within the process, their speech acts are spilling over to public speech. In their defense, perhaps the parties haven't realized that they have left the suspended context of the negotiation room, where certain kinds of deception are countenanced. In this section I will offer an alternative explanation. We can make sense of the intuition that the process of compromise can improve a piece of legislation.[74] Negotiation can produce a law mildly worse on the substance, but better in the process. It can raise a law's democratic credentials. There's nothing mysterious about the idea that a practice can honor a process-related value that would not exist but for the actual give and take of participants. Consider elections. The process of citizens submitting ballots needn't get its value solely from its tendency to produce results that are good or right. We think that electoral procedures themselves can invest authority in a political system.[75]

Once we accept that substance and process-based reasons make up "two distinct and irreducible points of view," as Thomas Christiano holds, we can see a chronic mistake in the literature on compromise. On the prevailing view, if parties to a negotiation come to see the package as all-things-considered better by their own convictions, then they haven't really engaged in a compromise. The process has been epistemically productive. It has led to the *correction* of false beliefs, not an authentic compromise. But this overlooks the two distinct dimensions by which we assess a piece of legislation. It treats negotiation as functionally equivalent to a seminar room, where the central business is the rooting out of mistaken convictions. On this model, successful negotiation often doesn't produce compromise but correction. It leads to one party coming to see it was in error. But, like elections, negotiation seems to have the potential to be a normativity-conferring process. If conducted according to certain rules, the process can seem to change our valuation of a proposal or law. This can explain what the sincere lawmaker means when she insists that the process made the bill better. The legislation really is morally better, all things considered. But it doesn't follow that the law is now better on every dimension, each considered in insolation. To see how this argument might work, let us start with schematics and descend to concrete cases of policy.

Two Bills. Suppose Bill X is somewhat more likely to fully satisfy your first-order principles than Bill Y. For Bill X, the only concessions extracted were those strictly necessary to attain the bare 51 majority in a body of 100 members. Bill Y is the upshot of an extended negotiation that, through non-strategic concessions, ends up eliciting near universal support—say 98 of 100 legislators. At this point, strategists have heard enough. They don't need to know anything more about the pedigree of these two bills. Their approach doesn't give them any resources to place weight on the value of the respective processes behind these two bills. Their sole criterion for selection is the bill's substantive merits. Of course, if strategists become convinced that Bill Y is less likely to be overturned, they can take that as a reason to support Y. They could sign on to a negotiated compromise that is more likely to be politically sustainable, even though somewhat less effective.[76] Now practitioners aren't yet ready to lend support to either bill. They will need to engage in a process of weighing the substantive and procedural considerations at stake. Were the non-strategic concessions worth their price? To answer this, we'll need to clarify what is valuable about a bill that receives this level of consensus. But first let's put one more case into memory.

The Omnibus. Next consider an omnibus spending bill. Suppose the majority party offers non-strategic concessions to secure bipartisan support. There are billions of dollars at stake in the negotiation process. The minority party agrees to support the bill if certain projects receive more funding than the majority party thinks is likely necessary for their success. On the merits, the bill sent out of the committee has been made somewhat worse by the negotiation process—by the lights of the majority party. This kind of negotiated compromise doesn't just frustrate the strategist. It *baffles* her. How could members of the majority party justify this kind of overfunding? This strikes her as an injustice. Without a story about how this concession serves their long-term electoral strategy, there just isn't any reason to have made these concessions in committee. The minority party, in contrast, has reason to think that the bill is doubly improved. It is mildly better on the substance *and* on the process.

What, then, is the procedural value that is being honored here? I am proposing that we place value on legislators "co-owning" statutes that they enact together. The democratic value of *co-ownership* captures the sense in which large-scale social legislation can become a kind of public property. It can explain the force of the elusive political virtue of two-party systems: bipartisanship.[77] The idea isn't that there is value somehow inherent in two parties agreeing on something. The mere alignment of policy preferences across the aisle doesn't make a virtue. Indeed, for modern-day Schumpeterians, this picks out a negative value. They see bipartisan agreement as probative evidence of inter-party collusion. If we confine the good at stake to the valuable relationship that holds when lawmakers decide together, we are missing the deeper location of value. On my view, it's a constitutive part of legislative compromise that legislators are our agents in a large-scale principal-agency relationship. Thus, when a non-strategic concession is offered to members in the minority party, by extension this concession is offered to the principals who authorize them to stand at the negotiating table. It is offered to you and me. The legislator we have placed in power is offered a concession that convinces her to sign on to the bill.

The value of co-ownership, then, doesn't ultimately lie in lawmakers standing in relationships of mutual, non-instrumental concern. We locate it in the relationships among democratic citizens. In claiming that legislators speak in the name of a subset of citizens, I'm departing from views that suppose that legislators stand in a principal-agent relationship with society as a whole. Jeremy Waldron takes this line when he worries about the purist. "[P]rincipled opposition to compromise at the level of partisanship," he argues, "may seem blinkered, self-centered, and obtuse when one is acting in the name of the whole society."[78] If lawmakers stand in an agency relationship with a subset of citizens, they have reason to value practices that put their principal in valuable democratic relationships. In contrast, I think that ordinary citizens have a prerogative to be purists—to place considerable weight on their doings.

We can now defend an asymmetry in how lawmakers and citizens relate to compromise. Suppose a citizen faces an initiative that contains three policy choices: the first satisfies, more or less, his full set of moral principles, the second is an attempt to approximate a compromise option, and the third is the policy that flies in the face of his principles. I think it can be perfectly justified for this citizen to select the policy option that most purely expresses his political principles. This holds, I think, even if he realizes that this pattern of voting, conducted by his fellow citizens, could well lead to the enactment of the unjustified policy. My explanation for this position should now be predictable. The practice of compromise, with the regulative rules that I've sketched, *wasn't available to this citizen.* He was handed a ballot with a pre-packaged set of options. He never had an opportunity to be part of the process of crafting these options.

This verdict departs from prevailing defenses of compromise in two ways. First, it can explain the conditions under which

legislators have a stronger presumptive moral reason to make concessions than ordinary citizens. This obligation does not emerge
out of the lawmaker's official role.[79] There's nothing in their official oath or even implicit in their agency relationship that delivers
this weightier obligation. What ordinarily distinguishes the citizen
from the official who speaks for them is the latter's access to the
practice of compromise. This won't always be a clean line. Think
of a citizen who joins a committee assigned the task of participatory budgeting. Within this emerging practice, now in place in
more than 1,500 municipalities worldwide, community members
are given considerable discretion about how public funds are to be
spent.[80] A role-based view would experience pressure to reclassify
this citizen as a part-time legislator. But this wouldn't be enough to
justify this conceptual redistricting. A practice-based view offers a
simpler explanation of how our citizen acquires a weightier moral
reason to engage in mutual concession.

Second, my approach avoids role gerrymandering. We can
explain why lawmakers don't have the purist's prerogative without altering the usual terms of representation. We needn't assume
that a lawmaker's paradigmatic agency relationship is to the whole
community. If legislators must aim to "name" all citizens in their
decision-making, they may experience pressure to take concessions seriously in their deliberative framework. This is the route
that Waldron takes. My worry is that it provides the right answer
for the wrong reason. Let's grant, for the sake of argument, that
executive officials may have reason to act under this banner: to see
themselves as "acting in the name of the whole society."[81] I think
that this is a highly revisionary description of the role of the legislator.[82] My account of compromise took the unfashionable view
that the central agency relationship of the legislator is organized
around one's constituency. I refrained from taking a line on precisely how this power-sharing arrangement between principal and
agent is to be worked out.

We've seen how co-ownership gives parties a reason to offer
non-strategic concessions. Now we can switch perspectives. How
does the value bear on whether a party offered a non-strategic
concession has reason to accept it? Consider a case based on a
major piece of social legislation. Suppose members of two political parties spend more than a year in iterated negotiations over a

universal health insurance program. Bipartisan "gangs" spring up and concessions are made in both sides in the process. Each side is placing weight on making mutual concessions. The social policy fundamentally changes in the process. Its final form has taken on board a remarkable number of provisions from the minority party, in the hope that there will be substantial bipartisan floor vote. But suppose that, despite this genuine process, there isn't any co-acceptance. This series of compromises fails to generate enough support to get any votes from the minority party, whether in committee or on the floor, for the piece of legislation. If we based our analysis of co-ownership on roll call voting, we'd conclude that no legislator in the minority party bears any liability for the ensuing law. But on my account of the practice, this would be a mistake. Making offers and having them incorporated into a statute is undeniably a liability-accruing activity. If this transaction was performed behind closed doors, it is not always datable and checkable, but this doesn't undermine the force of the verdict.

This distinction will strike purists as casuistry. On their view, if you refuse to accept a compromise or even engage in the process of give and take, you can "disown" any legislation downstream. The law didn't pass through your hands. If you participate in the process of concession and eventually accept a compromise, you become a kind of moral co-sponsor of the resulting law. There is no sense in which some constituent parts of the package are more or less identified with any given party. This "lumping" derives from their athletic conception of joint activity, which we located in their Cooperation Premise. For them, there's no way around the idea that compromise is a robustly cooperative activity that makes all of us share responsibility for each and every line item. Our responsibility is all or none. On the flip side, strategists never saw compromise's give and take as a shared activity. The admissibility of concession and accommodation depended on first-order judgments about the acceptability of a policy. They ask whether giving up anything of substance, however small, would advance their principles of distributive justice. We can now see more clearly the dimension of democracy that they are indifferent to. They don't place any independent value on a distinctively democratic consideration: the value of legislators co-sharing in the responsibility for legislation. We ask them the usual questions about the process of negotiation: Who demanded what? Who gave up what? They don't think that answers to these questions will be morally revealing. Instead of focusing the causal processes that produced this law, they direct our attention to the gains they have made in service of our first-order principles.

There are two ways legislators can stand in relation to a concession. Let's say that a party is *responsible* for some aspect of the law when she proposed or supported it in the negotiation process. This makes them co-authors or sponsors of a provision, exposing them to moral complaint from individuals wronged by the law, including the negative reactive attitudes of blame, resentment, and indignation. In contrast, a party who co-accepts a compromise is morally *liable* for all of its provisions, including the concessions that they made to a disagreeing party. But they need not bear strong moral responsibility. When you raise a moral complaint against a concessionary provision, the lawmaker can point out that she *accepted* this provision, so she bears a kind of secondary responsibility for it. But her acceptance doesn't alter her belief that that provision was unjust. This notion of liability isn't inert. It acknowledges that in going with the compromise, warts and all, the signing parties take responsibility for its contents. When a lawmaker accrues liability for their accommodations, this can affect her future agenda-setting. It may shift the policy profile of legislators, putting pressure on them to prioritize a concern that has been neglected in the negotiation process. A negotiation begins, with strategists placing no weight on accommodation and offering nothing to parties in a minority position of power. They rely upon a bare majority to pass the bill when they could have ensured much broader support with a small concession. Notice that the out-of-power party to compromise wanted to share in some kind of ownership of the law. If their offer had been accepted, they would have accrued narrow responsibility for the provisions they actively supported and broad liability for accepting the whole package. But when their offer is altogether rejected by the strategist, the outvoted party can rightly claim that this wasn't our doing. The strategists have now put themselves in a situation where they and their principals solely bear responsibility for this law. The possibility of sharing in liability has been closed off.

Now let's add a twist to this case. Suppose our strategists were mistaken about the substance of this issue. They passed a bill—their opponents would say they "rammed it through"—that made their shared political institutions more unjust. If you reject the democratic value that I'm calling co-ownership, you will dwell on their substantive mistake. Simon May suggests that attending to their first-order mistake can explain our reaction to the uncompromising individuals who push through unjust legislation: "Those who refuse to compromise unjustifiable positions are acting improperly, not because they refuse to pursue principled compromises, but because their positions are unjustifiable from the beginning. The error lies at the first order, not the second."[83] On my view, there is a compound error here. Imagine addressing these strategists at a town meeting. Even if they were blamelessly mistaken about the moral status of the law, there still seems to be a remainder. They refused to enter a relationship with legislators whose small concessions would have altered the terms of their moral liability for the law. The charge that they neglected the value of co-ownership is compatible with criticism on the substance of the law.

Precisely how liability gets shared is crucial for this picture. It will partly depend on what this practice is like. The underlying ontology may make all the difference. The purist assumed, without argument, that compromise must be a cooperative activity. She flinched at the thought of merging into a group subject with rival legislators, given the commitments that thought seems to have carried with it. We unearthed the nested assumption that all joint intentional activity must be cooperative. But this may be false. I'm assuming cooperative activity is a moralized idea that rules out background coercion and deception,[84] and includes the idea of sharing responsibility for our endeavor. A cooperative activity needn't involve the equal sharing of responsibility, but an equal division may serve as a default setting.

How does participation with other parties in the production of a compromise bear on the participants' moral liability? Purists are convinced that either avoidance of the practice or bare-knuckled obstructionism within it can block them from liability.[85] They think that their hands-off posture allows them to insist: "we had no part in the making of that law." Conversely, strategists can't understand why you'd ever pass on the chance to make your political institutions less unjust. They might say to their brethren: "Take the deal."

Their view of shared liability might put considerable weight on the *negative responsibility* of a lawmaker with a causal opportunity to accept a reforming statute who takes a pass. For him, interposing yourself in a compromise reduces or even eliminates your liability for a prevailing injustice by mitigating it. Practitioners can accept this claim. They can hold, sensibly, that legislators can be responsible for their doings and allowings. The practitioner owes us an answer to the puzzle of concession and accommodation. How does liability shift when a concession is made that isn't strictly necessary for the long-term promotion of their principles? When they can plant the flag of their convictions as far as possible with impunity, why shouldn't they? The purist and strategist altogether miss the procedural side of justice.

We can close this section with two limitations of this argument. First, the conclusion may seem too weak. If you continue to doubt that lawmakers can be *required* to compromise, my argument is compatible with the weaker conclusion that they can be *permitted* to engage in this practice. This lighter weight conclusion follows from granting any weight at all on the policy of Shared Deliberation and Co-Acceptance. This unofficial position treats the posture of the practitioner as *permissible*, if not generally required. Lawmakers who value co-ownership are not acting wrongly when they offer non-strategic concessions. This may sound like a relatively weak position, but it is enough to refute those who reject the entire space of principled compromise.[86]

Second, the conclusion of my argument may seem too strong. Am I assuming that any legislator, whatever their institutional backdrop, has a reason to engage in non-instrumental compromise? I'm not. The overall institutional design and internal organization of lawmaking bodies can affect the valance of moral compromise. My argument has taken for granted a first-past-the-post system. For a system of proportional representation, compromise may be induced through other means. This reveals a contingency of my argument that I welcome. My claim isn't that there is a universal moral reason to engage in this kind of accommodation whenever one is producing statutes. Institutional mechanisms can alter the terms of this practice, shifting sites of concession within the system.[87] But in the absence of these concessionary features, an informal practice of compromise may be necessary to honor our democratic values.

IV. COMPROMISE'S DEFEATERS UNDER UNJUST CONDITIONS

Nearly every piece of legislation contains substantive unjust. This holds true in legislative systems that enact law in a sprawling, omnibus form.[88] So lawmakers face a persistent question: Should I support a bill that introduces certain substantive injustices while remedying status quo injustices? Some pieces of legislation are, of course, more grievous than others. And the species of substantive injustices will surely matter in our reckoning. This is what made the purist's position problematic under conditions of actual politics. I've defended non-strategic concessions that honor a procedural value. This value of co-ownership, on my view, exerts a presumptive pull on the give and take of negotiations. When a concession can create broad "buy-in" across the legislature, co-ownership explains how the compromise process can make legislation more justifiable. Still, to the conceding party, the ensuing law is less justifiable on the substance. Hence, while the product is, all things considered, a morally better law, the process creates a moral remainder. In this final section, I will describe two compromise defeaters, and then answer two objections that draw their force from this remainder.

Critics of non-strategic compromise have fed off a one-sided diet. That is how Ludwig Wittgenstein characterized philosophical approaches that "nourish one's thinking with only one kind of example."[89] Objectors have selected negotiation topics that make their case—with the most grievous concerns on offer. The leading rejection of non-strategic compromise is built entirely around a single example of abortion policy.[90] We shouldn't be surprised that when confronted with this degree of moral gravity acknowledged by both sides, the substance of negotiations swamp the relatively modest weight assigned to being accommodating. The conclusion that neither side should offer non-strategic concessions is precisely what we would expect. It provides no evidence that a value like democratic co-ownership is inert. Opponents have made their case too easy, relying on cases that ensure their conclusion. A distinctive feature of my account of compromise was that parties don't offer concessions without reason. If certain conditions of negotiation have been met, they share a policy of placing weight on giving accommodations if and only if they bring on board the other party. We won't be able to observe this weight directly in a range of cases. We won't know, for example, if each party shared this weighing policy only to have substantive considerations override it. Recall the analogy from earlier. Suppose the admissions director who has a personal policy of placing weight on legacy candidates rejects a candidate who is far below the bar. This isn't evidence that there wasn't any weight placed on this consideration in her deliberations. It's entirely consistent that this policy of weighting has been overridden by substantial considerations.

There's a second way that injustice can serve as a compromise defeater. The means or ends of a negotiating party can directly affront the democratic value of co-ownership. In these cases, the weight a party should assign to accommodation is voided. Consider Lyndon Johnson's stripping down of the Civil Rights Bill of 1957. Hubert Humphrey accused him of "gutting" the act by conceding the voting rights section. When pressed to justify this concession, Johnson's reason is strictly instrumental: "You can't pass a Civil Rights bill with Voting Rights intact! Not this year. Not now." There wasn't any non-instrumental reason "leftover" in these negotiations. For in this case, the tactics and ends of the bill's Southern opponents serve as paradigms of compromise defeaters. Their "hardball tactics" included an array of deception and outright lies, procedural violations documented by the Senate parliamentarian, and chronic stalling with the hope that white backlash would lead the Majority Leader to stand down. What's more, their substantive principles directly targeted the value of citizens relating to each other as equally sharing authority. Therefore, when a party to a legislative compromise holds aims that affront this democratic value, the ordinary weight placed on non-strategic concessions is silenced. In negotiation, the substantive injustice of a party's proposal doesn't *outweigh* the procedural value of deciding together; it *cancels* the moral reason to offer non-strategic concessions.

With these two defeaters in place, let us consider two objections. The strategist takes up the point of view of victims of substantive injustice. How can lawmakers who make a non-strategic concession answer this moral complaint? The first thing to stress is that both substantial and procedural considerations matter to us. Let's see how these two distinct values may enter into a compromise. Suppose a legislative committee is distributing $100 million within a larger farm bill. You believe that roughly half of these funds should be distributed to more sustainable crops like soybeans, while the other party to the negotiation believes that only one-third of these funds should be distributed in this way. But if you offer a concession, in this case literally meeting them half-way, they will support the farm bill in its entirety. Now imagine the moral complaints of the soybean farmers who receive less federal aid than they are due. You can grant the substance of their complaint but appeal to the procedural value that this compromise has respected. Whether your appeal to the value of a broad swath of legislators—and by extension citizens—co-owning the farm bill will be convincing to them is an open question. But notice that in this kind of case, if the lawmaker had not made a non-strategic concession, there would be "victims" as well. If citizens value relating to each other as sharing in the momentous task of legislating, then they will have a moral complaint when lawmakers treat compromise like the strategist. I want to stress two features of this case. First, the farmer's moral claim isn't silenced by the lawmaker's answer, but it has been permissibly overridden. One virtue of my account is that it can explain the moral remainder that compromises leave in their path. They tend to look "ragged and unsatisfactory" in retrospect.[91] A theory shouldn't make them look any better than this. Second, to see where non-instrumental compromise makes a difference, we should look for the run-of-the-mill legislation that makes up the bulk of what lawmakers attend to, not moments of higher lawmaking.[92] The democratic value of co-ownership is, I've argued, a workhorse virtue, but it does little work in the high-gravity legislating that critics of non-strategic compromise have focused on.

A second objection to non-strategic compromise comes from the purist, who fixes on the unjustifiability of checkerboard solutions. We know that legislative compromises produce statutes that are theoretically incoherent. They may clash with components of existing laws on the books. Or their internal workings may stand in tension with each other. They may draw distinctions without reasons. In a system where omnibus bills are standard fare, this concern is only heightened. Consider the checkerboard legislation that only subjects women born in even years to criminal sanction for abortion.[93] This reductio marks out a series of cases that are

alleged to violate a master-value of lawmakers. I think our reasons
for worrying about checkerboard laws are diverse—they may be
inconsistent, incoherent, or even unintelligible. I doubt that they
fall under a unified objection. My point can be put more strongly.
I think we shouldn't appeal to legislative integrity as an independent ideal. My answer holds for two independent reasons. First, we
don't strictly *need* it. There are more economical ways to account
for our intuitive worries about the checkerboard than to discover
our Neptune, a planet whose presence was inferred because of the
orbits of its moons. And second, assigning integrity-independent
value generates implausible verdicts. It is an oversensitive compromise *defeater*, condemning perfectly innocent legislative compromise. At the same time, it can induce compromises that are pro
tanto objectionable. To make the first point, consider a law that
looks incoherent on the books, but can have a rationale that is
acceptable. Consider the heavily brokered deal that produced the
National Breast and Cervical Cancer Early Detection Program.
The law funded screenings for poor women. But a rough and
tumble conference compromise stripped funds for treatment for
women who received positive test results. Now tens of thousands
of poor women were learning about their diagnosis with no ability
to do anything. Nine years later, Congress approved funding for
women. As some of the legislators who went along with a deeply
incoherent law anticipated, the effect of this law was to develop a
constituency where it didn't exist before. Once poor women had
this knowledge, they organized and pressed legislators to render
the law coherent.

Integrity can also induce compromises that can't sustain justification. Consider an actual, if even more fantastical case, where
legislative integrity seems overvalued. A legislative compromise
scheduled elimination of the estate tax in 2010. On January 1,
2011, it was scheduled to return to its 2001 level of 55 percent,
providing a disturbing incentive structure for affected individuals and their families. The decision to add a sunset clause to this
tax cut was a peculiar kind of compromise that repays reflection.
Those lawmakers who pursued a shift in tax law came to believe
that it was morally less acceptable to compromise on the essential
principle. Notice the self-reported attitude toward compromise
that exercised the bill's supporters:

If you oppose a tax on the grounds that it is wrong and should not exist at all, a sunset clause that might bring the tax back in the future must seem profoundly unsatisfying. However, as many of the moral crusaders told us, any of the compromises that might have secured permanent legislation were simply unacceptable. A moral argument that a tax is wrong does not permit distinctions among farmers, small businesses, and large businesses . . . The same moral commitments that held the group together made it difficult for them to compromise.[94]

We can take two points from this interpretation of opponents of the "death tax." First, this case shows the difficulty of unpacking the lawmaker's moral reason to make the whole of the law as morally coherent as possible. Without guidance on how to weigh incoherence in the law in a synchronic and diachronic way, we are left without direction-guidance in this kind of tradeoff. This suggests that ordinary political morality has an uneasy relationship with the demands and the strength of integrity-based considerations.[95] Second, these moral crusaders appeal to the distinction between *internal* and *external* compromise.[96] Opting for an ideologically pure law with a sharp sunset over a pared-down law that was permanent was seen as a clear decision. They saw themselves as having stronger reasons to reject internal compromises—for these were seen as more direct threats to their principles. This may be especially true in this case, where a single principle about the unconditional wrongness of the estate tax appears to be doing all of the work.

CONCLUSION

If compromise didn't exist as a part of our politics, we'd have a reason to invent it. And if the practice becomes a sham, brought down by purists, strategists, and ruthless tacticians, we'd have reason to rebuild it. Against the deliberative picture of negotiation, I've defended "sharp dealing" within the practice of compromise. When another party resorts to bluffing or threats, this can license actions that would not normally be permitted by compromising parties. Such tactics can also diminish the weight that parties must place on accommodation. My approach, in this way, runs counter to the rigoristic treatment of compromise in democratic theory.

Instead of developing principles ported from purely deliberative settings, I've tried to develop an account of compromise from the ground-up, from within a more empirically based picture of what parties to compromise see themselves as doing. Building the account from this direction reveals the fragility of the practice. Good-faith legislators may find themselves within a practice so corrupted that the moral reason to accommodate is frustratingly weak. In these cases, a legislator's reason to compromise won't be enough to inform their actions, since competing moral reasons will outweigh their policy of adjusting their position in response to a rival position. My account has the resources to explain how rebuilding the practice can be morally permissible, if not required. The process of restoring integrity to the practice of compromise will be an inherently risky one. It will demand that legislators commit together to be more open to concessions than they strictly must be. This kind of joint supererogation is particularly difficult in electoral settings, where one's attempt to accommodate can lead to charges of spinelessness and hypocrisy. This is a reminder of the enduring advantage of parties that reject the spirit and letter of the compromise practice. They can insist they are "dupe-proof."

Most of us think that a culture of compromise is a core part of a working democracy. We're already in the market for a conception of democracy that can explain this. We've met a cast of characters and have gotten to know their underlying rationales. A system that gives purists and strategists the power to block or stall legislation makes them into obstructionists. The two of them can end up feeding off each other's vices, with the purist chastening the strategist for abandoning their principles by their flexibility, and the strategist accusing the purist of undermining their principles by their rigidity. In this downward spiral, both sides insist that the political crisis they create is "not on my hands, but my opponent." Each may refuse to take any kind of responsibility for a system that they inevitably co-own. Deadlocks like this remind us that the problem of clean hands cannot be wished away.

Notes

1. Bernard Williams, "Politics and Moral Character," *Public and Private Morality* (Cambridge, UK: Cambridge University Press, 1978).

2. Michael Walzer, "Political Action: The Problem of Dirty Hands," *Philosophy & Public Affairs* 2, no. 2 (Winter 1973), 160–180. Though Walzer went on to eliminate most of the problem in later writings: "dirty hands aren't permissible (or necessary) when anything less than the ongoingness of the community is at stake, or when the danger that we face is anything less than communal death" (46). Dennis Thompson places the problem in a democratic setting in *Political Ethics and Public Office* (Cambridge, MA: Harvard University Press, 1987). Jeremy Waldron accepts the dilemmic character of democratic dirty hands in "Dirtying One's Hands by Sharing a Polity with Others," draft paper for Office and Responsibility Conference, Fall 2012. Unlike the view I am proposing here, Thompson and Waldron suppose that the problem survives in representative democracies.

3. I'm not eliminating the problem by denying the possibility of moral dilemmas. My suggestion is that we can reveal this as a non-problem simply by looking at its picture of democratic agency.

4. Eric Beerbohm, *In Our Name* (Princeton, NJ: Princeton University Press, 2012).

5. Charles Beitz, *Political Equality (Princeton, NJ: Princeton University Press, 1990)*, 113.

6. Thomas Schelling, *The Strategy of Conflict* (Cambridge, MA: Harvard University Press, 1960).

7. John Rawls, "Two Concepts of Rules," in *Collected Papers*, ed. Samuel Freeman (Cambridge, MA: Harvard University Press, 1999).

8. Rawls stresses that it is "logically impossible" to perform a series of actions without the background practice in play. Here I shift our focus from the individual actions of baseball—striking out, fouling—to the forms of joint agency that social practices make possible. Rawls, "Two Concepts of Rules."

9. On my view, in some cases it can be procedurally acceptable for a majority to, in the end, enact a law without concessions.

10. Michael Bratman, *Shared Agency: A Planning Theory of Acting Together* (Oxford: Oxford University Press, 2014), 4–29.

11. Mark Greenberg's moral impact view avoids the traditional divide, but flips the way that law creates obligations: "[Legislators] do so by changing the morally relevant facts and circumstances, for example by changing people's expectations, providing new options, or altering what has been chosen by democratically elected representatives," Mark Greenberg, "The Moral Impact Theory of Law," *Yale Law Journal* 123, no. 5 (2013), 1290.

12. Williams, "Politics and Moral Character," 59.
13. Daniel Kahneman and Amis Tversky, "The Framing of Decisions and the Psychology of Choice," *Science* 211, no. 4481 (1981), 453–458.
14. G.E.M. Anscombe offers a version of this character: "[S]uppose I were convinced that B wished to deceive me, and would tell the opposite of what he believed, but that on the matter in hand B would be believing the opposite of the truth. By calculation on this, then, I believe what B says, on the strength of his saying it—but only in a comical sense can I be said to believe *him.*" "What Is It to Believe Someone?" in C. F. Delaney, ed., *Rationality and Religious Belief* (University of Notre Dame Press, 1979), 9.
15. Jay Wallace, "Hypocrisy, Moral Address, and the Equality of Persons," *Philosophy & Public Affairs* 38, no. 4 (Fall 2010), 307–341.
16. Bernard Williams, "Deciding to Believe," *Problems of the Self* (Cambridge, UK: Cambridge University Press, 1973).
17. Matthew Boyle, "Active Belief," in D. Hunter, ed., *Belief and Agency* (Calgary: University of Calgary Press, 2011), 119–147.
18. Robert Nozick offers the parent warning the child: "If you do *A* I'll have a heart attack." See Nozick, "Coercion," in White Morgenbesser, ed., *Philosophy, Science, and Method: Essays in Honor of Ernest Nagel* (New York: St. Martin's Press. 1969), 440–472.
19. Robert Kaiser, *Act of Congress: How America's Essential Institution Works, and How It Doesn't* (New York: Vintage Books, 2014), 161.
20. Schelling, *The Strategy of Conflict,* 45.
21. Schelling, *The Strategy of Conflict,* 45–56.
22. Terrence McConnell, "Moral Blackmail," *Ethics* 91:4 (1981), 544–567.
23. The basic form of this argument has been mounted by both political parties, with our current president having voted for default as a senator, so it cuts ice in both directions.
24. G. A. Cohen, *Incentives, Inequality, and Community* (Stanford: Stanford University Press: Tanner Lectures in Human Values, 1991), 280.
25. Tamar Schapiro, "Compliance, Complicity, and the Nature of Nonideal Conditions," *Journal of Philosophy* 100, no. 77 (2003), 350.
26. This case is loosely based on the nine months of negotiations over the Affordable Care Act, which involved a Gang of Six and, later, a Gang of Eight. Eventually the charge was made that one side was going through the motions of the practice of compromise, but wasn't actually taking up accommodating stances.
27. From the movie, *The Godfather: Part II,* written by Frances Ford Coppola and Mario Puzo.
28. The special wrong of this kind of threat may be in the neighborhood of A. J. Julius's account of wrongful threats. *See* A. J. Julius, "The Possibility of Exchange," *Politics, Philosophy, & Economics* 12, no. 4, 2013.

29. Seana Valentine Shiffrin, *Speech Matters: On Lying, Morality, and the Law* (Princeton, NJ: Princeton University Press, 2014), 143.

30. David Lewis, "Scorekeeping in a Language Game," *Journal of Philosophical Logic* 8: 339–59.

31. J. L. Austin, *How to Do Things with Words* (Cambridge, MA: Harvard University Press, 1975), 143.

32. Amy Gutmann and Dennis Thompson, *The Spirit of Compromise: Why Governing Demands It and Campaigning Undermines It*, Updated Edition (Princeton, NJ: Princeton University Press, 2014).

33. Carlo Muñoz, "Budget proposal 'not my ideal plan,' Obama says in weekly address," *The Hill*, March 6, 2013.

34. Kaiser, *Act of Congress*, 195.

35. While I understand legislative compromise as a distinctive subspecies of negotiation, many theorists have dismissed the exchange of demands in negotiation as mere "haggling." Joshua Cohen warns that "collective decision-making ought to be different from bargaining, contracting, and other market-type interactions, both in its explicit attention to considerations of the common advantage and in the ways that that attention helps to form the aims of the participants," "Deliberation and Democratic Legitimacy," *The Good Polity: Normative Analysis of the State*, Alan Hamlin and Phillip Petit, ed. (New York: Blackwell Press, 1989), 17. For defenses of compromise that see it as part of the architecture of bargaining, see Andrew Sabl, *Ruling Passions: Political Offices and Democratic Ethics* (Princeton, NJ: Princeton University Press, 2002). Nancy Rosenblum also accepts this view: "Deliberation is not an animal different from negotiation and compromise," *On the Side of the Angels: An Appreciation of Parties and Partisanship* (*Princeton, NJ:* Princeton University Press, 2008), 147. Cass Sunstein, for example, holds that civic republicans should be "hostile to bargaining mechanisms in the political process and will instead seek to ensure agreement among political participants." Cass Sunstein, "Beyond the Republican Revival," *Yale Law Journal* 97, no. 8, 1549.

36. Jane Mansbridge and Mark Warren, "Deliberative Negotiation," in Jane Mansbridge and Cathie Jo Martin, ed., *Political Negotiation: A Handbook* (Washington, DC: Brookings Institution Press, 2016), 166.

37. Mansbridge and Warren, "Deliberative Negotiation," 166–167.

38. Thomas Gilligan and Keith Krehbiel, "Asymmetric Information and Legislative Rules with Heterogenous Committee," *American Journal of Political Science*, 33:2 (1989), 459–490.

39. In his murderer example, even Kant sought to distinguish dissembling and lying. See *Lectures on Ethics*, J. B. Schneewind, ed., Peter Heath, trans. (Cambridge, UK: Cambridge University Press), 27:700.

48 ERIC BEERBOHM

40. Contrast this view with Amy Gutmann and Dennis Thompson, who leave more wiggle room in *The Spirit of Compromise*.

41. This kind of purism about speech contexts takes what Austin calls a "constative utterance," upholding "the ideal of what would be right to say in all circumstances, for any purpose, to any audience, etc." Austin, *How to Do Things with Words*, 146.

42. Schelling, *The Strategy of Conflict*, p. 45.

43. Robert Caro, *Master of the Senate (New York:* Knopf Doubleday Publishing Group, 2002).

44. Amy Gutmann and Dennis Thompson, *Democracy and Disagreement* (Cambridge, MA: Harvard University Press, 1996).

45. T. M. Benditt, "Compromising Interests and Principles," in J. R. Pennock and J. W. Chapman, ed., *Compromise in Ethics, Law, and Politics, Nomos, XXI* (New York: New York University Press, 1979), 26–37. Also see Gutmann and Thompson, *The Spirit of Compromise,* and Henry Richardson, *Democratic Autonomy: Public Reasoning about the Ends of Policy* (Oxford: Oxford University Press, 2002).

46. C. A. J. Coady and Onora O'Neill, "Messy Morality and the Art of the Possible," *Proceedings of the Aristotelian Society, Supplementary Volumes* 64 (1990), 269; Benditt, "Compromising Interests and Principles."

47. I'm grateful to Alex Zakaras for stressing this point about selective or inauthentic purism.

48. Samuel Scheffler, "Doing and Allowing," *Ethics* 114: 2 (2004), 215–239.

49. John Ferejohn and Charles Shipan, "Congressional Influence on Bureaucracy," *Journal of Law, Economics, and Organization* 6 (1990), 287–335.

50. I leave it open whether purists accept a moral catastrophe clause that allows them to budge when the circumstances are existential. Robert Nozick's rider is limited to "catastrophic moral horror." Robert Nozick, *Anarchy, State and Utopia* (New York: Basic Books, 1974).

51. David Luban, "Bargaining and Compromise: Recent Work on Negotiation and Informal Justice," *Philosophy & Public Affairs* 14, no. 4 (1985): 415.

52. Robert Schenkkan, *All the Way: A Play* (New York: Grove Press, 2014), 63.

53. G. A. Cohen, *Rescuing Justice and Equality (Cambridge, MA: Harvard University Press, 2008).*

54. "[W]hen we reflect on a principle, and ask ourselves what that principle requires, we are always engaging in moral reasoning, not just deriving a conclusion from some given rule. T. M. Scanlon, *Being Realistic about Reasons* (New York: Oxford University Press, 2014), 119.

55. John Searle, for instance, thinks these two ideas come pre-packaged together: "the notion of collective intentionality implies the notion of cooperation." "Collective Intentions and Actions," Philip R. Cohen, Jerry Morgan and Martha Pollack, ed., *Intentions in Communication* (Cambridge, MA: MIT Press, 1990), 406.

56. Margaret Gilbert, *Joint Commitment: How We Make the Social World* (Oxford: Oxford University Press, 2014), 420.

57. Sen. Olympia Snowe (R-ME), participated in healthcare negotiations, members of her constituency accused her of committing an act of treason.

58. Immanuel Kant, *Practical Philosophy*, ed. Mary J. Gregor (Cambridge: Cambridge University Press, 1996 [1785]), 27:700.

59. "Uncompromising extremism" because it lacks a "commitment to getting the public business done" and represents an "abdication of responsibility for governing." Gutmann and Thompson, *The Spirit of Compromise*, 127.

60. Avishai Margalit, *On Compromise and Rotten Compromises* (Princeton, NJ: Princeton University Press, 2009).

61. Thomas Hobbes, *Leviathan*, Richard Tuck, ed. (Cambridge, UK: Cambridge University Press, 1991), 33.

62. Ronald Dworkin, *Law's Empire* (Cambridge, MA: Belnap Press, 1988), 211.

63. Nolan McCarty and Michael Barber, "Causes and Consequences of Polarization," in Jane Mansbridge and Cathie Jo Martin, ed., *Political Negotiation: A Handbook*.

64. Rosenblum, *On the Side of the Angels*.

65. Simon May defends the strategist as the only justifiable approach to moral compromise. For him, even the slightest concession must pass the instrumental test: "only ever warranted for pragmatic reasons," "Principled Compromise and the Abortion Controversy," *Philosophy & Public Affairs* 33:4 (2005), p. 317.

66. Philippe van Parijs describes this state as one "where there is unconditional surrender or submission of one party to domination by the other." "What Makes a Good Compromise?" *Government and Opposition* 47:3, (2012), 469.

67. Simon May puts it this way: "As participants in political decision-making, citizens share responsibility for reaching correct decisions through deliberative processes in which all have equal standing," Simon May, "Moral Compromise, Civic Friendship, and Political Reconciliation," *Critical Review of International Social and Political Philosophy* 14, issue 5 (2011), 596.

68. Beerbohm, *In Our Name: The Ethics of Democracy*.

69. This point about participation and nonparticipation arose in the Olympic trials for badminton in 2012. Eight athletes were disqualified for exploiting a matched system that encouraged early losses. The charge was that they were acting a "in a manner that is clearly abusive or detrimental to the sport," "Olympic Ideal Takes Beating in Badminton," *New York Times*, August 1, 2012.

70. In *The Spirit of Compromise*, Amy Gutmann and Dennis Thompson note that the means and ends of a compromise with both play a justificatory role.

71. Theodore M. Benditt draws a distinction between the means and ends of a compromise in "Compromising Interests and Principles." What I'm claiming is that these two dimensions of compromise function together, helping us generate defeators and enablers.

72. Joseph Carens, "Compromises in Politics," in *Compromise in Ethics, Law, and Politics*, ed. J. Roland Pennock and John Chapman (New York: New York University Press, 1979), 135.

73. B. van Fraassen, *Laws and Symmetry* (Oxford: Clarendon Press, 1989), 143.

74. This is not an unusual diagnosis, but it has been a kind of dangling modifier. It's not clear how this argument works. See, for instance, Patrick Dobel, *Compromise and Political Action: Political Morality in Liberal Democratic Life* (Savage, MD: Rowman & Littlefield Publishers, 1987).

75. Christine Korsgaard, "Kant on the Right to Revolution," in *The Constitution of Agency (Oxford, UK: Oxford University Press, 2008)*, 247.

76. As A. John Simmons notes: "Is a politically popular but likely less effective policy to be preferred to one that has questionable political support but is more likely to be effective?," "Ideal and Nonideal Theory," *Philosophy & Public Affairs 38, no. 1 (Winter 2010)*, 18.

77. Bipartisanship is a much discussed value in ordinary political morality, but almost never acknowledged in democratic theory. The concept only comes up in Nancy Rosenblum's treatise on parties as synonymous with anti-partyism. But on the gloss I'm giving it here, we needn't assimilate these two concepts.

78. Jeremy Waldron, *Law and Disagreement* (Oxford: Oxford University Press, 1999), 205.

79. Here my view contrasts with Andrew Sabl's role-based defense of compromise in *Ruling Passions*.

80. See, for instance, Andrea Cornwall and Vera Schattan P. Coelho, *Spaces for Change? The Politics of Participation in New Democratic Arenas* (Chicago: Chicago University Press, 2006).

81. In the 2000 presidential election, candidate Al Gore often reminded his audience that the presidency was the only constitutional position where one is obligated to represent every member of society.

82. My view is consistent with the claim that the law, in some metaphorical sense, speaks on behalf of the whole community. What I'm resisting is the assumption that our representatives represent every member of our polity. In *Law and Disagreement*, Waldron has a footnote that personally addresses candidate reviewers of this book, warning them that he is not proffering an account of political representation.

83. May, "Principled Compromise and the Abortion Controversy," 325.

84. Bratman, *Shared Agency*, 37–38.

85. And purists derived this from what I claimed was an overly strong reliance on the doing/allowing distinction.

86. See May, "Moral Compromise, Civic Friendship, and Political Reconciliation."

87. "Political scientists study the internal rules of legislatures that encourage or inhibit negotiation 'across the aisle.' Rules for agenda-setting, committee assignments, and the degree of independence of committee chairs, the possibility of amending bills, cloture, and so on make it more or less likely that the dominant party will be able to avoid hearing out the minority (or factions within its own ranks), much less make concessions." Rosenblum, *On the Side of the Angels*, 404.

88. For an analysis of this relatively new norm, see Barbara Sinclair's *Unorthodox Lawmaking: New Legislative Processes in the US Congress* (Washington, DC: CQ Press, 2011).

89. Ludwig Wittgenstein, *Philosophical Investigations*, edited by P. M. S. Hacker and Joachim Schulte (New York: Wiley-Blackwell Press, 2009), 593.

90. To be fair to Simon May's impressive challenge, proponents of noninstrumental concessions had advanced this case as a useful starting point. But I think this is among the worst possible cases for a defense of nonstrategic compromise to work with. May's argument is *conceded* by Dennis Thompson and Amy Gutmann in *The Spirit of Compromise*. "In our view, mutual respect . . . does not provide a sufficient reason to compromise, nor does it give compromise an independent intrinsic value. The general value of compromise, as we defend it here, does not alone determine whether the content of any particular compromise is acceptable" (225). I accept that the "appeal to mutual respect" isn't enough to serve as a compromise enabler. But Gutmann and Thompson mistakenly conclude that there is no available enabler that can serve this role. Here I take myself to be offering a distinctive defense of non-strategic concession.

91. Waldron, *Torture*, p. 92.

92. Bruce Ackerman, *We the People: Volume 1* (Cambridge, MA: Harvard University Press, 1993).

93. Ronald Dworkin, *Law's Empire* (Cambridge, MA: Belknap Press, 1986), 182.

94. Ian Shapiro and Michael J. Graetz, *Death by a Thousand Cuts: The Fight over Taxing Inherited Wealth* (Princeton, NJ: Princeton University Press, 2005), 261.

95. Ronald Dworkin holds that "it is part of our collective political morality that such compromises are wrong, that the community as a whole and not just individual officials must act in a principled way." Dworkin, *Law's Empire*, 182. I am here raising doubts about his confidence in this claim.

96. "A compromise must be external, not internal; it must be a compromise about which scheme of justice to adopt rather than a compromised scheme of justice." Dworkin, *Law's Empire*, 179.

2

THIRD PARTIES TO COMPROMISE

ANTON FORD

I. Introduction

When political theorists write about political disagreement, they tend to focus attention on the parties to a disagreement. And when they discuss compromise, they tend likewise to focus on the parties to a compromise. In the simplest case of compromise, as in that of disagreement, there are two such parties. The two are engaged in a process of joint decision-making. Because they disagree, because neither can persuade the other, and because they must resolve their disagreement, concessions are offered by each until they arrive at something that is acceptable to both. From either point of view, the result is less than optimal, but not as bad as it might be, and better than it would be if it were left to the other party.[1]

Accounts of political compromise often address themselves to questions such as these: Is the back and forth between the compromisers a species of bargaining?[2] How is it possible to compromise without sacrificing one's own moral integrity?[3] What is the difference between compromising one's interests and compromising one's principles?[4] Must the resolution to a political disagreement be internally coherent in order to be acceptable?[5] Does political compromise require political friendship, civic trust, or mutual respect?[6] If so, are there non-instrumental reasons for offering up concessions?[7]

Questions such as these pertain to the relationship between the compromisers. That is, of course, a fine thing to discuss. But it tends to be discussed in isolation from another relationship that one might have expected to hear about: the relationship between a compromiser and whatever third party is in danger of being wronged by the decision on which a compromise is sought. Third parties are not normally mentioned in accounts of political compromise—not even by political theorists writing about "political ethics." This is remarkable. In any event, compromising is a decision-making process. Decisions of all kinds are liable to affect people. And, they are liable to wrong the people whom they affect. The liability of decisions to affect people is not an incidental feature of theirs: it is part of what makes them decisions—as distinct from, say, hopes, wishes, and prayers. Moreover, the liability of decisions to wrong those whom they affect is part of what makes decisions important in any domain of life where justice is at stake.

Meanwhile, if justice requires anything, it requires one not to wrong people. The requirement is in force when one is making a decision. If one is making a decision that has the potential to wrong people, one is obliged to keep those people in mind, to avoid wronging them. This is the case whether the decision is public or private, and whether it is unilateral, bilateral, multilateral, or omnilateral.

It follows that, if one is party to a joint decision that has the potential to wrong someone, one stands in (no fewer than) two relationships that constrain one's action in the decision-making process: one relationship with one's fellow decision-maker(s), and one relationship with whomever is in danger of being wronged. Nothing about one's preferences, values, principles, or interests (e.g., their being reasonable), nothing about the character of the decision-making process (e.g., its being fair or democratic), and nothing about one's relationship with one's fellow decision-makers (e.g., its being respectful, tolerant, and inclusive) releases one from the obligation not to wrong the people who are affected by a decision that one is helping to make.

Since compromising is a process of joint decision-making, all of this applies to it. In any decision where justice is at stake, a party to a compromise stands in relations of right to (no fewer than) two other parties: namely, (1) the other party to the compromise, and (2) whatever third party the decision threatens to wrong.

The central contention of this chapter is that the kind of disagreement that motivates an interest in political compromise is such that there is always someone in danger of being wronged by the decision over which there is a disagreement, and that, consequently, the relevant constellation of duties is tripolar, not bipolar. The standard bipolar model systematically erases one of the three poles and two of the three relations that constitute the predicament of anyone making a joint decision where justice is at stake.

In section II, I situate the topics of political disagreement and political compromise in the broader theoretical context of bilateral decision-making. First, I will distinguish between two kinds of bilateral decision: those that threaten to wrong a third party and those that do not. Then, focusing on the former, I will consider the tripolar relation that holds between the two parties to a bilateral decision and the party threatened with injustice. Finally, I will argue that the political decisions that animate an interest in political disagreement and political compromise are of this kind.

I argue in section III that, in the relevant kind of political decision, political agreement—like political disagreement—is a tripolar affair.

In section IV, I consider how this tripolarity inflects various themes from democratic theory, the themes that provide the usual setting for discussions of compromise.

Then, in section V, I will explain how a bipolar conception of political disagreement can distort one's understanding of the value of compromise. If one focuses exclusively on the parties to a disagreement, one is liable to form the impression that political compromise is, not just a necessary evil, but somehow inherently good. This is in fact the view of a number of political theorists, who defend what has come to be known as "principled compromise."[8] The doctrine recommends that one should sometimes offer unforced concessions to political opponents in matters of dispute where justice is at stake. That is, it recommends offering concessions that are not necessitated by balances of power or by any strategic consideration about how to advance justice, and that are, in one's view, counterproductive to that end. In doing so, it inadvertently counsels one to wrong a third party. The injustice of the recommended action would be obvious if the relevant third party were in view.

Recent events in US electoral politics and the surrounding conventional wisdom about the value of bipartisanship lend credence to the doctrine of principled compromise. I will conclude, in section VI, with a word about this.

II. POLITICAL COMPROMISE AS A SPECIES OF BILATERAL DECISION

II.1. Decisions That Threaten to Wrong No One

Some decisions affect other people without threatening to wrong them. If I am deciding where to eat dinner and choosing between restaurants, the proprietors of the restaurants between which I am choosing will all be affected by my decision, but none of them will be wronged by it, no matter what I decide. For, I do not have an obligation to eat in any restaurant. No restauranteur has a right against me that I do so.

A decision of this kind can also be made bilaterally. If you and I are choosing a restaurant together, neither *I*, nor *you*, nor *we* will wrong any restauranteur. Still, we might behave badly with respect to one another. Even though no third party is exposed to injustice, there are two parties to the decision, and one of them could wrong the other in the process of decision-making. For example, recognizing that we have different preferences, I might try to bully, blackmail, threaten, or otherwise manipulate you into going where I want to go. Alternatively, one of us might graciously indulge the other's preference. Or we might agree to flip a coin. Or we might compromise, picking a restaurant that, from either point of view, is less than optimal, but that is acceptable to both of us, and that each of us prefers to the other's first choice.

Such a decision might be made by two groups, rather than by two individuals. If your family and my family are deciding between restaurants, neither *your family*, nor *my family*, nor *our two families together* will wrong any restauranteur. But the families may treat each other well or badly in the process of decision-making. As before, there are many of ways of coming to a decision. One family could manipulate the other or indulge the other's preference. The two could agree to flip a coin. Or the two could compromise.

Nothing much changes if you and I have been delegated by our respective families to decide where to eat dinner together, with you expressing the preference of your family for one restaurant and me that of mine for another. The only difference is that, in addition to the bipolar relation between the two parties, there is now also a fiduciary relation within each of the parties. But there is still no danger of anyone's doing any injustice to any third party. Since there are still two parties to the decision, there is still the potential for one of the two to treat the other badly in the process of decision-making. Moreover, there are the same possible routes to a decision: e.g., manipulation, indulgence, coin-flipping, and compromise.

All of these cases are structurally similar to one in which two parties negotiate over a price. The parties to such a negotiation may be individuals or they may be groups (e.g., corporations). Whatever one might want to say about how the parties should treat each other in the process of negotiating, there is no third party to consider. For, no matter what the result of the negotiation turns out to be—whether a low price, a high price, or a fair price—no third party will be wronged by it. It does not cease to be a two-party transaction if the buyer and the seller both hire lawyers to do the negotiating. One lawyer will have fiduciary duties to the seller and the other to the buyer. But what are being negotiated are the interests of two parties. There is no third party whose interest is at stake.

Not all disagreements that arise in joint decision-making spring from conflicting desires. The parties to a joint decision might have conflicting opinions about how to achieve a common goal, one that does not threaten to wrong any third party. Perhaps they disagree about how to save their jointly controlled crops. Neither party to the dispute need be moved by any desire apart from the desire to solve this problem. If they must act together, but neither can persuade the other, various things could happen: one party might manipulate the other; one might defer to the other's judgment; the two might flip a coin; or the two might compromise. As before, they could treat each other well or badly. Moreover, the parties to such a dispute could be individuals or groups; and, if groups, they might or might not have spokespeople to argue their position. This case is like the previous ones in the following respect: whatever the two parties decide to do, however they reach their decision, and whether or not they wrong each other in the course of reaching it, no third party is involved.

II.2. Decisions That Threaten to Wrong Someone

Though not all decisions have the potential to wrong someone, many do. If I need to dispose of an old flowerpot, the easiest thing to do might be to push it off the balcony. Deciding to do so is one thing if the balcony is that of a ship in the middle of the sea. It is different if the balcony hangs over a crowded street. In the latter case, pushing the flowerpot off the balcony would gravely wrong the people in the street below. It would not merely affect them. And it would not merely harm them. It would wrong them. It would treat them in a way that they have a right not to be treated.

My relation to those whom I could wrong is not that of an agent to its principal. I do not represent them or act on their behalf. They are not my clients or constituents. I am not their counselor or delegate. We do not constitute a person, legally or otherwise. Insofar as I could wrong them, we are other to each other. I have duties *to* them. They have claims *against* me.

But my relation to those whom I could wrong is also not that of a benefactor to a beneficiary. To decide against wronging those affected by my decisions is not an act of charity or altruism. I am not doing them a favor. They do not owe me gratitude. What I must respect is not their preference but their right. I owe it to them not to do them wrong.

All of this is true if the decision is bilateral. The question of what to do with an old flowerpot is one I might decide with a second party. If my partner in the decision proposes that we push it off the balcony, I still have a relationship to those in the crowded street below. Whatever my past, present, or future relationship to my fellow decision-maker might be, we are suddenly now at odds, provided that I recognize that the people in the street below have a right against me that I refrain from dropping, or helping anyone drop, flowerpots on them.

Of course, these people also have this same right against my partner, and against the two of us insofar as we act together. If I say so to my partner, I am not acting as the benefactor of those in the street below, but neither am I acting as their spokesperson. I am speaking for myself as one party to a decision the outcome of which threatens to wrong them. What I am saying—on my behalf, not theirs—is what we, my partner and I, the decision-makers, should do in view of their right not to be wronged by us. The structure is the same if the decision is made, not by two individuals, but by two groups. If one group advocates pushing the flowerpot off the balcony, and other opposes this course of action on the grounds that someone would be wronged by it, and so advocates an alternative, there are, as before, two parties to the decision, and a third party, which may be wronged by that decision.

Little changes if we suppose that each of the two groups has a delegate representing its position in discussions of the balcony question. The delegate for the anti-balconists will speak on behalf of the anti-balconists, but she will not speak on behalf of the people in the street. For, the delegate is not delegated by the people in the street, but by the anti-balconists. The people in the street below constitute a third party whom the anti-balconists (including their representative) see themselves as having a duty not to wrong.

The two groups on the balcony might disagree about whether to push, not a flowerpot, but one from among own their ranks into the street below. If the street below is crowded, as we have been imagining, then the relevant third parties—the ones at risk of being wronged—include both the people in the street below and whoever is in danger of being thrown off the balcony. On the other hand, if the street empty, the only third party is the latter. And again, both sides of the dispute could be argued by representatives delegated by those who disagree.

If a joint decision must be made, and if neither side can persuade the other, then, whether the parties to the disagreement are two individuals or two groups—and, if they are groups, whether they have delegates or not—the conflict could be resolved in various ways: one side could manipulate the other; one side could defer to the other's judgment; they could flip a coin; or they could make a compromise. Whatever decision they come to, however they come to it, and no matter how well or badly they treat one other, a third party is involved.

II.3. Tripolar Relations of Right

As we have seen, a unilateral decision may or may not threaten to wrong anyone. If it does not—because, say, one is choosing between restaurants, or between possible means to an end (where neither the means nor the end is unjust)—one is unconstrained by relations of right: as far as concerns justice, one is free to do as one pleases, or as one thinks is most efficacious. On the other hand, if a unilateral decision threatens to wrong someone, one's decision-making is constrained by one's relation to whoever is potentially wronged by one's decision. This is a bipolar relation of right between the one who makes the decision and the one who could be wronged by it.

A bilateral decision is like a unilateral decision in that it may or may not threaten to wrong anyone. One difference between unilateral and bilateral decisions is that, even if a bilateral decision threatens no injustice, a party to it is constrained by a relation of right. For, even though there is no one external to the decision-making who could be wronged, there is such a person internal to the decision-making.

Another difference between unilateral and bilateral decisions is this: if a bilateral decision *does* threaten to wrong someone, a party to the decision is constrained by a relation of right to whomever is in danger of being wronged, but—and this is the difference—the relation between this decision-maker and that third party is not merely bipolar. For, the second decision-maker is also constrained by a relation of right to the same third party, and the relation of the decision-makers to one another is partly constituted by the relation in which each stands to that third party.

An example will make this clear. If one is standing on a balcony with a second person, who announces his (unilateral) decision to push a flowerpot into the crowded street below, his intention to wrong the people in the street affects one's own relation to him (i.e., to the second party). Arguably, one has an obligation to try to stop him, if not physically, then by means of persuasion.[9] Even if one does not have an obligation to stop him, one is certainly obliged to not help him. For, if one party chooses to help a second to wrong a third, the first wrongs the third.

Notice that it does not matter *why* the second party intends to do what would wrong the third. It might be as a joke, in anger, for money, because it is inconvenient not to, because it is necessary to advance a worthy cause, or for the sake of lofty principle. It simply does not matter. If the first party recognizes that the second proposes to wrong a third—*for any reason whatsoever*—the first wrongs the third in choosing to help the second.

Moreover, it does not matter *why* the first party chooses to help the second. It might be out of friendship with the second, out of malice toward the third, for money, because it is inconvenient not to, because it is necessary to advance a worthy cause, or for the sake of a lofty principle. Whatever the reason, the first party wrongs the third. If the reason is base, it is a base reason for choosing to wrong someone. If it is high-minded, it is a high-minded reason for choosing to wrong someone. In any case, it is a reason for choosing to wrong someone.

This is how things stand in a case where one is a mere bystander to someone else's unilateral decision to wrong a third party. Even in a case where one is a mere bystander, one's practical relation to a second person is affected by that person's decision to wrong a third.

The three-way relation is more intimate when two of the three are deciding together. If one is party to a decision and one's partner in the decision-making proposes a course of action that one knows would wrong a third, one is obliged, not merely not to support that proposal, but to oppose it. In this case, it is not a matter of intervening in an injustice that a second person inflicts on a third. It is a matter of one's not inflicting an injustice. For, in this case, one co-authors the decision.

II.4. Political Decisions That Threaten to Wrong No One

Having said something on the general topic of bilateral decisions, let's now turn to those decisions that are, specifically, political. These can be made by different kinds of political agent—e.g., by political parties, activist organizations, trade unions, public officials, and private citizens. But there is a certain ambiguity in the idea of a political decision, and hence also in that of a political disagreement and a political compromise. One might understand the idea of a "political decision" so broadly as to cover any decision, on any question, made by any political agent—including, say, any decision made by any public official in any official capacity. So understood, there are many political decisions, many political disagreements, and many political compromises that affect people,

and that are of significant public concern, but that do not threaten
to wrong anyone.

For example, a committee exercising public authority may have
to decide how to use a given fund of money in order to achieve
an uncontroversial good. It is possible to have a genuine disagreement about what course of action would be most effective. Suppose the question is how to improve road safety. One faction of the
decision-making body may favor the introduction of roundabouts,
while another favors stop signs. Or suppose the question is how to
advance the treatment of some disease. There might be a disagreement about which research program, or which research team, to
support.

If the goal is important—if lives are at stake—then it is important to make a good decision. However, there need not be anyone whom a poor decision would wrong. No one will have been
wronged if the committee decides to fund one research team
rather than another, but later, in hindsight, this is seen to have
been a poor decision. It is not as though either research team had
a right to be funded. And while the general public has a right that
public officials make their best effort, and use their best judgment,
to serve the public interest, doing so is consistent with making an
honest mistake. It is not as though the public has a right that public officials be correct in all their judgments.

The parties to a dispute about the relative merits of roundabouts
and stop signs could treat each other well or badly. For, there are
various ways that their dispute could be resolved. One side could
manipulate the other. One could defer to the other's judgment.
The two could flip a coin. Or the two could compromise.

However, disagreement over the relative merits of roundabouts
and stop signs is not what one would call a political controversy,
even if the dispute is between elected public officials acting in the
public interest. For, the decision itself has no political content. In
arguing for or against a position, no one will appeal to any political principle. This is not the kind of decision that animates an
interest in political disagreement or political compromise.[10] It is
worth mentioning these decisions only in order to set them aside.

II.5. *Political Decisions That Threaten to Wrong Someone*

Interest in the topic of political compromise is animated by a concern with decisions that have political (and not merely technical) content. This is clear from the examples that political theorists give. No one mentions traffic patterns or any of the myriad logistical questions that public officials settle in the execution of their official duties, even though there can be disagreement on such questions, and even though such disagreement can be settled through compromise. The disagreements, decisions, and compromises that matter to political theorists are those in which justice is at stake. Their paradigms of disagreement concern issues like abortion,[11] same-sex marriage,[12] healthcare,[13] taxes,[14] slavery,[15] apartheid,[16] and war.[17] In disagreements such as these, there is always someone in danger of being wronged by the decision.

This is why I said, in the introduction, that it is remarkable that discussions of political compromise tend to frame the topic in bipolar terms. The standard picture is one on which there are two disputants with opposing convictions (or values, or principles, or interests, or preferences). The questions asked within this framework are always a version of this: "Given their opposing convictions, how they should treat each other?" The total number of parties is two, and of relations, one.

The objection to this model is not that it fails to record the fact that justice is at stake, but rather that it records this in the wrong way. The fact is not recorded by depicting a decision-maker as having two obligations to two other parties. Bipolar accounts only depict one relationship to one other party. The would-be third party and all obligations to that party are shoved into the content of someone else's convictions—as though they were only figments of the imagination.

Of course, in any political controversy, there is apt to be a dispute about the identity of the third party. This does not mean that there is no third party, or that the relations of right and of mutual respect are merely bipolar. It simply reveals the character of the dispute. Consider, for example, the abortion controversy. Activists on both sides of the controversy take themselves to stand in two important relations: one to those one the other side; and one to a third party that is vulnerable to injustice. Those who defend abortion see women as the third party, while those who oppose it see fetuses as the third party. Even if one believed that, for the purposes of providing an account of political compromise, it was necessary to remain impartial on the substantive question in dispute, such impartiality would not recommend narrowing one's theoretical focus to the two disputing parties. For, that is not how either disputant understands its own predicament. That there are exactly three relevant parties is one point on which both sides should agree.[18] Whichever side is right, a bipolar account is wrong.

As we have seen (in sections II.1 and II.4), there *is* a kind of disagreement for which a bipolar model is perfectly adequate: a bilateral decision that threatens to wrong no one. Two individuals or groups of people (with or without representatives) can disagree about where to go to dinner. In order to act together, they need to work through their conflicting desires. Or again, two individuals or groups of people (with or without representatives) can disagree about how to improve traffic safety. In order to act together, they need to work through their conflicting their beliefs. In cases like these, the number of relevant parties is two, rather than three, because the decision is one that does not threaten to wrong anyone.

But since, in the only kind of decision that matters in political theory, someone is in danger of being wronged, the decision-makers always stand in tripolar relations of right. The parties to a decision have duties to each other, yes. But they also have a duty not to wrong those who are affected by their decision. The objection to the bipolar account of political compromise is that it misrepresents the kind of decision that motivates an interest in political disagreement: it represents decisions in which justice is at stake as though they were decisions about restaurants or roundabouts.

III. POLITICAL DISAGREEMENT AND POLITICAL AGREEMENT

Theorists who write about political disagreement tend to say little or nothing about political agreement. However, agreement and disagreement are both possibilities when political agents act together, and they must have the same, or a similar, structure. This suggests a further reason for thinking that political disagreement is a tripolar affair: namely, that political agreement is.

When one person acknowledges the right of people in the street below not to have flowerpots dropped on them, and when she acts accordingly, there is a bipolar relation between that one person and those in the street below. When a second person agrees with the first, and when they act accordingly together, the two agree in acknowledging the same right of the same third party. The parties to the agreement agree with one another, and that is one relationship. But each also stands in (and sees herself as standing in) a relation to the party whose right she acknowledges.

Similarly, political agreement relates the agreers (the minimum number of which is two) both to one another and to a third party whose right the agreers agree in affirming. Unlike abortion, women's suffrage is no longer controversial, so this is an example of unquestioned agreement. Any two parties to this agreement acknowledge, and agree in acknowledging, someone's right. The political judgment on which the agreers agree refers itself to a class of persons—in this case, to women—who are owed something, and who would be wronged by opposition to that about which the agreers agree.

There is also agreement between agents on the same side of a controversy. Even as they disagree with opponents of abortion, defenders of abortion agree with one another. They agree *in* their joint recognition and defense *of* someone's right. The relation of two agreers to one another and to the class of persons whose rights they acknowledge and defend is the same whether the right in question is controverted or not. Whether it is a right to vote or a right to abortion: the structure is tripolar either way.

But now, returning to our main subject, where such a right *is* controverted, those who recognize it find themselves in relations both with some whose right it is, and with others who are wronging them. This is the predicament of anyone who makes a political judgment on a topic of controversy. It is therefore also the context of political compromise.

IV. LIBERAL DEMOCRACY

IV.1. Institutions

I have so far said nothing about liberal democracy, a theme that often frames the discussion of political compromise.[19] My attempt to reframe the topic by placing it in the context of bilateral decision-making might seem to ignore all of the complexities that characterize political disagreement—and therefore also compromise—in societies with democratic pretensions. I do not deny that such disagreements are much more complicated than one about how to dispose of a flowerpot. My only claim is that they are not *less* complicated—they are *at least* that complicated. There is nothing about the context of a liberal democracy that transforms what would otherwise be a tripolar relation of right into a merely bipolar relation.

One sort of complexity mentioned in the literature concerns the institutions of political representation. In the introduction to their recent book on legislative compromise—a book that focuses on the machinations of the US Congress—Amy Gutmann and Dennis Thompson write:

> The character of legislative compromise is shaped by its distinctive democratic and institutional context. It takes place in an ongoing institution in which the members have responsibilities to constituents and their political parties, maintain continuing relationships with one another, and deal concurrently with a wide range of issues that have multiple parts and long-range effects. The dynamics of negotiation in these circumstances differ from the patterns found in the two-agent, one-time interactions that are more common in most discussions of compromise.[20]

Gutmann and Thompson are sensitive to a legislator's obligation to those across the proverbial aisle, with whom she and her associates (her party and her constituents) need to compromise. What they do not mention here is any obligation, on the part of a legislator (or her party or her constituents), to those who are vulnerable to unjust legislation.[21] It does not belong to the "democratic and institutional context" of legislative compromise, as Gutmann and Thompson present it, that people are affected, potentially unjustly, by the laws that result from the back and forth between the compromisers.

This is a clear example of the bipolar model. As Gutmann and Thompson frame the issue, there are only decision-makers, who have moral convictions, and who compromise with each other to reach a decision. In reality, though, in addition to the decision-makers, there is someone on the receiving end of every such decision. Gutmann and Thompson's leading examples of legislative compromise pertain to taxes and healthcare. These are matters in which justice is at stake. They concern the distribution of benefits and burdens of social cooperation. Depending on how such an issue is resolved, someone could be wronged.

In the passage quoted above, Gutmann and Thompson mention three features of the institutional context in which legislative compromise takes place. These features do indeed distinguish legislative compromise from "the two-agent, one-time interactions that are more common in most discussions of compromise." But acknowledging these complexities is compatible with recognizing genuine obligations to genuine third parties.

First, Gutmann and Thompson allude to the relation between a representative, her political party, and those whom she represents. These three terms—party, representative, constituent—are terms for roles in a decision-making process, or in a decision-making institution. It is in a process of decision-making (e.g., law-making), or in the context of a decision-making institution (e.g., the legislature), that a representative is supposed to represent her constituents. Her role is to act on their behalf while the decision (the law) is being made—not to suffer on their behalf once it is in place. Meanwhile, the relevant sort of political party is an organization of decision-makers: its membership is exhausted by those who represent and those who are represented in the decision-making process. Acknowledging the complex relations between various roles in a decision-making process is compatible with thinking that this decision-making, like all decision-making, carries with it the obligation, on the part of the decision-makers, not to wrong those who are affected by the decision.

Second, Gutmann and Thompson allude to the fact that legislators—who are, after all, career politicians—"maintain continuing relationships with one another." But this is not a reason to think that legislators (or those whom they represent, or their parties) have no responsibility to those who are affected by the law. In general, the fact that two individuals (or two groups) have a long-term and mutually beneficial relationship to one another does not mean that it is impossible for them to wrong third parties when they make decisions together. If anything, the duty not to wrong those affected by one's decisions would seem to be especially weighty for legislators, whose decisions are enshrined in law and violently enforced by a coercive state apparatus.

Finally, Gutmann and Thompson note that the legislators "deal with a wide range of issues that have multiple parts and long-range effects." But since these long-range effects affect people—people who could be wronged by being so affected—such people should have a role in a theory of what, when, why, and how it is legitimate to compromise.

IV.2. Democracy

There is nothing about the context of democratic decision-making that exempts one from the duty not to wrong the people who are affected by the decisions that one is helping to make.

If three people on a balcony agree to hold a vote on whether to dispose of a flowerpot by pushing into the street below, and they vote, and it is fair, this does not nullify the participants' obligations to the people in the street below. The people in the street below did not participate in the decision-making process, but that is not the point. The point is that they are the ones in danger of being wronged by the decision. A person can be wronged by a decision in spite of having had a role in the decision-making. If three people on a balcony decide by voting that one of them—the tall one—is to be pushed over the edge, the fact that there was a vote does not make the outcome anything other than murder. "But we voted" is not a defense.

The same applies to the democratically instituted policies of a state. Some such policies affect non-citizens. A state's military exploits, environmental policies, immigration and asylum laws, international trade agreements, embargoes, gifts of foreign aid, etc., affect people in other parts of the world. Such people do not participate in the decision-making process, and they are not represented by anyone who does (on *any* theory of representation). But that they are not represented is not the important point: the important point is that they are the ones affected. And they can be wronged.[22] Others of the democratically instituted policies of a state primarily affect its citizens. Someone might wonder whether citizens can be wronged by such policies. The answer is that they can, if the policies can be unjust: for, there is no such thing as an unjust law that is not unjust to someone. The question therefore reduces to this: Can a democratically made law be unjust? One could claim that so long as the decision-making process is fair and democratic, the outcome is necessarily just; however, this is an extreme position, which not many theorists, and not many others, will find remotely plausible.[23] It is enough for my purposes to observe that this position is the only way to avoid the conclusion that there is a third party—a party exposed to injustice—in democratically made decisions. Given that there is such a party, there is someone whom the decision-makers have an obligation not to wrong.

IV.3. Respect

The liberal refrain that we must live on terms of mutual respect with those with whom we disagree (provided their position is sufficiently reasonable) is another important theme in the literature on compromise, and it is part of what suggests the standard bipolar model. But if there is a second party with whom one disagrees on a matter of public concern where justice is at stake, then there is also a third party whom, in one's own eyes, the second party is wronging. For, as one sees it, the second party supports an injustice against that third party.

This is not to deny that one owes respect to the second party: the liberal refrain is fine as far as it goes, but it is only half of the story. For, even if one must live on respectful terms with those who *support* (what one regards as) injustice, still, one must also live on respectful terms with those who *suffer* (what one regards as) injustice.[24] It is not a coincidence that one regards oneself as living among both groups of people. There could not be anyone who suffered injustice, unless there were those who supported it. Conversely, there could not be anyone who supported injustice, unless there were those who suffered it.

Acknowledging this is neutral with regard to substantive conceptions of justice. It does not presuppose anything about what the important injustices are, or who suffers them, or who supports them. Any substantive conception of justice orients one with respect to *two* distinct parties, and it dictates that one treat them *both* with all due respect. The tripolar relations of right, discussed in section II.3 above, are mirrored in relations of respect, reciprocity, and mutual recognition.

V. POLITICAL COMPROMISE AS A NECESSARY EVIL

V.1. Though Evil, Necessary

Having situated political compromise in the broader theoretical context of bilateral decision-making, having noted its connection to tripolar relations of right, and having observed that these relations are a feature of democratic decisions, let us now consider the kind of good that compromise is.

Common sense suggests that political compromise is the kind of good that is normally called a necessary evil. It suggests that making a concession to one's political opponents is like throwing one's cargo overboard in a storm: it is something one should sometimes do, but only if one is forced to—that is, only if it is required to avoid something worse. There are two positions opposed to this. The first is that one should never make even forced concessions. The second is that, in addition to making forced concessions, one should sometimes also make unforced concessions.

To adjudicate between these three valuations of compromise, it is helpful to adopt the perspective of someone who is in danger of being wronged by the decision on which a compromise is sought. (Remember, we are only interested in cases where there *is* such a person.) The perspective of a third party provides a useful vantage point from which to survey the competing views.

Suppose that one is in danger of being wronged by a decision where a political compromise might settle a dispute. Suppose, further, that one is presented with an array of potential political allies of one kind or another—e.g., political parties, activist organizations, trade unions, legislators, elected officials, fellow citizens. And suppose, finally, that these political agents all recognize the injustice to which one is exposed, and that all of them deplore it, but that among them there is this difference: some will countenance no concessions; some only forced concessions; and some both forced and unforced ones. Who should one choose as an ally? It would be foolish to choose as an ally someone who stands aloof from any effort that promises less than perfect justice. For, even if things are bad now, it might require significant effort to keep them from getting worse. And, all things being equal, improvements to the status quo are welcome. (Of course, improvements can be offered with conditions that make them unacceptable; but if the conditions were removed, it would always be preferable to suffer less injustice.) In that case, one wants an ally who is willing to fight for all forward progress. This will not be someone who sniffs at every compromise. Concessions are often necessary to avoid losses, and to make gains. For someone on the receiving end of injustice, they are—unfortunately—a genuine necessity.

V.2. Though Necessary, Evil

Theorists who deny the commonsense view of compromise tend to do so from the opposite direction. They do not deny the necessity of making concessions to political opponents. Rather, they claim that it is sometimes good to offer up concessions even though one is not forced to do so.

This position circulates as the doctrine of principled compromise. The doctrine recommends that political agents make unforced concessions on the supposed grounds that there is something good about accommodating the opposing side of political disputes. Patrick Dobel offers a compendium of reasons for making unforced concessions:

> Principled compromise can occur for good reasons separate from a sheer concern with another's power. Individuals can compromise because they respect the personal autonomy or dignity of other citizens, or because the compromise ethos extends and strengthens liberal and democratic life. Humility and conscientiousness can justify compromise. People also can compromise to protect a system of institutions and practices that give life to liberal and democratic ideals.[25]

It is easy to see why, if one focused exclusively on the parties to a compromise, it might seem positively virtuous to make unforced concessions; and conversely, why it might seem "ruthless" to refuse ever to do so.[26] But as soon as one considers the perspective some-one exposed to injustice, things look otherwise.

A principled compromiser is the last ally that one would choose if one found oneself on the receiving end of injustice. Those who fail to appreciate the necessity of compromise, and who hold themselves aloof from anything less than a perfectly just resolu-tion, are useless most of the time, but at least they will not betray you: there is no danger that they will freely and voluntarily throw their own weight behind the injustice to which you are exposed. By contrast, the principled compromiser does that sort of thing as a matter of principle. Even when it is clear that a concession will contribute nothing to a just resolution of this or any other conflict (either immediately or in the long term); even when it is clear that it is a step in the wrong direction; and even when it is clear that the concession could be avoided—even then, the principled compro-miser thinks it is sometimes right to accommodate the opposition.

Why? "Because it is good to accommodate the opposition." Why? *It does not matter.* It does not matter what reason a politi-cal agent provides for offering unforced concessions in a matter where justice is at stake, whether it be to demonstrate respect for those with opposed convictions,[27] to acknowledge the moral com-plexity of the issue,[28] to spread the spirit of compromise,[29] or to promote some democratic value.[30] Anyone who thinks it is in prin-ciple good to accommodate the opposition—for any reason, no matter how lofty—is an ally to beware of, if one finds oneself on the receiving end of injustice.

The point is not merely that unforced concessions are unwel-come to those who are on the receiving end of injustice. Unforced concessions are unwelcome to those who are victims of injustice because unforced concessions are an additional injustice against them. There is, after all, a political agent who is freely and know-ingly lending its support to a measure that does them wrong.

This is also clear if we consider the question from the point of view of a person who is deciding whether or not to accommodate the opposition. If what one's political opponents want is a wrong against a third party, and one sees this, then one cannot give one's opponents what they want without wronging that third party. It is one thing to be forced to give it up. If one is not forced—if it is a gift—then, no matter why one offers it, one is wronging the third party. For, again, if one party freely helps a second to wrong a third, the first wrongs the third. It makes no difference *why* the first helps the second: the reason can be as high-minded as you like.

Where justice is at stake, political compromise is a necessary evil, as common sense suggests. The doctrine of principled compromise, which recommends offering unforced concessions, only seems plausible if one forgets about (or denies) the existence of third parties. Once third parties are acknowledged, the injustice of such a recommendation should be obvious.

VI. Bipartisanship

The doctrine of principled compromise is sometimes an expression of the intuition that it is good if public policy has a broad base of support.[31] In the context of US politics, a similar intuition manifests itself in the valorization of bipartisanship. There is a grain of truth in this intuition, which needs to be acknowledged. However, once we have identified the relevant grain of truth, we will see why it does not suggest that any political agent should think of compromise as anything but a necessary evil when justice is at stake.

The grain of truth is this: while partisan justice is good, bipartisan justice is better. It is good if just legislation is in place. And it is good even if it is held in place by the majority party alone, against the will of the minority. But it is *even better* if both parties support it.

The good in question here is not merely instrumental. If women do not have the right to vote—as was the case until recently in the United States (1920)—then achieving women's suffrage is good, even if, when it becomes an established right, it remains a contested political issue, and a significant portion of society still opposes it. But so long as a significant portion of society still opposes it, the victory is incomplete. This is so for two reasons, the first of which is instrumental and the second of which is not: first, because a decision that lacks broad support is vulnerable to countercurrents that might reverse it; but second, because no one wants to live in a society where such rights are observed only grudgingly by a significant portion of one's fellow citizens—one might settle for it, but no one hopes for it.

Someone who supports a law because the law is just does not aspire merely that it become law, and so, does not aim to win the minimum amount of political support necessary to carry the day—a bare majority, as it might be. A just law is justifiable to anyone, and one's aim is to win the support of everyone, so that the law will express the will of all or most of one's fellow citizens. The fulfillment of such an ambition might take years, decades, or centuries, but that is the ambition. Admittedly, not all laws codify a right. But such cases bring out something that is true in general. If one supports *anything* on the grounds that it is just, then one's aim is not to win the bare minimum support necessary to carry the day. One's aim is to win as much support as possible—unanimous support, if possible. It is inherently good to live in a society where justice not only prevails, but is supported by all or many.

That is the grain of truth in intuition that there is something good about broad-based and bipartisan support of public policy. The problem is that the opposite is also true. While partisan injustice is bad, bipartisan injustice is worse. It is bad if unjust legislation is in place. And it is bad even if it is held in place by the majority party alone, against the will of the minority party. But it is *even worse* if both parties support it. In a two-party system of government, bipartisan support of a just policy is the best possible state of affairs, but bipartisan support of an unjust policy is the worst possible state of affairs.

And notice, the latter is not merely instrumentally bad. It is, of course, instrumentally bad if there is widespread opposition to something that is just. It is instrumentally bad because it will be difficult to rectify the injustice. But that is not all. It is inherently bad to live in a society where a prevailing injustice is supported by all or by many of one's fellow citizens.

The value of bipartisanship cannot be assessed in abstraction from the matter on which the two parties agree. The same holds more generally. Broad support is, alternatively, the crowning achievement or a damning indictment of multilateral decision-making. Its value is conditional on the justice or injustice of the substantive matter at hand. Since uncontested justice is better than contested justice, since contested justice is better than contested injustice, and since contested injustice is less bad than uncontested injustice, the absence of contestation (partisanship, faction, conflict, strife, polarization, and so on) may be either bad or good. Justice sets a double standard.

This accounts for the intuition that it is good for public policy to have a broad base of support. It *is* good—and inherently good—provided the policy is just. On the other hand, and no less important, it is bad—and inherently bad—if it is unjust. Since the relevant good is conditional on the justice of the substantive matter at hand, it cannot provide a reason to accommodate political opponents by making unforced concessions on decisions in which justice is at stake. Moreover, since the justice of the substantive matter is determined by reference to third parties, the value of bipartisanship can only be assessed in the context of tripolar relations of right.

NOTES

1. For a more precise articulation of the core features of compromise, see Simon Căbulea May, "Moral Compromise, Civic Friendship, and Political Reconciliation," *Critical Review of International Social and Political Philosophy* 14 (2011): 581–602, pp. 582–585.

2. David Luban, "Bargaining and Compromise: Recent Work on Negotiation and Informal Justice," *Philosophy & Public Affairs* 14 (1985): 397–416.

3. Arthur Kuflik, "Morality and Compromise," in *Compromise in Ethics, Law, and Politics: NOMOS XXI*, ed. J. Ronald Pennock and John Chapman (New York: New York University Press, 1979), 38–65; Martin Benjamin, *Splitting the Difference: Compromise and Integrity in Ethics and Politics* (Lawrence: University Press of Kansas, 1990).

4. Theodore M. Benditt, "Compromising Interests and Principles," in *Compromise in Ethics, Law, and Politics: NOMOS XXI*, ed. J. Ronald Pennock and John Chapman (New York: New York University Press, 1979), 26–37.

5. Ronald Dworkin, *Law's Empire* (Cambridge, MA: Harvard University Press, 1986), 177–224; Samantha Besson, "Four Arguments against Compromising Justice Internally," *Oxford Journal of Legal Studies* 23 (2003): 211–241.

6. Amy Gutmann and Dennis Thompson, "Mindsets of Political Compromise," *Perspectives on Politics* 8 (2010): 1125–1143.

7. Simon Căbulea May, "Principled Compromise and the Abortion Controversy," *Philosophy & Public Affairs* 33 (2005): 317–348.

8. Perhaps the most developed defense of principled compromise is J. Patrick Dobel, *Compromise and Political Action: Political Morality in Liberal and Democratic Life* (Savage, MD: Rowman & Littlefield, 1990). Support for some version of the doctrine is often found in discussions of abortion: see Amy Gutmann and Dennis Thompson, *Democracy and Disagreement* (Cambridge, MA: Belknap Press, 1996); and see George Sher, "Subsidized Abortion: Moral Rights and Moral Compromise," *Philosophy & Public Affairs* 10 (1981): 361–372. Gutmann and Thompson and Sher are among the many authors discussed by Simon Căbulea May in "Principled Compromise and the Abortion Controversy," the most prominent criticism of principled compromise. May's criticism of the doctrine appears to accept the bipolar framework that is the main target of my own discussion. (At any rate, May does not appeal to third parties as such.) This is worth noting for two reasons. On the one hand, it suggests that the bipolar framework does not lead one inexorably to the doctrine of principled compromise. On the other hand, it alerts us to the possibility that the bipolar framework may yet be the source of the problem: for, it may present the issues in such a way that principled compromise is, though not inevitable, nevertheless a natural place to end up. That is in fact my suspicion. For the latest endorsement of principled compromise, see Eric Beerbohm, "The Problem of Clean Hands" (this volume).

9. This would appear to be Cicero's verdict: "Of injustice there are two kinds, — one, that of those who inflict injury; the other, that of those who do not, if they can, repel injury from those on whom it is inflicted . . . [H]e who does not, if he can, ward off or resist the injury offered to another, is as much in fault as if he were to desert his parents, or his friends, or his country." *De Officiis*, trans. Peabody (Boston: Little Brown and Company, 1887), Bk. I, Ch. 7.

10. As Isaiah Berlin put it: "If men never disagreed about the ends of life . . . the studies to which the Chichele Chair of Social and Political Theory is dedicated could scarcely have been conceived. For these studies spring from, and thrive on, discord. . . . Where ends are agreed, the only questions left are those of means, and these are not political but technical, that is to say, capable of being settled by experts or machines, like arguments between engineers and doctors." "Two Concepts of Liberty," an inaugural lecture delivered before the University of Oxford on October 31, 1958 (Oxford, UK: Clarendon Press, 1959).

11. Amy Gutmann and Dennis Thompson, *Democracy and Disagreement*; Sher, "Subsidized Abortion: Moral Rights and Moral Compromise"; Roger Wertheimer, "Understanding the Abortion Argument," in *The Rights and*

Wrongs of Abortion, ed. Marshall Cohen et al. (Princeton, NJ: Princeton University Press, 1974), pp. 23–51.

12. Andrew Lister, *Canadian Journal of Philosophy* 37 (2007): 1–34.

13. Amy Gutmann and Dennis Thompson, *The Spirit of Compromise* (Princeton, NJ: Princeton University Press, 2013).

14. Ibid.

15. Thomas Smith, "The Compromise Principle in Politics," Edmund J. James Lectures on Government, Second Series (Urbana: University of Illinois Press, 1941), 29–49. See also Richard Bellamy and Martin Hollis, "Consensus, Neutrality and Compromise, *Critical Review of International Social and Political Philosophy* 1 (1998): 1, 54–78.

16. Gutmann and Thompson, *Why Deliberative Democracy?* (Princeton, NJ: Princeton University Press, 2004), pp. 160–187. See also Simon Căbulea May, "Moral Compromise, Civic Friendship and Political Reconciliation," *Critical Review of International Social and Political Philosophy* 14 (2011): 581–602.

17. Avishai Margalit, *On Compromise and Rotten Compromises* (Princeton, NJ: Princeton University Press, 2010).

18. The point on which I say that both sides should agree is stated clearly by Robert P. George, an opponent of abortion: "When it comes to issues such as abortion, no moral compromise is possible without doing injury to someone's rights (that is, the rights of the fetus if, in truth, abortion violates the rights of the unborn, or the rights of the woman if, in truth, women have a right to abortion)." See "Democracy and Moral Disagreement: Reciprocity, Slavery and Abortion," in *Deliberative Politics*, ed. Stephen Macedo (Oxford: Oxford University Press, 1999), pp. 184–197, at p. 192.

19. Bellamy and Hollis declare that "compromise is the lifeblood of liberal democracies," adding that "compromise is the stuff of both democracy, with its concern that everyone has a stake, and liberalism, defending individual and group freedom." See "Consensus, Neutrality and Compromise."

20. Gutmann and Thompson, *The Spirit of Compromise*, 11.

21. At one point, Gutmann and Thompson express concern about the effects of legislation on those, such as immigrants, who are not represented in the legislative process (ibid. 47–48). But what raises special concerns about immigrants is not the fact that they are vulnerable to unjust laws. There is nothing special in that: on any plausible view, *citizens* are vulnerable to unjust laws. What raises special concerns about immigrants is, apparently, that they are vulnerable to laws that no representative of theirs had a hand in making. Gutmann and Thompson do not suggest any reason for thinking that a person's having a representative in the legislature

should make a non-issue of that person's vulnerability to unjust laws. Else-where Gutmann and Thompson say that public officials "cannot credibly deny their primary and direct responsibility for securing the well-being of their society, according to some combination of their own and their constituents' best moral lights," which might suggest that lawmakers (and their constituents) stand in relations of right with those whom their deci-sions affect (108). But it is not at all clear whether Gutmann and Thomp-son mean that public officials are responsible *to* the affected people, or merely *for* them. (A gardener may have a responsibility *for* securing the well-being of a rosebush without having responsibility *to* the rosebush.) However such passages are to be read, they are asides in a book about the ways in which compromisers should think about each other.

22. Can they not? Someone might say "no" on the grounds that any-thing goes in international relations. But, notice, that is not a view about democracy. If two states—one a democracy, the other a monarchy—ally to invade a third, in order to plunder and divide its natural resources, there is no plausible reason for saying that the actions of the monarchy are an injustice, but that those of the democracy are not: it was the same action (invasion), for the same reason (plunder), performed by both.

23. Dworkin writes: "Some say that justice has no meaning apart from fairness, that in politics, as in roulette, whatever happens through fair procedures is just. That is the extreme of the idea called justice as fair-ness. Others think that the only test of fairness in politics is the test of result, that no procedure is fair unless it is likely to produce political de-cisions that meet some independent test of justice. That is the opposite extreme, of fairness as justice. Most political philosophers—and I think most people—take the intermediate view that fairness and justice are to some degree independent of one another, so that fair institutions some-times produce unjust decisions and unfair institutions just ones." Dwor-kin, *Law's Empire*, 177.

24. The same could be said about the value of inclusion. Just as those with whom one disagrees are not the only ones toward whom one needs to demonstrate respect, they are not the only ones whose inclusion one needs to secure.

25. Dobel, *Compromise and Political Action*, 80.

26. Dobel likens T. V. Smith to Machiavelli on the grounds that "Smith argued that one should never compromise unless forced by necessity" (80). For the charge of ruthlessness, see Beerbohm, "The Problem of Clean Hands," this volume.

27. Colin Bird, "Mutual Respect and Neutral Justification," *Ethics* 107 (1996): 62–96, p. 92; Bellamy and Hollis, "Consensus, Neutrality and Compromise," pp. 54–79, at p. 76.

28. Dobel, *Compromise and Political Action*, 89-90.
29. Gutmann and Thompson, *The Spirit of Compromise*.
30. Beerbohm, "The Problem of Clean Hands," this volume.
31. Beerbohm defends principled compromise partly on the ground that "we place independent value on broad agreement as to the content of the law" (6). He suggests that "the democratic value of *co-ownership* [of the law]" might "explain the force of the elusive political virtue of two-party systems: bipartisanship" (33). See Beerbohm, "The Problem of Clean Hands," this volume.

3

THE MORAL DISTINCTIVENESS OF
LEGISLATED LAW

DAVID DYZENHAUS

Of Persons Artificiall, some have their words and actions *Owned* by those they represent. And then the Person is the *Actor*, and he that owneth his words and actions, is the AUTHOR: In which case the Actor acteth by Authority, and as the Right of possession, is called Dominion; so the Right of doing any action is called AUTHORITY and sometimes *warrant*. So that by Authority, is always understood a Right of doing any act; and *done by Authority*, done by Commission, or Licence from him whose right it is.[1]

In this passage from chapter 16 of *Leviathan*, "Of Persons, Authors, and things Personated," Hobbes set out the nub of one of his main innovations in political philosophy, which I shall refer to as "the authorization argument." The argument is that citizens are the authors of all that their lawmakers do, because the lawmakers represent or personate the state, and the individuals have given their authorization to the state "without stint"[2] to make judgments about right and wrong on their behalf. Since the law made by the sovereign lawmaker is made with right, Hobbes, relying on the etymology of *ius/iustitia*, asserts that the citizens whose right is the foundation of the authority of the legislative actors are disentitled from accusing their sovereign legislator of injustice. The right with which lawmakers make law is the citizens' right. Hence, citizens as authors own the sovereign's acts as if these acts had been done by themselves, though only in the sense that these acts will and should be attributed to them.[3]

Hobbes is generally reputed to be a kind of legal positivist, an early exponent of the command theory of law according to which the law is no more than the commands of a legally unlimited sovereign. If that reputation is right, the authorization argument seems to make him a moral as well as a legal positivist. All there is to law is the positive law made by our lawmakers, and all there is to morality, or at least to that part of morality which citizens must regard as compulsory or not up to them to decide for themselves, is to be found in the commands.

In *In Our Name: The Ethics of Democracy*,[4] Eric Beerbohm relies on Hobbes's authorization argument in order to get to the conclusion that in a democracy we own what our lawmakers do.[5] "If," he says, "I consent to be personated by another agent, I own her words and actions."[6] However, Beerbohm departs from Hobbes because in his hands the authorization argument is meant to bring home to citizens that they are complicit in the injustices wrought by their lawmakers. He thus rejects Hobbes's moral positivism since on his view there are standards of justice independent of the content of the law to which we as citizens have access.

In Our Name thus deliberately creates a tension that Hobbes regarded as excluded by the logic of the authorization argument. We own the law that our lawmakers make even when it is unjust. Indeed, Beerbohm's version of the authorization argument is meant in part to get citizens to see that because they own what their lawmakers do, they should be spurred to make themselves into better citizens—availing themselves of existing democratic mechanisms, perhaps even creating new ones. In other words, if there is a disjunction between your moral ideals and the legislation you cannot disown, you should pay better attention in the future to your civic responsibilities. Given this difference between his position and Hobbes's, as well as an argument that the degree of individual complicity can vary,[7] he need concede only a "grain of truth" to Hobbes's version of the authorization argument.[8]

I shall try to show that one needs to take more than a grain from Hobbes's authorization argument if one is going to take anything at all and that Beerbohm's own position is weakened because he does not take enough, as becomes apparent in his "The Problem of Clean Hands: Negotiated Compromise in Lawmaking," chapter 1 of this volume. There Beerbohm elaborates another argument

he had sketched in *In Our Name*—that lawmakers can't help but
compromise their moral ideals in order to get legislation enacted.
In a paragraph that foreshadowed "The Problem of Clean Hands,"
he states, quoting Barbara Herman, that politics "requires deep
compromises and shady alliances . . . Individuals acting as the
agents of the larger entities can't hew to moral principles and
serve the ends of their office."[9] He goes on:

> Law making is a collective enterprise defined as much by the give-
> and-take of working out the contents of a bill as the final act of vot-
> ing for its passage. If lawmakers are to be constrained by a subset
> of principles, how are they to act in settings where horse-trading,
> logrolling, and other brands of compromise—moral, tactical, and
> strategic—are normative?[10]

By "normative," Beerbohm seemed to mean that lawmakers are
morally justified, perhaps even under a moral duty to compromise,
and that this is the case both when they have to act immorally in
order to achieve their moral ideals and when they have to compromise those very ideals. They are required, in other words, to make
moral compromises both with respect to process and to substance,
procedural compromises and substantive compromises.

This interpretation is confirmed by "The Problem of Clean
Hands" in which he argues that compromise of one's moral ideals in the legislative process is a fact of political life, but is to be
welcomed rather than deplored since "compromise can, given
certain background conditions, make a piece of legislation more
democratic."[11] Moreover, it is "necessary for sustaining valuable
democratic relationships."[12] "The practice of compromise . . . is
a response to the value we place in deciding together, even when
serious disagreements remain. Democracy's value can only be captured relationally in the equal sharing in authority over our political institutions."[13]

These ideas, Beerbohm notes, will repel "purists," those who
refuse to take part in the activity of compromise "as a way of cancelling their moral connection to an objectionable policy."[14] The
ideas will also be rejected by "strategists," who are willing to make
compromises, but only those that are strictly necessary for them to
get their way to the greatest extent possible. There is, however, a

third character available, who shows the way between unrealistic purism and the too realistic or pragmatic strategist, the "practitioner," who "attempts to comply with the letter and spirit of the constitutive rules of compromise."[15] "This follows not from 'a calculation of her long-term political goals,'" but because "of the value of relating to her co-citizens on justifiable terms."[16]

Beerbohm also argues that legislators have "a weightier moral reason to countenance compromise than ordinary citizens."[17] It is morally legitimate for you as a citizen to be a purist, but your legislators are morally bound to consider compromise. This argument might come as a relief to some, as only the legislators must get their hands dirty with compromise, thus leaving the citizens morally untainted. But Beerbohm does not let citizens off the moral hook. On the basis of his own version of the authorization argument, he proposes that citizens co-own their political institutions. Legislators stand to citizens in an agency/principal relationship such that if legislators must be practitioners of moral compromise, the citizens on behalf of whom they act own their actions.

If it were immoral for legislators to compromise, we the people would then have to insist that legislators be purists. But the argument that legislators have a moral reason to compromise, perhaps even a moral duty, permits Beerbohm not only to retain the argument of *In Our Name*, but also to suggest that the two arguments work in a democratic tandem. Legislators must compromise because they co-own the statute that is the product of their activity. But citizens cannot insulate themselves from this practice. They share "moral liability" for the compromises: "The problem that emerges is *ours*. It's owned by democratic citizens concerned with complicity in legislated injustice."[18]

It is, however, not that clear what citizens are supposed to do with this realization, nor precisely what the moral stakes are. Beerbohm does say that the "admirable feature of purists is their recognition that there are genuinely 'rotten' compromises,"[19] thus adopting Avishai Margalit's distinction between political compromises for the sake of peace that are justifiable and compromises that can never be justified because they "establish or maintain an inhuman regime."[20] And I take it that Beerbohm does not consider it permissible for legislators to make rotten compromises, even though it is the case (as he makes clear in *In Our Name*) that immoral and inhuman laws, whether the product of compromise or not, are laws that citizens might have to accept were enacted in their name. In such cases, the prescription follows that citizens should act to ensure that what lawmakers do is more in line with what citizens think should be done, or, perhaps, act to ensure that what lawmakers do cannot be attributed to them, because the citizens have effectively disowned the lawmakers' acts. However, if what I called above procedural or substantive compromises of moral ideals are either morally permitted or required for legislators, it is difficult to understand why citizens should be worried about the fact that they have to own the compromises made in their name, unless the issue is (as he appears to suggest at times) that lawmakers must do what citizens should not morally speaking do, but still the citizens have to own what the lawmakers do.

In addition, there is an important issue that his argument fails to confront, at least insofar as it is meant to illuminate the practice of legislative compromise in democracies in general. For the practice of compromise that he describes might be rather localized, shaped as it is by the peculiarities of the US political system.

Consider, for example, Philip Pettit's point in an essay, "Varieties of public representation," that the "representational priority adopted in a system of government is going to have an enormous influence on how the system and the society as a whole works."[21] Pettit contrasts the Westminster and the Washington systems to show that in the latter, lawmakers are much more subject to local pressures, more tempted to grandstand, more subject to lobby pressure, and less responsive to general (as opposed to local) public opinion.[22] The point I want to extract is, however, bigger than that the practice of compromise will be different in Washington from Westminster. For it also the case that the legislative outputs of Washington are likely to be botched in a way that looks strange to those accustomed to the Westminster system.

In this light, we might need to take into account another kind of compromise—the "botched compromise." This category has to be divided into at least two subcategories, according to the substance/process distinction: substantively botched compromises, in which there is some incoherence in the moral goals that are the product of the lawmaking process; procedurally botched compromises, in which the goals plausibly advance the public interest, but the means provided are insufficient or even undermining of the goals. Of course, some compromises might be botched in both ways. But they differ from legislation that is not botched on either of these dimensions, but whose moral goals fall short of some moral ideal, perhaps so short as to be considered a rotten but unbotched compromise.

My claim is not that the outputs of the Westminster system are going to be morally less compromised in the sense of not being the product of compromised moral ideals. Indeed, the Westminster system might make easier the passage of what we can think of as morally dramatic legislation, legislation that effectively changes the moral course of a society. Consider how the *minority* Conservative government in the United Kingdom was able to force through legislation that has radically changed higher education, a change that many view as a radical compromise of moral ideals, but which was not subject within the legislative process to Washington-style pressures that might have mitigated that compromise, perhaps by deliberately botching it. We might say that in one sense of moral compromise—the dramatic compromise of moral ideals—the Westminster system is more vulnerable than the Washington system, since it is not as subject to compromise within the legislative process. But, on the other hand, it is more capable at delivering morally beneficial legislation than the Washington system.

Now one could respond that these remarks go wrong in supposing that there is some set of moral ideals that stands outside of the democratic legislative process and which we can use to measure the extent to which a law either compromises or advances morality. And to the extent that Beerbohm suggests that there is "a widespread commitment to the idea that healthy civic life involves some accommodation of the sincerely-held views of others,"[23] he might be taken to be suggesting that morality is the output of an appropriately designed legislative process, rather than the set of standards that we use to assess the outcomes of the process. In other words, the more views that are included in and that have an impact on the process, the better it will be from the standpoint of a democratic moral theory. With that established, you as citizen should ensure that the product that you will under certain conditions own is a product that you feel morally comfortable with. And if there is a disjunction between your moral ideals and the legislation you cannot disown, you should pay better attention in the future to your civic responsibilities.

If Beerbohm were to be tempted by this kind of response, he would come closer to the Hobbesian position I described above as moral positivism. We have to own as just whatever our legislative representatives churn out. His position would differ from the one usually associated with Hobbesian authoritarianism only in that it is qualified by his commitment to democracy, indeed, to a much more vibrant democracy than any that exists today. In other words, because we own these legislative products, we should ensure that what we own is what we want to own; and democracy makes that possible.

Notice in this regard that Hobbes does not require citizens to believe that the sovereign's laws are morally sound—that they do represent "right reason," but rather, only that they act as if the laws were morally sound.[24] In addition, that the citizen is barred from accusing the sovereign of injustice does not mean that the sovereign's laws are immune to moral scrutiny. While the sovereign cannot commit injustice, he can, Hobbes takes pains to point out, commit iniquity, thus offending against one of the laws of nature, which as a package make up the "true and onely Moral Philosophy."[25] Finally, Hobbes is not averse to arguments that show how institutional arrangements might serve to align the sovereign's determination of the public interest with the citizen's sense of what is appropriate. His argument in chapter 19 of *Leviathan* for the superiority of monarchy over democratic and aristocratic forms of government rests partly on the claim that in a monarchy it is more likely that the public interest and the private interest will coincide. He is therefore open to an argument that we should adopt the political structure that is most likely to make the laws that we own the laws that we in fact want to own.

Two features of Hobbes's argument in chapter 19 are worth emphasizing. First, it is a different kind of argument from the authorization argument. The latter is normatively prior in that it tells us why citizens own the laws their lawmakers make whatever the form of government, while the former is more a prudential argument about how best to ensure that the laws have a content of which we approve. Second, Hobbes raises a concern about the democratic form of government. It can invite factional disputes, and the number of individuals who make up the sovereign body makes the democratic sovereign much more prone to lobbying.[26] My point here is not to endorse these prudential arguments. Rather, I aim to highlight that Hobbes wanted to avoid fracturing the unitary nature of sovereign authority that one risks if one gets the prudential argument wrong. And I believe that this kind of concern is directly raised by Beerbohm's book and by "The Problem of Clean Hands."

In *In Our Name*, Beerbohm emphasizes a "considerable" "gap" for us, that is, for us democrats, between authorization and authorship. Just as it is the case that I do not coauthor the biography that I authorize you to write, so I do not necessarily coauthor the legislation that my legislature writes.[27] There can be authorization, that is, without control. Hence, I am a coauthor to the extent that I exercise control over those I authorize to act in my name, including legislators.

I think that something has gone wrong here. If I give my lawyer a blanket authorization to negotiate a contract on my behalf, even though I do not write a single term of the contract and exercise no control over the process, each term will be attributed to me. That people might know that I did not write a word of the contract does not get in the way of their treating each term as if I had written it. In contrast, authorizing a biography has more to do with granting an author privileged access to material and to people, including often the subject of the biography. Authorizing it does not attribute the content to the subject, as is especially clear when the family of a deceased subject authorizes a biography. If the subject authorizes, at most one can infer some advance stamp of approval, but we know that on occasion such subjects have indignantly withdrawn that stamp.

The legislative role seems, then, more like that of the lawyer with blanket authorization than like that of the authorized biographer. The clients might fire the lawyer who makes a contract whose terms are not to their liking, just as citizens in a democracy can try to kick out or otherwise punish legislators who made a law that they think unjust or wrong in some other way. But the clients own that contract and the citizens own that law. Moreover, while the clients can in the future narrow the scope of the authorization they give to their lawyers, citizens must continue giving blanket authorizations to legislators. A legislator or group of legislators might come into office on the basis of a promise to implement a very specific set of policies. But that promise does not constrain their authority to use their independent judgment even if breaking it means that they will be turfed from office at the first available opportunity.

Moreover, it might be the case that the distinction between authorization and authorship on which Beerbohm relies, so that he can drive a wedge between authorization and authorship/control, is one that Hobbes explicitly and for good reason rejects. It is not, as Beerbohm puts it, that "even Hobbes refuses to treat authorship and authorization as coextensive terms."[28] Rather, Hobbes insists that they be treated as coextensive despite the fact that there is no actual control or authorship. As Beerbohm knows, regarding them as coextensive requires adopting a fiction.[29] But without that fiction, certain kinds of important legal and political relationships would not be possible. I can give my lawyer an explicitly limited mandate, and in a democracy, mechanisms exist for control over legislators. But the point of these relationships is that they make possible the attribution of actions to me even when I have in fact done nothing to control and could do nothing. In the legal context, a bridge or a hospital or a minor can have action attributed to them, and, in the political context, so can an abstraction like the state, which as Hobbes emphasizes, is by itself but "a word, without substance, and cannot stand."[30]

Indeed, because the state is an abstraction, it needs to be personated. No laws could be made were it not for the fact that there is a sovereign lawmaker, who represents the state, and in representing the state the legislator also represents the unity that is "we, the people." The important distinction for Hobbes is between authorization and representation, not between authorization and authorship. Individuals authorize the state. But that authorization has to be a blanket one, "without stint,"[31] in order for the state to be born, because the state is a fictitious unity that makes possible a kind of political relationship that could not otherwise exist—the relationship whereby I have to own what my lawmakers do because they represent the unity that I have generated through my agreement of authorization.

I suspect then that Beerbohm's argument from *In Our Name* conflates authorization and representation. In addition, as I think the argument of "The Problem of Clean Hands" shows, he might fragment that conflation in a way that corresponds to the actual situation of Washington-style politics, but which has the effect of losing the normative force of the authorization/representation nexus that was one of Hobbes's most important innovations for modern political philosophy. As Beerbohm says, "In claiming that [lawmakers] . . . speak in the name of a subset of citizens, I'm departing from views that suppose that legislators stand in a principal-agent relationship with society as a whole."[32] This departure risks making authorization turn on the actual degree of individual or group complicity. Law is no longer owned by the individuals who authorized the state, nor do lawmakers represent the unity of the people. Rather, lawmakers represent particular constituencies of individuals who exercised or who could have exercised some control over them, and only discrete constituencies own particular laws.

As David Runciman argues, Hobbes's theory of representation offers a way of reconciling "the claims of political representatives to take decisions on behalf of individuals with the rights of individuals to judge how well they are being represented." Hobbes does this by insisting that it is the state—not the individuals—that is represented.[33] Runciman points out that if democratic theorists give up on Hobbes's account of representation, they face rather "stark choices." They either have to abandon the "language of representation" and employ "other terms to describe the relationship between governments and electorates" or they must abandon the "idea of national collective identity."[34] The problem with Beerbohm's argument is that it might want to hang on to the language of representation at the same time as abandoning the idea of the unity of the people and the state.

The problem is not confined to the tension this strategy creates. For there is also the issue that with this abandonment there is a loss of the normative force that accompanies the idea that politics is, as Runciman puts it, "more than a battleground of individual wills."[35] And with the loss of that normative force we can no longer maintain a grip on the idea of a jural and moral community, one in which we own the laws that our lawmakers make for us. We thus have to give up on the thought that the content of the law makes up, as Hobbes put it, a kind of "public conscience,"[36] despite the fact that we know that legal content is in some sense the product of moral compromise. And it is significant that Beerbohm levels a similar objection against the strategists—that "lawmakers aren't haggling over prices; they are engaged in a process that ends in authoritative demands backed by armed men and women."[37]

I stated "in some sense the product of moral compromise" because we can recognize, even applaud, the fact that the road to legislation is paved with moral compromises and yet think that the content of the legislation cannot be read off that legislative history. Indeed, in Westminster systems, judges for a long time totally barred themselves from looking to the history of parliamentary debates in order to get clues about how to answer questions of statutory interpretation, and even in the Washington system it is controversial in what way such history is relevant to interpretation. More important for the present discussion is that Beerbohm acknowledges that legal content must be more than the product of mere political compromise when he asserts in "The Problem of Clean Hands" that legislative compromise is qualitatively different from ordinary practices of compromise. It is, he says, "easy to see the moral distinctiveness of *legislated law*."[38] He continues:

> That a group of people can gather together, write some words down on sheets of paper, and by their communication alone have changed the law is a brazen thought. Now what constitutes "the law" is furiously contested, and we would be wise to avoid taking a position here. So long as positivists and nonpositivists accept that legislatures take actions that change our moral obligations, we can leave open precisely how legislators make the law what it is.[39]

Beerbohm is right that "we can leave open precisely how legislators make the law." But he goes wrong in the claim that "we can leave open precisely how legislators make the law *what it is*." For the suggestion that there is an "is" there takes sides in the debate he thinks he can avoid between positivists and nonpositivists. Moreover, only the nonpositivist side accepts the "brazen thought" that legislated law is *morally* distinctive and that its distinctiveness resides in the fact that it changes our moral obligations.[40] As H.L.A. Hart put it on behalf of the positivist tradition, "the idea of a moral legislature with competence to make and change morals, as legal enactments make and change law, is repugnant to the whole notion of morality."[41]

It is not, of course, only legal positivists who will reject the idea that law is morally distinctive in this way, or, as I described it above, the position of moral positivism, according to which not only is the content of the law simply the content of what is validly posited by lawmakers but that content must be taken by legal subjects as moral, as representing right reason. Liberals and others will concede that one can make a case for an obligation to the law of one's sovereign when the law is the product of a democratic process; but in that case, liberals will insist, the legitimacy of the law derives from the fact that the process is democratic and not from its quality as law. In addition, a concession that there might be such a case does not entail conceding that the law should be thought of as a public conscience, since the resistance to thinking of the law in this way extends to democratically made law. Even if there are reasons to obey law because it is democratically made, these are reasons independent of the content of the laws; the reasons pertain, that is, to the merits of the democratic process. It remains for the individual conscience to judge the merits of the content and, if it is morally offensive, conscientious objection becomes an issue. In other words, if private conscience is to have the priority it should enjoy, it must rely on standards of justice that are independent of the will of the state or of the collective, no matter that the will is both expressed in law and that the law is democratically made.

Hobbes's position is thus distinctive since it is neither compliance with independent moral standards that makes law legitimate nor with the particular procedures required for its enactment, but something else. Beerbohm wishes to set a similar course for his argument and, as we have seen, he thinks there is at least a "grain of truth" in Hobbes's view that authorization shapes that course.[42] But, as I have indicated above, Beerbohm takes a different course, since he rejects the view that "legislators stand in a principal-agent relationship with society as a whole" and thus a view that stretches from Hobbes through to the present that something important turns on the claim that lawmakers act "in the name of the whole society." On Beerbohm's account, the "central agency relationship of the legislator is organized around one's constituency."[43]

Here it is instructive to note what Pettit describes as "an inherent tension between two sets of forces" in the Washington system.

> There are pressures on individual members of Congress to represent their different constituencies responsively, on pain of not being reelected. And at the same time there is pressure at the group or system level to generate and maintain a body of law that has the coherence required, and the fit with system-wide public reasons, to pass as the voice of the people (Dworkin 1986).[44]

The reference here is to Ronald Dworkin's *Law's Empire* and to the idea that legislated law forms part of a public record that requires justification when any particular law is enforced and a question arises about how it is to be interpreted. Judges are the officials we charge with providing the justification and they must seek to uncover the theory that shows the relevant parts of the public record in its best moral light. The process is not such that one works out the answer to that question and then supplies the justification. Rather, the answer is supplied by the theory. A crucial assumption in all of this is that the judge must suppose that the public record can be explained as the record established by one master lawmaker, who speaks in one voice to a community of individuals unified by the moral principles that underpin that record. In other words, the pull toward coherence or "integrity" in terms of public reasons follows from something like the authorization argument. As Dworkin puts it, "it is inconsistency in principle among the acts of the state personified that integrity condemns."[45]

Dworkin suggests at times that two principles of integrity are in play— an adjudicative one and a legislative one. The adjudicative principle of integrity instructs judges "to identify legal rights and duties, so far as is possible, on the assumption that they were all created by a single author—the community personified—expressing a coherent conception of justice and fairness."[46] However, the legislative principle does not appear to require anything different, since it "asks those who create law by legislation to keep that law coherent in principle."[47] Hence, it seems that judges have to do their bit on the assumption that the lawmakers did theirs, whether or not the latter tried or succeeded. Hobbes, we should note, has much the same view. Judges are to avoid coming to unreasonable interpretations of legislative intention and must indeed work on the assumption that the sovereign intended his laws to comply with the laws of nature, in particular equity, because to assume otherwise would be a great insult to the sovereign.[48]

In "The Problem of Clean Hands," Beerbohm seems tempted to reject Dworkinian integrity,[49] as he did in chapter 8 of *In Our Name*. In the latter, he contrasts a "super lawmaker," Pericles, with Dworkin's super judge, Hercules.[50] But it is unclear to me exactly what the points of contrast amount to, other than the fact that Pericles takes into account citizens' actual views and tries to make principled sense of those, whereas all that Hercules cares about is the data in the public record of law and seeks to make moral sense of that data. Recall that Beerbohm says, "Lawmaking is a collective enterprise defined as much by the give-and-take of working out the contents of a bill as the final act of voting for its passage."[51] But while lawmaking is surely shaped or determined (though perhaps not "defined") in the way he describes in both *In Our Name* and "The Problem of Clean Hands," the question remains what to make of the product. More particularly, how are citizens to understand the law that makes up the public record of the political community as supplying them with moral reasons if all there is to law is not something morally distinctive, but merely the outcome of power struggles—of "deep compromises and shady alliances"?

As I have indicated, one can always deny with legal positivism of the sort advanced by Hart that there is anything morally distinctive about legislated law and argue that it is morally healthy for citizens to see that such law is no more than the outcome of power struggles and as such does not offer citizens moral reasons. That the law is democratically made can then be argued to provide the reasons or that the law happens to be substantively just. As we have seen, Beerbohm rejects both of these options. Like Hobbes, he wishes to steer a path between those that contend, "on one side for too great Liberty, and on the other side for too much Authority,"[52] in Beerbohm's case, between the liberals who suppose that law supplies moral reasons only if its content happens to be just, and the democrats who suppose that compliance with democratic procedures suffices to make law moral. But as far as I know, the only way to steer that path is via something like the authorization argument.

With that argument, as one can see from both Hobbes's and Dworkin's very different legal theories, travels the assumption that law is morally distinctive and that the judicial role is in part to ensure that law lives up to its moral aspirations. One important respect in which their legal theories differ is that Dworkin neglects the institutional nature of law and the principles specific to legal government that Hobbes termed the laws of nature and that in the twentieth century Lon L. Fuller called "the internal morality of law."[53] For both Hobbes and Fuller, the commitment to governing through law entails a commitment to governing in accordance with these principles and the principles by themselves—that is, whatever the political form of government—exercise a kind of moral force.[54]

The force is centrifugal in that it requires, among other things, that laws be general, not inconsistent, capable of compliance, that it have, in other words, a form that makes it possible to understand law as the expression of "a single author—the community personified." But it is also centripetal in that these and other principles—in particular those that attach to the role of a judge (for example, impartiality, equity)—require that the law be justifiable to the individuals to whom it is applied.

Here Fuller emphasized the importance of impartial adjudicators in a rule-of-law order, in which the issues submitted to the adjudicators "[tend] to be *converted* into a claim of right or an accusation of guilt. This conversion is effected by the institutional framework within which both the litigant and the adjudicator function."[55] The process of reasoned argument requires the person making the argument to present it as more than a "naked demand." It has to be presented as a "claim of right," that is, as "supported by a principle." And that has the consequence that "issues tried before an adjudicator tend to become claims of rights or accusations of fault."[56] Thus, Fuller regards courts and other adjudicative institutions as "essential to the rule of law." The object of the rule of law is to substitute for violence peaceful ways of settling disputes. Obviously, peace cannot be assured simply by treaties, agreements, and legislative enactment. There must be some agency capable of determining the rights of the parties in concrete situations of controversy.[57]

But notice that for this adjudicative conversion process to take place, the law must be convertible, and that requires a prior conversion process. Legislation requires the reduction of a political program to the explicit terms of a statute and thus a conversion of policy into public standards, which produces a kind of legal surplus value. By this I mean that the legitimacy of official action in compliance with the statute is not simply that of compliance with a political policy that the demos or polis has determined to be appropriate. It is also the case that this conversion process adds value because it brings into being a particular type of *public* standard, one that permits the operation of the principles identified by Fuller as the principles that give law its moral quality and that enables claims of right based on legal principle to be adjudicated. If the law is not convertible in this way, a problem is raised that is internal to legal order and that requires those charged with maintaining the legal order in good shape to consider reform.

This requirement, generated by principles intrinsic to legal order, has the result that judges must try to the extent possible to avoid understanding the content of the law as representing a botched compromise, since such compromises resist both the centrifugal and the centripetal aspects of the moral force of government according to law. Laws that reflect botched compromises will exert contradictory demands on individuals or make them promises that can't be fulfilled. As such, they will create tensions in the practice of government according to law that have to be resolved if legal order is not to be undermined. But the requirement also has the result that the law must be interpretable to the individuals it affects in a way that plausibly shows that the community in whose name the law speaks regards her as a full member of that community. The content of the law must, to use Dworkin's slogan, be such that the individual can think of herself as treated with equal concern and respect.

Lawmakers can make life more or less difficult for judges either by enacting botched compromises into the law or by compromising moral ideals to the extent that the law can't be interpreted as exhibiting equal concern and respect. In doing that, they undermine not only the relationship whereby the political community is represented by the law that the lawmakers make, but also the relationship of authorization between discrete individuals and the community. Thus, lawmakers have a duty to avoid compromises of the sort that will render law incapable of doing the task that we ask it to do.

I want to end by suggesting law that is not compromised in a way that makes it difficult for judges to do their interpretive duty does make up a public conscience of the sort Hobbes envisaged. I think it is also the case that democratic controls on the law that lawmakers make in our name can go a long way to ensuring that the law we own is the law that we want to own. Hobbes was likely right that democratic lawmaking invites and requires political compromise and that an attendant risk is the fracturing of the political community into particular constituencies that undermine the authorization argument. My claim here is that government under law shows us that the legal form itself will resist certain kinds of compromise in order to maintain the idea that we all belong to one jural, moral community.

Perhaps—a dismal thought to some—we live in a world that is doubly disenchanted. Not only, as Hobbes advised, have we had to give up the idea that there is some ultimate moral telos that unites us as a community. But we also have to give up on the only telos he thought still available after the first wave of disenchantment: the telos of peace, stability, and liberty under law enjoyed by a community unified by their recognition that for them the law is a public conscience. If that second wave has happened, we are living in a world where our moral community is coterminous with something like a "constituency" or perhaps some overlapping constituencies. Law could then be no more than the outcomes of particular political battles, and it would almost always compromise at least one constituency's moral ideals. Moreover, if one had the Washington system in place, it would be likely that many laws would reflect botched compromises as well as compromises of moral ideals.

I do not think Beerbohm supposes that we live in that world, one stitched together by fragile and uneasy compromises between constituencies that are deeply divided by different visions of the morally ideal. And much of his argument in both *In Our Name* and "The Problem of Clean Hands" could be understood as advice about how to avoid the transition to it by getting us to see that we do own what our legislators do. But that advice will work only if there is more to the idea of "in *our* name" than he most of the time allows. For if the "our" reduces to the constituency I happen to belong to or to identify with, it loses the kind of normative force that he suggests when he tells us of "the moral distinctiveness of legislated law."

NOTES

1. Thomas Hobbes, *Leviathan* (Cambridge: Cambridge University Press, 2013), 112.

2. Ibid., 114.

3. Hobbes, to be clear, does not think that the citizens have transferred their right to the sovereign, but have laid aside their right to judge for themselves how best to secure their preservation, thus freeing up the sovereign to make such judgments on their behalf.

4. Eric Beerbohm, *In Our Name: The Ethics of Democracy* (Princeton, NJ: Princeton University Press, 2012).

5. Ibid., 26, 45, 46, 226.

6. Ibid., 45.

7. See ibid., ch. 9, "Democratic Complicity."

8. Ibid., 226.

9. Ibid., 223.

10. Ibid.

11. Beerbohm, opening section of chapter 1, "The Problem of Clean Hands," of this volume.

12. Ibid., "Three Players" section.

13. Ibid.

14. Ibid.

15. Ibid.

16. Ibid.

17. Ibid.

18. Ibid., his emphasis.

19. Ibid., "Three Players" section.

20. Avishai Margalit, *On Compromise and Rotten Compromise* (Princeton, NJ: Princeton University Press, 2010), 2–3.

21. See the appendix by Philip Pettit and Rory Pettit, to Philip Pettit, "Varieties of public representation," in Ian Shapiro, Susan C. Stokes, Elisabeth Jean Wood, and Alexander S. Kirshner, eds., *Political Representation* (Cambridge: Cambridge University Press, 2009), 61, 87. I would not of course think this point is news to Beerbohm, but as it happens, he is one of the people whose help Pettit acknowledges in the essay, at 61.

22. Ibid., 85–87.

23. Beerbohm, opening section of chapter 1, "The Problem of Clean Hands," of this volume.

24. See, for example, Hobbes, *Leviathan*, ch. 37, 306.

25. Ibid., 110.

26. Ibid., 131–32.

27. Beerbohm, *In Our Name*, 45.

28. Ibid.

29. Ibid., 46.

30. Ibid., 245.

31. Ibid., 114.

32. Beerbohm, "The Problem of Clean Hands," chapter 1 of this volume, Co-Ownership as a Civic Value section.

33. David Runciman, "Hobbes's theory of representation," in Shapiro et al., eds., *Political Representation*, 15, 32. See also David Runciman, *Pluralism and the Politics of the State* (Cambridge: Cambridge University Press, 1997). It would, I think, be instructive to compare Beerbohm's departures from Hobbes with those wrought by the English pluralists Runciman discusses, especially Harold Laski.

34. Runciman, "Hobbes's theory of representation," 32–33.

35. Ibid., 31.

36. Hobbes says that "the law is the publique Conscience, by which . . . [the individual] hath already undertaken to be guided"; *Leviathan*, 223.

37. Beerbohm, "The Problem of Clean Hands," chapter 1 of this volume, section on Legislative Compromise as a Practice.

38. Ibid., his emphasis.

39. Ibid.

40. Note that this claim is true only of the contemporary debate. Certainly Bentham thought that legislated law is morally distinctive and wanted to get rid of "judge made law." And this kind of political preference for legislated law as morally superior survives into the work of Jeremy Waldron, who at times seems to place himself in the positivist tradition.

41. H.L.A. Hart, *The Concept of Law* (Oxford: Clarendon Press, 1994, 2nd edition), 177.

42. Beerbohm, *In Our Name*, 226.

43. Beerbohm, "The Problem of Clean Hands," chapter 1 of this volume, section on Co-Ownership as a Civic Value.

44. Pettit, "Varieties of public representation," 83.

45. Ronald Dworkin, *Law's Empire* (Fontana: London, 1986), 184.

46. Ibid., 224.

47. Ibid., 167.

48. Hobbes, *Leviathan*, ch. 26, 194.

49. Beerbohm, "The Problem of Clean Hands," chapter 1 of this volume, section on Compromise's Defeaters under Unjust Conditions.

50. Beerbohm, *In Our Name*, 201–202.

51. Ibid., 223.

52. Hobbes, *Leviathan*, 3.

53. Lon L. Fuller, *The Morality of Law* (New Haven, CT: Yale University Press 1969, revised edition).

54. See David Dyzenhaus, "Hobbes on the Authority of Law" in Dyzenhaus and Thomas Poole, eds., *Hobbes and the Law* (Cambridge: Cambridge University Press, 2012), 186.

55. Lon L. Fuller, "The Forms and Limits of Adjudication," in Kenneth I. Winston, ed., *The Principles of Social Order: Selected Essays of Lon L. Fuller* (Oxford: Hart Publishing, 2001), 101, 111, emphasis added.

56. Ibid., 111.

57. Ibid., 114.

4

ON COMPROMISE, NEGOTIATION, AND LOSS

AMY J. COHEN

INTRODUCTION

This chapter began as an effort to think through a question: why is a robust theory of compromise missing from legal negotiation and related fields within alternative dispute resolution (ADR)—fields that are devoted to informal, consensual, and collaborative forms of dispute resolution and problem-solving? If compromise were to have an institutionalized home in law and legal practice, surely it would be here. Its absence, the chapter argues, reflects the particular history of ADR's emergence as a legal field.

ADR has made famous the insight that disputants negotiate in the shadow of the law.[1] But it is equally the case that ADR itself has developed in the shadow of legal—and the legal turn to economic—process. Adjudication is characteristically envisioned as an adversarial contest between formally equal parties, and one that is governed by ideals of judicial objectivity, neutrality, and a winner-take-all logic.[2] Legal negotiation and mediation offer a voluntary alternative to this idealized model of adjudication as the imposition of foundational reason from above. They enable disputants to fashion intermediate remedies that are shaped, yet not determined, by judicial authority.[3] But paradoxically much of ADR theory invokes a different kind of objectivity and neutrality—instead of the judge's interpretation of truth and right we have the economist's aspiration for optimal allocation.

As we shall see, foundational contributions to the prescriptive field of legal negotiation describe interpersonal exchange via the liberal economic ideals of growth and distribution (grow the pie before cutting it). To put the point bluntly, negotiation theorists speak of generating maximally efficient exchange—that is, trades that involve the least possible cost to produce the greatest possible gain. On this view, negotiation does not involve compromise at all. To the contrary, it represents mutually beneficial encounters where cost represents a consensual, and thus compensated, calculation made in return for gain. But because negotiation theorists of course recognize that parties often will not agree on how to divide the surplus produced through exchange, they also offer a set of strategies and techniques to help parties allocate value based on reasoned deliberation. That is, growth is followed by a series of distributional choices that parties are encouraged to work out by applying rational and jointly agreed-upon standards.

As a model for consensual dispute resolution, legal negotiation thus combines a particular economic rationality for growth with a particular legal rationality for distribution—all translated into lay terms and popularized through how-to manuals, training exercises, and pedagogical instruction for law students, dispute resolution professionals, and judges. In this model, compromise appears in precisely two ways: first, as an impediment to growth and, second, as a last-resort strategy for distribution. That is, when parties have opportunities to create value from exchange, compromise describes a failure to negotiate sufficiently far out on a Pareto frontier—that is, compromise refers to dividing a pie that is smaller than it otherwise could be. But if parties have exhausted all possible gains from trade *and* if they have developed competing but equally reasoned distributional positions, then compromise is recommended as a neutral mechanism to split the difference among the allocations suggested by these positions.[4]

In this chapter, I consider how and why negotiation and related fields in law developed through the language of growth and distribution rather than also through a theory and practice of compromise. To flesh out what I see as the distinctions, I suggest two alternative modes of compromise that I compare to growth and distribution: *compromise shaped by principle* and *compromise shaped by constraints.* In brief, compromise shaped by principle is an effort to capture how people experience loss not as a strategy to produce gain but rather as a practice of caring—at a cost to themselves—for the values or well-being of another or caring for values or principles in the abstract. In the clearest cases, sharing, sacrifice, and sometimes even altruism are more apt metaphors for dispute resolution here than reciprocal exchange.[5] I use the phrase "compromise shaped by principle" to describe how, in these moments, parties often appeal to principles—be they moral, political, or procedural—to which they ascribe and which they experience as transcending the conflict at hand. These principles make loss feel justified, sometimes even virtuous, in a particular dispute.

A second way negotiators experience loss that is also not fully captured by the idea of growth and distribution is what I am calling *compromise shaped by constraints*. Here negotiators experience the effects of material and social power that make loss feel not justified but rather structurally compelled. Unlike compromise shaped by principle, the negotiator is trying to advance her own interests and values as best she can but within structural and social contexts that mean these interests and values are already deeply constrained. Thus, in the clearest case of compromise shaped by constraints, subsistence or survival is a better metaphor for dispute resolution than voluntary wealth-maximizing exchange.

As constructs, "growth and distribution" and "compromise shaped by principle and constraints" are thus different approaches to making sense of social practice. That is, they are different approaches to making sense of what people do—and of what theorists and practitioners of ADR think people should do—when they negotiate with one another. To be clear, this approach to studying compromise in negotiation is not methodologically tight: neither construct is derived from a stable set of empirical data or presented as conceptual categories that are logically complete.[6] To the contrary, I anticipate that in actual negotiations, settlements will often reflect modest forms of principles, constraints, and self-interest promoted through trade. If it is useful nonetheless to contrast growth and distribution with compromise shaped by principles and constraints, it is because these constructs allow us to investigate the variety of human practice involved in dispute resolution *alongside* the social and historical development of one particular model that today dominates instruction in consensual dispute resolution in law.

Or, to put the point differently, in a field like legal negotiation that constantly engages with real people and conflicts, theoretical constructs gain power when they can be articulated as practical advice, skills, and techniques. Growth and distribution—far more than compromise—has become an attitude and practice—a privileged way of being in a problem—to teach and reproduce in law schools and legal practice. To illustrate what I mean, consider two approaches to beginning settlement negotiations facilitated by mediators. From the perspective of ADR practice, the first will sound entirely familiar; the second, strange if not in-credible.

First:

We think it is possible for all of you to leave this negotiation better off than you currently are. Too often people leave value on the table when they try to resolve a conflict because they are angry, hurt, or committed to abstract principles. Our goal in this out-of-court settlement is to help all of you maximize what you want at the least cost to the other sides—that is, our goal is to help you make a bigger pie and also to help you each find what you think are fair and reasonable ways to get a slice.

Versus:

We think it is unlikely for all of you to leave this negotiation feeling fully compensated or "made whole" given the loss, harm, and feelings of injustice that this conflict has produced. The best we can do is try to help you work out a compromise to share or manage this loss. Our aim is to work out a compromise in a principled fashion that expresses your own concrete values, sense of self, and social commitments even if we can't achieve an allocation that will appear to all of you as fully reasoned "on the merits." At the same time, we know this allocation, like all allocations, will be shaped by background power and social and structural constraints. We will therefore try to make visible and critically analyze the constraints at work in this negotiation and investigate how they are shaping your decisions as you strive for a fair settlement or as you decide that a settlement is not in your interests.

These two "opening statements" reflect different assumptions about human motivations and experiences in conflict; the latter insists on a critical evaluation of social exchange that foregrounds the reality of managing loss rather than the possibility of creating gain. That said, I do not venture any general conclusions about the politics or effects of adopting one approach over the other. In different contexts, both of these discursive frames can produce progressive or conservative, empowering and disempowering effects on the ground. I thus approach compromise in this chapter not as the subject of normative prescription, moral theory, or institutional design, but rather as a tool of social and historical investigation and normative critique. That is, my aim is not to propose a full-blown theory of compromise around which to reorient the field of extralegal dispute resolution. Rather, it is to use two suggestive human experiences of compromise in order to make visible how ideas of growth and distribution arrested the development of a more pluralistic praxis—one that is more fully engaged with the kinds of values and conditions that people experience as legitimating (or alternatively compelling) loss—not simply how people do or should strive for gain.

But even this is a tricky aspiration. Like the broader law and economics framework from which it borrows, legal negotiation is agnostic to ends. As such, it offers a model for dispute resolution that is extremely capacious—willing to build in any and every party's subjective and normative preferences, including, we should presume, preferences for principled compromise.[7] In other words, there is nothing intrinsic to the theory and practice of legal negotiation that must refuse to accommodate compromises as I am describing them. Still, legal negotiation today offers a basic set of assumptions and prescriptions about how to resolve legal conflict through voluntary exchange that prioritize growth and interest maximization. Within this model compromise may emerge as an idiosyncratic preference to be assimilated as needed but is not a basic or coequal methodological category of problem-solving and dispute resolution in law.[8] In what follows I explore how and, more provisionally, why this came to be. But I leave it to the reader to decide whether the ascendency of growth and distribution as a dominant micro-practice of legal dispute resolution itself includes a kind of loss.

I. On Compromise Shaped by Principles and Constraints

Before turning to negotiation theory and practice, let me sketch definitions of compromise shaped by principles and constraints. I begin with a somewhat detailed description of compromise shaped by principle because there is a good deal of philosophical writing that understands compromise as a moral or ethical act.[9] I do not present this literature in any comprehensive way. Rather, I appropriate four of its recurring themes in order to propose a general category of compromise shaped by principle, and one that is distinct from what I define as compromise shaped by constraint.

First is the idea, borrowed from philosophers, that compromise is different from trade and market-based exchange. What compromise shaped by principle does not describe, in other words, is a process where parties jointly agree to ascribe a value to a commodity based on the price signals of a market or their own perceptions of supply and demand. Rather, it refers to a more narrowly defined subset of negotiation behavior.[10] Second is the related idea that compromise shaped by principle likewise does not describe what happens when parties surrender to threats, coercion, bluffing, or material need. On the contrary, parties compromise when they limit the pursuit of self-interest to some degree, not when they make concessions that reflect *only* relative bargaining strength.[11]

Third, philosophers argue that parties engage in compromise of this sort precisely because of the higher-order values they hold; be these abstract values or values placed on particular relationships with others. This is the view of compromise proposed, for example, by several contributors to the 1979 NOMOS volume on compromise. Martin Golding argued that when parties compromise, they acknowledge the moral legitimacy of their opponents as well as of their opponents' interests. Compromise, he therefore reasoned, "presupposes a commonality or, more exactly, a community."[12] Theodore Benditt put the point as follows: "compromising and (mere) bargaining differ" because compromise requires recognition of the other.[13] Arthur Kuflik likewise argued that rather than an expedient to manage the competitive assertion of self-interest, compromise is a moral response to the problems of reasonably competing values, perspectives, and resources that is grounded in a first principle of mutual respect.[14] Indeed,

Kuflik proposed to think of compromise as a principle of social organization "not among those who are roughly equal in strength and cunning, but among those who hold one another in equal regard as persons."[15] In these and other philosophical accounts, compromise follows from first-order dignitary and moral commitments. But because I want a category flexible enough to describe a range of human experiences, I describe compromise shaped by principle as motivated by a broad range of principles—that parties may experience as universalizing or particularistic, deontological or welfarist—but that, in all cases, they experience as transcending and thus serving to limit the more immediate interests and desires that inform a dispute.

Fourth, precisely because compromise expresses higher-order or extrinsic values in this way, it is also distinct from reasoned convergence on the merits of the dispute. That is, compromise does not happen when parties come together in their deliberations on a right answer to resolve a conflict or the best way to solve a problem.[16] It is more often an expression of value pluralism—a recognition that one's opponents' claims are also legitimate and therefore deserve a measure of accommodation. Such an accommodation, however, typically depends on an additional extrinsic source of justification—for example, moral respect, community, obligation, paternalism, solidarity, love. As Henry Richardson puts it, a "reasoner" does not compromise when she is convinced of the truth or soundness of another's argument; rather, she compromises when she agrees to change her position to one she "would not have accepted *but for* [a] kind of concern and respect."[17]

As an illustration of compromise shaped by principle, consider a classic, albeit fictional, conflict where ideas of justice are plural and there are no commodities or private legal entitlements to trade. In Sophocles' *Antigone*, Creon, the ruler of Thebes, and Antigone, his niece, are bitterly divided over the burial of Antigone's brother Polyneices—who is an enemy of the state.[18] For Creon, a proper burial would undercut national unity, social order, and state authority.[19] For Antigone, to leave Polyneices unburied would violate gods' laws as well as the deep pull of kinship commitments.[20] The nineteenth-century philosopher Georg W. F. Hegel represented this conflict as a contest between the law of the gods (and the family) *versus* the law of the state—both of which, he argued, as expressions of justice, are partial and incomplete. He wrote:

> Here, familial love, the holy, the inward, belonging to inner feeling, and therefore known also as the law of the nether gods, collides with the right of the state. . . . [Creon] maintains that the law of the state, the authority of government, must be held in respect, and that infraction of the law must be followed by punishment. Each of these two sides actualizes only one of the ethical powers, and has only one as its content. This is their one-sidedness. The meaning of eternal justice is made manifest thus: *both attain injustice* just because they are one-sided, *but both also attain justice.*[21]

On this legal pluralist account, a compromise would require Antigone and Creon to reconcile competing principles—which they would do, if at all, not only by rationalizing how the other's principle accomplishes justice, but also by experiencing a measure of respect, even solidarity, for the overlapping communities of kinship and state they share. Perhaps Creon would be motivated by the love of his son, who is betrothed to Antigone, and through his son, feelings for Antigone; perhaps Antigone would experience a countervailing set of familial commitments to support her uncle in his efforts to consolidate the state. And through these transcendent commitments they would bridge unshared values and positions and thus endure—but perhaps never resolve—feelings of loss.

This sort of compromise—perhaps a decision to bury Polyneices in a remote location outside the state[22]—resembles what Henry Richardson calls "deep compromise." This is an agreement that happens when rivals revise and modify their ends—a possibility, Richardson argues, that "by definition, exists only for groups of people in which mutual respect, concern, or shared identity is strong enough for them to try to work together."[23] It also resembles what Avishai Margalit calls a "sanguine compromise," an agreement that "involves painful recognition of the other side, a giving up of dreams, making mutual concessions that express recognition of the other's point of view, and that is not based on coercion of one side by the other."[24] For the side with more opportunities and means to influence the agreement, compromise shaped by principle may therefore entail sacrifice—as Margalit puts it, "deliberately decreasing my share compared to possible agreements that I might have extracted, had I insisted."[25] For the weaker side, this sort of compromise requires sufficient autonomy to ensure that an agreement is not coerced by economic or political power. Clearly, it is not a compromise shaped by principle if Antigone surrenders her position to evade punishment at Creon's hands. A "principled compromise," Patrick Dobel likewise insists, can be justified by a range of values "separate from a sheer concern with another's power."[26] Nor is it a compromise when Creon is persuaded by a prophet that his position was wrong-headed ("I've realized," he declares, "it's always best to live your life respecting well-established laws").[27] Again, as I am describing it, a compromise shaped by principle is defined narrowly to exclude agreements produced only through relative bargaining strength, the application of internal reason to reach a "correct" answer to a problem, or attention to the price signals of a market.

To be sure, this description of compromise shaped by principle, loosely borrowed from philosophers, represents more an ideal type than an actual institutionalized practice in law or politics operating on the ground. I suspect it is rare that people in legal disputes experience compromises as purely volitional, self-expressive acts. A second category—and also one that is undertheorized in ADR—is what I am calling compromise shaped by constraint. Again, in the clearest case of compromise shaped by principle, a negotiator experiences herself as deciding to relinquish some of her own values or interests in order to advance a higher-order end. In the clearest case of compromise shaped by constraint, she experiences herself as laboring to advance her own values and interests as best as she can against significant adverse conditions—conditions that may themselves shape and constrain a negotiator's values and interests.

What I am calling compromise shaped by constraints shares elements in common with what political theorists Amy Gutmann and Dennis Thompson recently described as classic compromise. A classic compromise is an agreement that parties reach because it serves their interests better than the status quo but also "an agreement in which all sides sacrifice something . . . and in which the sacrifices are at least partly determined by the other sides' will."[28]

Critically, this sort of sacrifice "involves not merely getting less than you want, but also, thanks to your opponents, getting less than you think you deserve," that is, less than you feel you should have received if only your opponents had been more reasonable.[29] Thus, in classic compromise, parties determine that relinquishing some of their commitments is the only available means to advance their other values and interests over their current positions. Moreover, Gutmann and Thompson ascribe a particular feeling to this decision: negotiators experience their concessions as undesirable or unfortunate, but, given a range of social, political, economic, legal, or interpersonal constraints, as also the best alternative under the circumstances.[30]

I take up compromises shaped by constraints in the final brief part of this chapter. But let me here simply acknowledge that principles and constraints will often bleed together. A negotiator may describe advancing a higher-order principle (love, community, moral obligation, democratic process) as equally an experience of volitional commitment and constraint. And as she makes concessions to advance that higher-order principle, she may simultaneously labor to advance her own self-interest. Still, as analytical categories to make sense of human experience, I think it is useful to maintain a provisional distinction. But this is not because I wish to suggest that there are principled compromises that operate outside of constraints (or that constraints are invariably negative and thus the proper subjects of resistance), but rather because I wish to use compromise shaped by constraint as an analytical tool to investigate qualitative distinctions in the forms and effects of coercion that operate on the ground. First, however, I describe the theory and practice of legal negotiation in order to compare it to a theory and practice of compromise shaped by both principles and constraints.

II. LEGAL NEGOTIATION

In the late 1970s and early 1980s, "problem-solving" negotiation emerged as a new field of legal pedagogy and practice. This was due largely to work pioneered at Harvard Law School—particularly the Program on Negotiation (PON) founded in 1983 and devoted to transforming dispute resolution "from 'win-lose' outcomes to 'mutual gains' solutions."[31] As I will suggest below, the field in part reflected a general turn in law to neoclassical economics. But what makes contemporary negotiation both important and intriguing is how it translated the economist's ideas of utility maximization and individual exchange *not* into truths of human behavior or ideas for the reform of legal rules but rather into skills, practices, and techniques. These are skills and techniques, moreover, designed precisely for people who often do not match the presuppositions economists ascribe to them. Thus, for example, legal negotiation theorists set out to help parties reframe conflicts over principle (whenever possible) into conflicts over fungible, hence tradable, goods, and to reframe conflicts over highly particular values into conflicts over values that could be made commensurate through appeals to common ground or, if not, bracketed to allow for more fungible exchange. Gabriella Blum and Robert Mnookin captured this aspiration well when they argued: "We are not claiming that the tendency to accentuate issues of morality or legitimacy is necessarily wrong, irrational, or 'biased,' although our intuition is that often disputants have not carefully considered alternative ways of framing their conflicts or the issues at hand."[32]

Legal negotiation theorists also aimed to reframe conflict resolution from a cost-filled legal procedure to one designed to minimize costs and maximize gains—cognitive, not only material, ones. Beginning in the 1990s, ADR scholars imported insights from behavioral economics to design process choices that would evade *feelings* of loss. Mnookin, for example, encouraged ADR scholars and practitioners to understand loss as an unstable perception: "whether something is viewed as a gain or loss—and what kind of gain or loss it is considered—depends upon a reference point, and the choice of a reference point is sometimes manipulable."[33] This subjective nature of loss, he continued, creates important opportunities for practitioners of ADR: "By emphasizing the potential gains to both sides of the resolution and de-emphasizing the losses that the resolution is going to entail, mediators (and lawyers) often facilitate resolution."[34]

I am thus describing a particular model of legal negotiation and ADR pioneered by Roger Fisher, Robert Mnookin, and others affiliated with Harvard Law School that oriented the field away from theories of loss and toward theories of gain. To be sure, there are scholars in the field that have diverged from this interest-based problem-solving model.[35] But as ADR is constructed and reproduced throughout American legal education and practice, it remains the overwhelmingly dominant one. Intriguingly, however, early theorists of legal negotiation, including Roger Fisher himself, identified compromise shaped by principle as a significant feature of why people do or should make concessions. In the following section, I therefore trace the roots of compromise in negotiation in order to illustrate the beginning of a more pluralistic practice that today has mostly receded from view.

A. On Compromise in Legal Negotiation

In one of the first serious works on legal negotiation, *Private Ordering Through Negotiation*, Melvin Eisenberg argued that compromise shaped by principle (although he didn't use this term) is an exemplary part of what actually happens in private dispute settlement.[36] He set out to challenge what he saw as a common distinction between adjudication as a process bound by norms and principles, on the one hand, and negotiation as a process governed by power and trade, on the other.[37] To be sure, Eisenberg's argument for a "norm-centered model of dispute-negotiation" is well known in negotiation.[38] But it is often read as a predecessor to the insight that parties bargain in the shadow of the law.[39] Bargaining in the shadow of the law is not compromise shaped by principle. As Mnookin and Kornhauser famously described the former practice, parties make demands and concessions based on their best calculations of their legal entitlements and their expectations of an adjudicated outcome.[40] Eisenberg, however, *also* wished to draw attention to parties in negotiations who made concessions that— precisely because they were not compelled or even encouraged by law—expressed independent recognition of the legitimacy of the other and her claims.

Equally intriguing (and, for his argument, surely unfortunate), Eisenberg explained that he could not find any domestic examples to illustrate this point.[41] He thus began his article with an anthropological account of a dispute in northern Tanzania where a relative refused to relinquish land owned by a deceased father to the father's son even though the son was entitled to the land under

customary inheritance law.[42] The relative argued that he had cultivated the land, cared for the father while the father aged, and that
the son already owned much more land than he. After a lengthy
process of community negotiation, the son agreed to divide the
farm "despite the clearly enunciated norm of inheritance."[43] On
Eisenberg's read, they divided the land affirmatively to express and
compromise among conflicting principles ("sons inherit," "a well-
off relative should not begrudge means of sustenance to a needy
relative," "one who voluntarily cares for an ageing relative until the
latter's death should share in his estate").[44] To be sure, this property division could have reflected a reasoned consensus between
the son and the relative about the correct way to weigh and value
these principles. But Eisenberg, it seems, interpreted this division
as a compromise—he used the word *accommodation*—where parties relinquished some of what they felt entitled to for the sake
of other community-wide norms: care, reciprocity, and material
need. That is, they made concessions for the sake of community
values (and perhaps also, we might guess, made some concessions
due to community pressure).[45]

As a second example, Eisenberg described a property dispute
between a tourist in Java and a manager of a hotel. The manager
claimed compensation when, after a tourist pulled a toilet cord,
a toilet tank came crashing down, damaging the bowl. From the
tourist's perspective, the manager's request was unreasonable. But
even though a judge agreed that he would not find the tourist liable under the relevant (no-fault) law, the tourist ultimately offered
(at the judge's suggestion) a small amount of compensation.[46]
Eisenberg again argued that we should see this case as an illustration of principled accommodation, *not* a reconciliation that stands
"in opposition to principle." The offer of money, he argued, could
plausibly be understood as a way for the tourist to acknowledge
that the manager made a good faith claim of right that deserves
some degree of recognition.[47] Here, compromise followed from a
higher-order dignitary commitment—namely, that sometimes it is
worthy to value another's assertions simply because they are made
in good faith—even in an arms-length and one-shot transaction.

In both these sorts of bread and butter disputes over land and
money routinely theorized in legal negotiation, parties declined
to maximize their legal entitlements at least in part on principled

grounds. Eisenberg suggested such principled concessions are common features of how people settle their differences. And although this descriptive hypothesis would not inform mainstream legal negotiation literature in any fundamental way, before he wrote *Getting to Yes*, Roger Fisher himself articulated a similar, albeit more prescriptive and utilitarian, claim. He argued that on the international plane, states—especially strong ones—should compromise for the higher-order end of a transnational legal system.

Although he would eventually become famous for the idea of mutual gain negotiation, as an international law scholar during the Cold War, Fisher presumed that conflicts of interest, authority, and ideology would invariably persist—a situation that made compromise both inevitable and urgently necessary. In his early work, he thus described negotiation less as an exchange in which both sides maximize their ends than as an ongoing and incremental process of mutual accommodation. In his words, "we must expect conflicts of interest to continue among the peoples of the globe as long as human beings survive."[48] And "we must expect to contend indefinitely," he argued, with differing "ideologies."[49] "Our object is thus not to impose upon the world a static, once-and-for-all solution. Neither should it be to impose a procedure in which the interests of the American people always come out ahead. . . . Rather we seek progressively to develop more orderly, moderate, and genuinely fair means of accommodating and adjusting the conflicts of interest which are bound to exist."[50] In other words, on the international plane, Fisher called for a process that would enable concessions and ongoing adjustments—not interest maximization or common ground.

To that end, Fisher's commitment to transnational legal process invoked the idea of compromise in two ways. First, he argued that legal process is an overarching normative value for which states should sometimes concede other substantive ends.[51] Second, and this point is more complex, he argued that legal process—and in particular adjudication—makes compromise not only desirable but possible. Adjudication, he explained, requires "fractionation"— that is, the breaking up of large and highly charged ideological claims into their "smallest components and dealing with them one at a time."[52] "Little issues can be adjudicated," he reasoned, "but big issues—that is, issues like democracy and communism, colonialism and independence—cannot.[53] Thus he wrote: "Viewed from this perspective, adjudication appears not as a process for settling big conflicts, but rather as one that is valuable because it tends to fragment conflict situations by cutting off and serving up for decision one small issue at a time."[54] In the absence of a single transnational hierarchy of authority, Fisher encouraged states to engage in a consensual system of negotiation that was *like* adjudication.[55] He ventured that if states could voluntarily fractionate their own disputes in similar ways, then they "will have a greater interest in keeping the game going than [they] will in winning what is involved in any particular piece," and they will therefore make modest concessions for the sake of the system.[56]

Although he did not use the term, for Fisher, compromise shaped by the principle of sustaining a transnational legal system was thus a critical normative feature of international negotiation. Indeed, he argued that "each player should regard his own losses as a reasonable and indispensable price to pay to keep the game going and, if need be, should *help make sure that such losses occur.*"[57] And he pressed upon American statesmen that although they naturally wished to win *each* dispute on its own strength and merits, they should not wish to win *every* dispute lest they erode the legitimacy of a consensual dispute settlement system.[58]

Compromise here thus follows from a commitment to a transnational legal community, albeit for Fisher a community that is rather thinly defined. Although Fisher encouraged national statesmen to "operate on the assumption that [their opponents] are sincere men who believe all things considered that they are pursuing a course of action which is morally right," he did not think it likely that statesmen would revise their ends simply for the sake of "shared values" or a robust "*sense* of community."[59] In his view, representatives of sovereign states needed a competing rational incentive; namely, a system that was to the benefit of all to support. Thus, for Fisher, sustaining a transnational legal system perhaps reflects an antecedent moral commitment to peace and legal process, but it clearly reflects an instrumental commitment to advance the welfare of all. I describe it as an example of compromise shaped by principle because it expresses an extrinsic justification for why loss should occur that stands apart from reasoning about the merits of a particular dispute and from internal calculations about what particular losses should offset what particular gains in order to maximize one's own immediate position. That is, this is not a case where negotiators are encouraged to specify equivalents, measure risk, and determine how much loss to trade for how much procedural legitimacy. In colloquial terms, rather than a bargained-for exchange we have a sacrifice for the sake of a system.

To conclude, both Eisenberg and Fisher, as they wrote about compromise and accommodation, proposed to blur distinctions between adjudication and negotiation—although they did so in different ways. Eisenberg was interested in how people used principles—competing moral, communal, as well as codified legal ones—in dispute settlement negotiations. Fisher called for a system of negotiation that, on his view, mimicked the conceptual processes of adjudication. Parties would represent large ideological conflict as discrete economic, legal, and political issues and, in this way, would more readily accept small losses alongside small gains (and for reasons that include fealty to a dispute settlement system).

Despite these beginnings, analogies between negotiation and adjudication faded and few other theorists ventured to describe compromise as a distinctive feature of either process. Here is a provisional sketch of why: Eisenberg and Fisher were writing in the late 1960s and early 1970s during a time that legal historians have characterized in two distinct ways—neither of which were particularly amenable to a legal praxis of compromise. First, as Larry Kramer has argued, this time period represented a highwater mark of rights-based judicial supremacy.[60] In the 1980s, defenses of judicial exceptionalism became all the more entrenched in the hands of a subset of liberal legal elites: think, paradigmatically, of Owen Fiss, who felt doubly assailed by critical legal studies and its language of rights indeterminacy on the one hand, and Reagan-style neoliberalism and the ascendancy of cost-benefit analysis, on the other.[61] For Fiss and scholars like him, adjudication was rights interpretation, *not* accommodation, adjustment, or compromise of any sort: "judges," he reasoned, "have no authority other than to decide what is just."[62]

At the same time, and as Fiss's defense of adjudication suggests, this period also marked the ascendancy of the law and

economics movement. In the 1970s, law and economics' fundamental assumption—that "[p]eople act as rational maximizers of
their satisfactions"—spread rapidly to inform the work of legal
scholars outside of an elite group at the University of Chicago
and into diverse non-market contexts, including whether people
should litigate or settle their disputes.[63] As I discuss in the following section, law and economics left an important imprint on ADR,
particularly the strand that developed to manage the delays and
costs accompanying what elite reformers described as a "litigation
explosion."[64] Beginning in the late 1970s and early 1980s, prominent legal negotiation scholars, including Fisher, created a field of
dispute resolution that was primarily about private voluntary trans-
actions. And they developed elaborate prescriptions to enable
individual actors to work out mutually advantageous arrangements
at the level of interpersonal exchange, turning efficiency principles into colloquial prescriptions.

ADR scholars, however, did not share law and economics'
radicalism; rather they moved between interest-based trades and
principled legal reasoning. They did so by distinguishing between
"growth" where efficiency principles governed, and "distribution,"
which they thought was properly subject to conventional forms
of legal reasoning. Parties in negotiation, they recognized, would
and should "invoke rules, cite precedents, and engage in reasoned
elaboration" to divide surplus value.[65] They also moved between
private disputes, where legal negotiation governed, and public disputes, which they made the subject of Fissian adjudication.[66]

Thus, even as it developed as an alternative to legal process,
ADR embraced two distinct logics that reflected the dominant
(albeit competing) approaches to liberal legalism of its time:
efficiency-maximization, on the one hand, and principled, rights-
based legal reasoning, on the other hand. In neither was compromise a salient category of analysis or practice.

B. *ADR in the Shadow of Law and Economics*

Before turning to the field of legal negotiation in the 1980s and
1990s, I want to highlight a few foundational presuppositions of
law and economics that, taken together, helped to reorient dominant perceptions and practices of how to resolve legal conflicts

about loss. First are the neoclassical ideas that preferences are subjective; that it is beyond the discipline of economic science to consider how preferences are formed;[67] and that it is impossible to compare preferences or "utilities" across individuals.[68] The neoclassical economist can simply use willingness to pay as a neutral medium to observe how actors themselves order and value their preferences in moments of exchange. Ronald Coase, who by many accounts "invented the modern discipline of law and economics,"[69] crucially added the idea that harms, like preferences, are subjective and indeterminate. In *The Problem of Social Cost*, he famously re-described prelegal harms as conflict of uses.[70] That is, what appears as harm to particular individuals or firms—for example, the farmer whose crops are trampled by the rancher's cows, the community that lives near a polluting factory, the fishermen whose fish swim in a river polluted with industrial contaminants—are, in fact, *joint* costs of coexistence,[71] or, in negotiation speak, "joint contributions" to a shared problem.[72] When harm is theorized as the parties' subjective experiences of joint costs, the challenge for dispute resolution becomes how to maximize parties' subjective experiences of net benefits. Loss (of crops or health or fish) is thus oriented away from, for example, principles that express community morality and toward rational calculations of what individual and social costs appear necessary to trade for what individual and social gains.

Richard Posner, likely the most important legal scholar to infuse neoclassical economics in American legal thought,[73] added the idea that there is no involuntary and no uncompensated loss in consensual agreements. In bilateral negotiated agreements, all loss is made in exchange for a gain, and such agreements by definition make parties better off (or at least not worse off) by virtue of the fact that the parties *consent* to exchange.[74] This is the case, moreover, regardless of the effects of these agreements over time. As Posner put it: "I contend, I hope uncontroversially, that if you buy a lottery ticket and lose the lottery, then . . . you have consented to the loss."[75] Notice that here that loss is made equivalent to risk of loss; because risk of loss is included as a commodity that is priced and thus compensated in exchange, loss itself is "fully compensated ex ante and hence [is] consented to."[76] Thus, as Robin West observes, for Posner "apparent losers in wealth-maximizing transaction" are not really losers—they consent to their loss because it "improve[s] their well-being."[77] Finally, constraints—such as social, structural, or environmental conditions that shape how and why and to what people consent—are irrelevant to this analysis. It then follows that "inequality of bargaining power" is, in Richard Epstein's words, an "incoherent" concept.[78] Posner likewise explained that "the argument of 'exploitation' based on 'unequal bargaining power' . . . lacks, so far as I can see, any economic basis."[79] The idea, in brief, is that people behave rationally to maximize their own subjective preferences, whatever their status or background conditions.

Taken together, these ideas—that loss, like preference, is subjective and unknowable except in moments of exchange, that loss is voluntary and compensated for by virtue of consensual exchange, and that exchange can be theorized without attention to constraints—suggest that analysts can conceive of dispute resolution as a market or bargaining situation where all parties seek to maximize gain.[80] And, indeed, these ideas informed the theory and practice of legal negotiation in important but also incomplete ways. In the shadow of law and economics, ADR did not simply set out to maximize the "private desires of individuals," as Fiss, for example, characterized the field.[81] Legal negotiation's own foundational texts and training materials suggest a practice that is more interesting and complex. Namely, these texts reveal how interest maximization and efficient exchange are not concepts that can be implemented wholesale into people's daily practices. These concepts come up against the reality of people's lives and their (potentially unstable and conflicting) desires in complex and challenging ways and must be translated and *taught*—and in a cooperative, dialogic fashion—so people can engage in relationships with others.[82] Thus, beginning with *Getting to Yes*, legal negotiation became devoted to helping people manage conflict by teaching them to internalize the logics of growth and distribution and, as we shall see, only secondarily or idiosyncratically the logics of compromise.[83]

C. Getting to Yes

It is hard to overstate the impact on the field of legal negotiation of Roger Fisher's and William Ury's 1981 *Getting to Yes*, with its circulation in the millions in 36 languages. In it, Fisher announced a scale-independent model of negotiation that would be equally relevant to "families, neighbors, couples, employees, bosses, businesses, consumers, salesmen, lawyers," as much as to representatives of nation-states.[84] *Getting to Yes* was thus unmoored from the particular problems of ideological struggle among nations that dominated Fisher's early work. As a result, it was also unmoored from any single normative measure of external justification that could redeem why and how compromise and loss should occur, such as creating and sustaining a consensual transnational legal system. In its place, Fisher offered a more minimalist and also privatizing account of dispute settlement and negotiation—a process that anyone and everyone can use by supplying their own interests, norms, and preferences and whose only transcendent aspiration is optimal allocation. In Fisher's and Ury's words: the "wisest solutions . . . produce the maximum gain for you at the minimum cost to the other side."[85]

As Mnookin and Kornhauser aptly observe, this sort of "optimal bargaining occurs when, in economic terminology, nothing is indivisible."[86] But how are ordinary people to go about understanding their desires as maximally divisible in this way? *Getting to Yes*—which as Fisher acknowledges purposefully "blurs a desirable distinction between descriptive analysis and prescriptive advice"[87]—set out precisely to teach people to learn how to articulate their interests in ways that would allow them to discover gains from substitution or trade.[88] Or, to put the point differently, Fisher's early emphasis on fractionation did not disappear; rather it was transformed into a practice of individual interest representation.

To that end, *Getting to Yes* introduced the idea of integration—that is, Mary Parker Follett's argument that what appears as a conflict can, in fact, reflect different kinds of discrete desires that are not actually opposed.[89] To capture the point, Fisher and Ury describe two sisters who, after dividing a single orange, discover one wants only the rind to bake a cake, the other only the pulp to make juice.[90] They use the story to argue that generating growth—or, in Fisher's and Ury's words, challenging "the assumption of a fixed pie"—depends on a practice of interest representation and substitution.[91] That is, parties "expand the pie" when they become willing to represent their primary desires or "positions" (the orange) as a set of secondary or underlying desires or "interests" (a cake, some juice) that can be satisfied through substitute means (the rind, the pulp).

In this model, *compromise* is the opposite of integration. It is the unreflexive and undesirable practice of dividing a fixed pie—that is, of too quickly cutting the orange in half for failure to engage in introspection, careful listening, and creative thinking. "Compromising between positions," Fisher and Ury explain, is unfortunate because it "is not likely to produce an agreement which will effectively take care of the human needs that led people to adopt those positions."[92] Nor is it likely, they argue, to uncover the multiple kinds of underlying interests including differences—in endowments, assessments, preferences (including preferences for risk), or predications—that can produce gains from trade.[93] Mnookin puts the point in a similar way: he suggests that "compromisers" have personality traits desirable for optimal problem-solving. But a "willingness to compromise may mean that [negotiators] aren't [as] effective [as] they might be" if they developed more cognitive and affective skills in empathy and assertion.[94]

Notice that in order to teach people to engage in economic exchange, negotiation scholars broke with a core analytical principle of neoclassical law and economics. As Posner explains, "economics does not seek to depict states of mind; it is concerned with what people (even animals) do, not what they feel or think."[95] But in order to help shape what people do, the scholar-practitioner of negotiation is often extensively involved in helping people reflect upon what they feel and think. That is, to encourage people to move from positions to interests, the scholar-practitioner of negotiation helps them interrogate what preferences they have, why they have them, what other ends those preferences may serve, and how these preferences can be served through other means. This analysis, however, often proceeds in highly particular and circumscribed ways. Negotiation scholars characteristically emphasize the psychological and affective determinants of preferences and not, as I shall argue below, the structural, environmental, or institutional ones. For example, emotions play a prominent role in negotiation literature. By acknowledging emotions as a significant element in human disputes, parties are encouraged to understand legal and economic conflict as reflecting, in part, the complex feelings that occur in social relations. And they are simultaneously encouraged to depersonalize their differences in order to engage in more effective exchange. The idea is that emotions have a logic of their own; when they are acknowledged and expressed, disputants understand the conflict differently and become better able jointly to focus their energy on the problem, not the people.[96] The behavioral turn in law and economics features in negotiation literature in much the same way: disputants can be taught about cognitive biases such as reactive devaluation, anchoring, confirmation biases, overconfidence, or endowment effects in order to evaluate how they can shape their preferences to make them more amenable to exchange.[97]

Here then, for example, is what Eisenberg's inheritance dispute would look like if it proceeded with a mediator or negotiation trainer steeped in this dominant problem-solving model. The son and the relative would be encouraged to move away from a debate about abstract principle (for example, does the son or the caretaker have a "right" to inherit). Instead, they would be asked to explain *why* they want the land and to represent their material interests as well as their deeper emotional needs and normative commitments in multiple ways. Perhaps the relative would answer that he desires compensation for some of his labor caring for the father as the father aged. And perhaps if pressed by the facilitator to dig a bit deeper, the relative might add that he also wants some appreciation from the son that includes some consideration of his more precarious economic position. Perhaps the son would assert that in addition to the land he desires a connection with his father as well as status in the community as his father's rightful heir. Even more, perhaps there are useful differences in needs and capabilities and economies of scale to exploit that could simultaneously meet the parties' material as well as their underlying emotional and psychological needs. What if the son invested in new farming machinery but, because he already owns a sizable plot of land, cannot himself cultivate both fields? Could the parties work out a long-term sharecropping arrangement that gives the son the right to own the land with the accordant status in the community, and that gives the relative the right to use the machinery and to farm and profit from the land and thus receive some compensation and recognition from the son? Would that leave them both better off according to their own standards of value—emotions, norms, and material interests all included—than dividing the land into separate parts?

Setting aside the (rather complex) answer to this question, let me here simply observe that this is a very different approach to negotiation than what the parties actually did. At least on Eisenberg's read, they divided the land to affirmatively express and compromise among conflicting principles that for the parties meant that "*each* had a right *to the land.*"[98] They thus based their negotiation on a logic of morality and right—but one that, via compromise, could accommodate a plurality of moral principles and understandings of right by people bound together in a kinship community. In this case, the task of the analyst of negotiation is, like Eisenberg, to try and make sense of conflicting moral economies rather than, like Fisher and Ury, to encourage parties to engage in an iterative process of interest representation in order to discover opportunities to reconcile interests and trade. To be clear, for Fisher, Ury, and others, "expanding the pie" is not an ethical mandate: parties can compromise, or be spiteful, or any number of things if they like. Rather, it is a mode of practice, a method to enculturate parties in a way of being in a problem that is presumed simply to appear to most disputants as a way that is better.

Other foundational works associated with the Program on Negotiation at Harvard Law School entrenched and expanded Fisher and Ury's trade-based model. Here, very briefly, are two examples. In *The Manager as Negotiator*, David Lax and James Sebenius offer a universalizing model for negotiation based on analyses of parties' preferences, forecasts, and endowments that they explain captures the basis "for *all joint gains.*"[99] Like all negotiation theorists, they define preferences broadly as "anything that the negotiator cares about" including process, relationships, and principles, but encourage negotiators to translate them, as best as possible, in commensurate terms susceptible to trade.[100] For example, a plaintiff may have interest in avoiding the anxiety of a trial but she can learn to represent that interest in a form open to substitution. Perhaps she could "imagine services one could buy to otherwise satisfy the same interest"—a magic pill that would eliminate her anxiety for a fixed sum of money.[101] In *Beyond Winning,* Robert Mnookin, Scott Peppet, and Andrew Tulumello likewise explain that the purpose of legal negotiation is to create value through exchange. Here too the key is uncovering all the secondary interests underlying initial positions that parties can learn to express— noncompetitive similarities, exploitable differences, and economies of scale—in the language of wealth-maximizing trade.[102]

Of course, none of these writers understand negotiation as simply a practice of value creation or integration. Trade ideally produces surplus value that can be divided in various ways. Thus, all these writers instead emphasize the relation between growth and distribution. As Lax and Sebenius put it: "No matter how much creative problem-solving enlarges the pie, it must still be divided; value that has been created must be claimed. And, if the pie is not enlarged, there will be less to divide; there is more value to be claimed if one has helped create it first."[103] Moreover, to varying degrees, all these writers disavow strategies of distribution based on only individual bargaining power and will. Fisher and Ury, for example, coined the phrase "principled negotiation" to encourage parties to divide surplus value according to what they call "objective criteria," that is, explicitly reasoned and mutually agreeable standards whose legitimacy would be obvious "to a great many people" and that are "fair and independent of either party's will."[104] In other words, they encourage negotiators to jointly rationalize why a distribution should proceed in a particular way by invoking widely accepted (indeed, quasi-universalizable) standards that are not clearly partisan to one's own side. These standards, they explain, can be any of "market value, precedent, scientific judgment, professional standards, efficiency, costs, what a court would decide, moral standards, equal treatment, tradition, reciprocity, etc." (they literally offer a list).[105]

Thus, if the aim for growth is interest representation and substitution (not compromise), the aim for distribution is jointly reasoned consensus (not compromise). When they discuss principled distribution, Fisher and Ury describe negotiators who agree to a particular allocation because they are persuaded that

an agreement is justified by some explicit standard of reason that
all parties accept or because it approximates the outcome they are
likely to receive in an alternative forum—for example, the agreement is based on "market value" or "what a court would decide."[106]
Indeed, Fisher and Ury use the term objective criteria precisely to
suggest a particular kind of *legal* rationality—an approach that is
aptly captured in their recommendation that negotiators "behave
like a judge" and consider and weigh reasons for and against various distributive standards including precedential ones. For example, they recommend: "[w]hen each party is advancing a different
standard, look for an objective basis for deciding between them,
such as which standard has been used by the parties in the past or
which standard is more widely applied."[107] *Compromise* is justified
if, after a reasoning process, parties reach two objective standards
that they "agree are equally legitimate" (their example is market
value versus depreciated costs).[108] This approach makes compromise a neutral principle to split the difference among the valuations suggested by indeterminate reasons.

Compromise shaped by principle, by contrast, more often
describes a negotiator who relinquishes a desire that she would
not otherwise rationally or objectively concede because she wishes
to express a (tacit or explicit) commitment to a higher-order
end—for example, respect, solidarity, community, obligation, or
love. When Fisher, Ury, and others recommend distribution based
on objective criteria—with compromise as a backstop solution—
they describe negotiators engaged in the deliberate application of
cognitive reason, more narrowly defined, as well as pragmatic cost-
benefit calculations.[109]

III. At Stake in the Difference

In the remainder of this chapter, I consider some of the stakes
of evolving dispute settlement mechanisms based on growth and
distribution rather than compromise. This is not an easy question to explore. All of these constructs (growth and distribution;
compromise shaped by principles and constraints) are efforts to
describe (or shape) social practice. And gaps invariably persist
between general constructs and the variability and multiplicity of
social practice on the ground. Hence my aim is not to offer an

abstract model or defense of compromise designed to compete with legal negotiation's general set of tools and prescriptions. To the contrary, I turn in subsection A (next) to specific examples of compromise institutions in order more concretely to explore some of the highly contextual normative debates that emerge when compromise shaped by principle is imagined as a salient feature of legal and extralegal dispute resolution institutions. In subsection B, I explore some of the social costs when, in legal and extralegal dispute resolution, compromise shaped by constraint is under-considered and under-described.

A. *Compromise Shaped by Principle*

I have argued that when people engage in compromise shaped by principle they limit (some of) their interests, values, and principles in order to advance an extrinsic or higher-order end. It follows that most institutionalized (rather than individualized) compromise procedures I could discover entail the establishment of a collective set of principles that inform when and why compromise should occur. In these institutions, compromise—like growth and distribution—embodies normative intuitions about how people should organize their social relations. But whereas growth and distribution present themselves as universalizing constructs—their higher-order commitments are interest maximization and "objectively" rationalized standards of distribution—the particular normativity of principles governing compromise appears immediately explicit. As we have seen, such principles may involve sustaining a transnational legal system, upholding community values that balance inheritance rights with care and material need, or advancing moral recognition (which for some philosophers of compromise is its own universalizing claim). Perhaps this is why Martha Minow recently suggested that the "crucial question" for analysts of compromise is a normative one: when should compromise "be resisted, and when instead . . . should compromise be advanced."[110]

Consider the following two very different examples of institutions that encourage compromise as a mechanism of dispute settlement. First, is the practice of "standing aside" in contemporary anarchist collectives. Because for anarchists non-hierarchical forms of self-organization are both a means and ends of a democratic society, collectives devote a great deal of energy to establishing their own consensual decision-making and dispute resolution procedures that "prefigure" the worlds they wish to create. These procedures are variously set forth in process- and skills-focused training pamphlets, websites, and books.[111] And they govern, for example, how a group should generate proposals to undertake various actions as well as resolve conflict on matters spanning how to allocate group resources to how to reconcile ideological difference about "diversity of tactics" (that is, the legitimacy of (non)violence) in protest actions. These procedures evolved from consensus-building practices deployed by Quakers and other directly democratic social movement activists (some of which have been popularized in the recent Occupy protests). Especially in smaller groups, they are often used in an effort to achieve consensus among all members.[112]

Despite a procedural norm of unanimous consent in intimate collectives, members may decide to "stand aside" if they personally disagree with the merits of an emerging consensus but nonetheless find it a good faith option for the group as a whole. The idea is that members should sometimes set aside their own desires and preferences simply because it is good to value the desires and preferences of others in a shared community—an idea that, on my account, is an example of compromising on principled grounds. For many anarchists, standing aside is made meaningful because participants often have the right to veto or "block" the actions of the rest if they feel the group decision violates the group's (or potentially one's own) ethical values. In other words, individual autonomy is made a precondition for group solidarity.[113] And activists who have adopted these practices report feelings of pleasure, even honor, in setting aside their own desires and rationalizations and accepting decisions out of respect and camaraderie for others—decisions that they would otherwise disagree with or dispute. For example, anthropologist David Graeber describes how members of a particular anarchist collective attempt to define consensus. As one explained, "it's supposed to be a process ... [u]nlike in majority voting, where you always end up with some alienated minority who voted against the proposal but then they just have to live with it anyway." A second followed to elaborate upon the distinction, "There is actually something kind of pleasurable . . .

in realizing what I think isn't even necessarily all that important, because I really respect these people, and trust them. It can actually feel good. But of course, it only feels good because I know it was *my* decision, that I could have blocked the proposal if I'd really wanted to. I chose not to take myself too seriously."[114] This activist thus describes standing aside as a self-expressive and individualized decision.

Here compromise follows from higher-order commitments to balancing individual autonomy with group solidarity. Sustaining these conditions for compromise, however, requires an incredible amount of labor to guard against hierarchy and inequality within a group. In fact, a good deal of training material discusses how to ensure that group dynamics do not silence diversity and individual dissent—and thus how to ensure that compromise and the consensus it can enable do not, in fact, reflect reluctant concessions to tacit forms of power and coercion. Suggestions typically include keeping and reviewing speakers' lists and moving members of traditionally disadvantaged groups to the front of the queue, appointing "vibe watchers" to attend to implicit power dynamics and to call out people on bad behavior, holding additional meetings to reflect on process, and conducting trainings on topics such as gender inequality.[115] Compromise is thus envisioned here as exceedingly fragile and time-intensive normative work. It is supposed to emerge out of feelings of group solidarity that, through procedural checks and group reflexivity, are protected from conformity and hierarchy. And it is simultaneously supposed to be sustained by guarantees of individual autonomy that entitle members to block group decisions—even if, at times, differences among members produce a voluntary division of the group along ideological or interest-based lines.[116] Precisely because anarchists relentlessly value voluntary social obligations, collectives are unlikely (or rather unwilling) to achieve any sort of permanent institutionalization (that might otherwise be sustained, for example, by enforcing majoritarian norms). Here, preserving the integrity of the process—including conditions to enable meaningfully autonomous compromises—means it is not always possible to preserve the integrity of the group.

Institutionalized compromise procedures are not, however, invariably (more or less successful) efforts to mediate among social commitments to solidarity, equality, and autonomy. To the contrary, disputants can use compromise shaped by principle purposely to mediate and thus maintain social rifts and hierarchies through higher-order commitments to paternalism and social harmony.[117] As an illustration, legal historian Amalia Kessler traces nineteenth-century debates among American lawyers and legislators over whether to adopt European-style conciliation courts.[118] In these courts, a third party—typically a lay citizen of high social standing—would encourage disputants to adopt an equitable compromise rather than apply formal rules of law.[119] On the heels of America's market revolution and the social dislocation it generated, proponents argued that importing similar kinds of conciliation courts would interject humanitarian considerations and values of benevolence and care into a new market-based order. Stronger parties could compromise to benefit weaker ones, thus adding a modicum of reciprocity and largess to otherwise unequal social relations. Proponents of conciliation courts were by no means against the practices of free enterprise and individual entrepreneurship transforming the country; they proposed to stabilize these practices by softening, via compromise, some of their effects.[120] By contrast, opponents worried that as an ideal of justice, conciliation courts would reward "communal harmony over and above the competitive assertion of self-interest" and were thus suited "to the inhabitants of hierarchical old world societies, rather than to modern, freedom-loving and market-oriented Americans."[121]

This early American debate about the role of compromise in legal procedure was thus a debate about the kind of social order best suited for a market-driven society. In this context, compromise was understood to follow from higher-order commitments to a certain kind of paternalism, care, and small discretionary measures of substantive redistribution. In rejecting conciliation courts, state legislators were rejecting precisely these values. As Kessler makes clear, they did not profess to prefer a legal system grounded only in rules that were general, neutral, and predictable. They also wanted a legal system that fostered an adversarial battle of wills and a spirit of formal equality, individual freedom, and competition rather than a spirit of sacrifice, benevolence, and dependence that they perceived as driving compromise forms of justice.[122]

In both anarchist process and debates about early American conciliation courts, compromise as a form of socio-legal organization reflects overarching ideals about the kinds of human relations and social conditions that should alternatively legitimate acts of altruism versus self-interest and acts of accommodation versus confrontation. And although these two institutions embody very different ideals, it is possible nonetheless to envision in both cases how the micro-practices and disciplinary processes of compromise procedures diverge significantly from the practices and processes of problem-solving negotiation. Legal negotiation encourages personal introspection in order to help parties more effectively externalize their conflict (not unlike what happens in a judicial process where conflict is ultimately abstracted from the parties themselves). Agreement then comes from discovering opportunities for commensurate trades and jointly reasoned standards for distribution. Compromise shaped by principle involves embedding conflict within the values and identities that disputants experience as constitutive of self and social relations. Here, agreement comes—if at all—from the variability and flexibility that is produced when values and identities are situated within social or community structures: for example, the anarchist commitment to balancing autonomy with solidarity so that members of collectives occasionally desire to "stand aside."

Whether either institution appears desirable, let alone practicable, in its own or other contexts will depend upon a host of factors including, of course, the underlying social relations of the parties to a dispute. By highlighting some of the normative debates driving different forms of compromise procedures, I wish to illustrate a more basic point; namely, how different approaches to allocating surplus in social exchange allow for different "becomings [and] ways of being" in a conflict.[123] Compromise is simply a different way of being in a conflict than the problem-solving that anchors legal negotiation: perhaps the most general thing to observe about it is that it entails (in its many possible iterations) explicit expression and social valuation of loss.

B. *Compromise Shaped by Constraint*

In this final section, I shift to compromise shaped by constraint in order to explore the ways loss can be made more or less salient in legal negotiation. Recall that, from the perspective of law and economics, there is only voluntary exchange regardless of constraints; parties trade revealed preferences and make themselves better off as a result. In legal negotiation theory and practice, however, parties are taught to interrogate and *represent* their preferences in ways that make them amenable to trade. This labor, in turn, engages the negotiation scholar in the murky analytical space of preference formation including choices about how broadly or narrowly to draw a contextual frame. In this part I ask: what if interest representation—that is, the voluntary decision of parties to render their desires into substitute forms of values— was described in negotiation not simply as a means of facilitating interest-maximization but also regularly as a practice of compromise potentially shaped by constraint? How would that change the way we see loss?

Recall Gutmann and Thompson's definition of classic compromise: in sum, they argue that in order to implement our principles and advance our interests, often we must trim them.[124] Two features strike me as worth emphasizing about Gutmann's and Thompson's definition. First, rather than the language of bargained-for exchange and calculating costs in exchange for gains, Gutmann and Thompson repeatedly use the term "sacrifice" to describe decisions that negotiators experience as simultaneously unfortunate but necessary to improve the status quo given one's constraints. Second, and perhaps for this reason, they do not turn to negotiation literature for skills and techniques to teach people how and when to "sacrifice" in this way. To the contrary, they distinguish themselves from "negotiation experts" who, they argue, favor the possibility of integration and joint gains and they cite the orange story as an exemplary illustration.[125] But the problem with the orange story as a metaphor for legal negotiation is not simply, as Gutmann and Thompson rather easily suggest, that the story implies that gains can be produced without sacrifice on any side— all theorists of negotiation understand that producing gains can require costs. Rather, from my perspective, the problem is that the orange story occludes the ways in which joint gains often depend on interest representation—which itself can involve compromise and loss.

Here, briefly, is what I mean. I suggested above that Fisher and Ury use the orange story to transform legal negotiation into a practice of representation and substitution. Primary desires are represented as secondary ones: positions are represented as underlying interests. In this account, autonomous individuals articulate their desires in complete and accurate ways. And negotiation theorists measure negotiated outcomes against these interests. That is, negotiation theorists trust that the sisters' desires are really for cake and juice and, as such, that the rind and the pulp stand in perfect substitution. This is how legal negotiation scholar Michael Moffitt could argue that "the single most important concept in modern dispute resolution literature [is] the idea that agreeing to an outcome at odds with one's position is not the same as compromising one's interests."[126]

But particularly under conditions of inequality, how people decide to represent the interests underlying their positions may be shot through with compromise shaped by constraint. Consider the following example. In *Getting to Yes*, Fisher and Ury illustrate the idea of integration not simply with the fabled sisters fighting over an orange, but with actual representatives of Israel and Egypt fighting over the land of the Sinai desert. Yet they tell the story in exactly the same way. Israel really wants security and Egypt really wants sovereignty, just as the sisters really want cake and juice. Thus, Fisher and Ury conclude that by agreeing to a demilitarized zone instead of physically dividing the land, Israel and Egypt "reconcil[ed] interests rather than compromis[ed] between positions."[127]

Yet this is what Anwar Sadat, president of Egypt, had to say in the Israeli Parliament in 1977, a year before the Camp David meetings took place: "[O]ur land does not yield itself to bargaining, it is not even open to argument. To us, the national soil is equal to the holy valley where God Almighty spoke to Moses. . . . None of us accepts ceding one inch of it, or accepts the principle of debating or bargaining over it."[128] From this perspective, we could see it as a compromise to transform what is represented as a sacred claim—an indivisible and principled right to land with all the entitlements, symbols, and attachments that includes—into an interest in possessing land within one's sovereign boundaries but with far fewer indicia and symbols of ownership and control. Equally as important: this compromise left Sadat with significant aspirations unmet. He wanted to negotiate not simply the end of Israeli occupation of the Sinai, but a comprehensive peace agreement to the Arab-Israeli conflict that restored Palestinian rights.[129] It may be a compromise that is in part shaped by principle, including recognition of Israel as part of a community of nation-states.[130] And it may be a compromise in part shaped by constraint—that is, an alternative preferable to the uncertainties of continued hostile relations. But in negotiation literature, Sinai stands for an agreement that involves the harmonization of interests, not an agreement produced through a significant degree of loss or compromise at all.

To describe this example as compromise rather than integration, the negotiation theorist would need to unpack and describe the interests expressed as "sovereignty" and "security" in broader historical, institutional, geopolitical, and structural terms.[131] I suspect that legal negotiation theorists rarely proceed in this way because to describe such a broad and diffuse set of constraints complicates the idea of maximizing a stable set of interests as far as possible whatever the conditions. Indeed, as an analytical construct, compromise shaped by constraints (with constraints broadly defined) suggests that in some negotiations parties may only ever experience different degrees and modes of coercion—that, in turn, become shaped and expressed as "interests" with different consequences for growth and distribution.[132]

Consider another example outside of negotiation literature; this one not between two sovereign states but rather between a Canadian mining company and a Peruvian agricultural village community. The company planned to purchase the villagers' farmland for its mining operations with payment in kind—a decision it announced in the shadow of state mining law that granted it particular (although also uncertain) expropriation rights.[133] As negotiations progressed and the company faced challenges producing suitable land for resettlement, the villagers became willing to represent their demand for land-based resettlement as an interest in compensation that could be satisfied by money. Exchange was thus made possible leaving both parties better off than any extant or likely alternatives given background bargaining conditions. Even more, the parties applied a seemingly fair and objective standard for distribution: the villagers received an amount of money that represented the full cost of resettlement to the mining company.[134] Under conditions of inequality, gains from trade happen precisely when lower-power parties become willing themselves to represent their desires as interests (e.g., money rather than land) that, if achieved, can also mutually serve the desires of higher-power parties better than any other set of alternatives. How, then, should the negotiation scholar describe this example? As compromise shaped by constraint or, as in the Sinai example, interest-satisfaction? Both are plausible interpretations for the negotiation scholar to offer. Perhaps an eye on compromise would invite analysis of background distributional rules and conditions that inform negotiating with state and corporate power when one's entire way of life and livelihood are at stake—including whether parties should seek to change or even break these background rules and thus whether any form of interest representation is desirable at all. Indeed, in the aftermath of this exchange, villagers found that they had traded a resource they were adept at sharing with others and using to generate income for a resource whose division among family members was highly contentious and, once divided, became more suitable for consumption than investment.[135] From this perspective, compromise versus integration (like growth versus distribution and surplus versus survival) blur: that is, when individual interests are placed into a mutually constitutive relation with social conditions, agreeing to an outcome at odds with one's position and compromising one's interests can appear more similar than distinct.[136]

CONCLUSION

In this chapter, I have argued that analysis of two significant human experiences of compromise in social exchange is peripheral within the mainstream field of legal negotiation. The first, compromise shaped by principle, is a sacrifice that in its clearest form is based not on competitive self-interest, bargaining power, or internal reason about the merits of a dispute or the best way to solve a problem. Rather, it is a performative act: an expression of higher-order values such as respect, recognition, paternalism, solidarity, or community, or an expression of higher-order purposes such as long-term peace and stability. The second, compromise shaped by constraint, is a choice to advance one's interests, but the choice is made against background conditions that mean one's interests are already deeply constrained. I also argued that the absence of compromise as a salient category of analysis in legal negotiation was not inevitable or conceptually compelled but rather reflects some of the practical ways in which mainstream ADR developed in the shadow of two liberal legal rationalities: growth shaped by efficiency principles and distribution governed by reasoned consensus or neutral (split-the-difference) criteria.

Consequently, as an analytical tool to think with and compare to legal negotiation, compromise shaped by principle allows us to foreground experiences that are not easily captured by the language of interest-maximization. To be sure, the economist may describe other-regarding behavior as internalizing someone else's utility or she may describe a decision to sacrifice an interest, value, or right for a higher-order end as equivalent to monetizing that end and making a rational trade.[137] But these descriptions do not, in my view, capture the phenomenology or personal psychology of invoking personal or communal values and principles to justify, even honor, potentially incommensurable loss. Compromise shaped by principle also allows us to foreground experiences that are likewise not easily captured by classic forms of legal reasoning: it reflects neither a worked out consensus between the parties nor an authoritative determination on the merits.

Compromise shaped by constraint, in turn, challenges the idea of loss as a voluntary and thus compensated calculation for a gain where all sides are made better off by virtue of exchange. In this sense, it offers a different approach to make sense of what actually happens in negotiation. As an analytical construct, it does not begin with revealed preferences—e.g., positions—that through self-reflection and self-regulation can be transformed into multiple and competing interests susceptible to trade that maximizes net gains. Rather, compromise shaped by constraint describes the ways in which parties compromise the ways in which they formulate and express their interests sometimes in a bid for their existence.

Perhaps because compromise does not therefore mimic the liberal discursive categories of adjudication or trade, it has remained mostly an outsider to legal process—in both its formal and, as I have argued here, its informal institutionalized forms. This is the case despite earlier efforts to make compromise an explicit topic of legal debate. For example, in 1979, the editors of our predecessor volume offered a guess as to why compromise was chosen as the annual theme by the members of the American Society for Political and Legal Philosophy and the American Association of Law Teachers.[138] They speculated that compromise stood to ameliorate a widely shared feeling that they were then "living at a time when interests tend to be denigrated and rights are sprouting from every tree."[139] Compromise, in other words, stood for a different way of doing things. It suggested an alternative to the "aggressive and competitive assertions of 'rights'" as the primary means of managing individual and group-based claims.[140] That is, compromise worked as a sociological imaginary to invoke against the legal mainstream.

Today, I would venture that many legal elites are less optimistic about the ability of rights, administered by courts and legislators, to resolve complex public controversies. In place of formal legal institutions, we have decentralized, even privatized, forms of dispute resolution "sprouting from every tree." And interests have supplanted, or become at least coequal with, rights as the predominant currency of public problem-solving and social well-being. Yet compromise is still not a salient category of legal analysis.

What would we gain with more analytical attention to compromise, if not in legal adjudication then in its rapidly proliferating consensus-based alternatives? Consider the field of new governance or democratic experimentalism, a reform movement in law devoted to expanding the role of stakeholder participation in dispute resolution and legislation. Among other legal process innovations, democratic experimentalists have revived earlier efforts to blur the boundaries between adjudication and negotiation—especially in complex cases where the welfare and expertise of a broad range of people is implicated.[141] Like Fisher, they see value in adjudication not because it can "teach a lesson or resolve big issues once and for all,"[142] but rather because it can incentivize ongoing and incremental processes of "stakeholder negotiation."[143] To that end, they advise judges to issue only general liability determinations against the status quo combined with penalties that no sides would prefer if the parties fail to reach their own negotiated agreements.[144] Because the shadow of the law is thus as procedural as it is substantive, democratic experimentalists anticipate that stakeholder negotiations will not simply approximate a process of interest-maximization that reflects each side's relative bargaining strengths.[145] Instead, they hope parties will open themselves to "broader moral and cognitive orientations,"[146] specifically by recruiting reason to articulate a common good across difference (a claim that is the subject of much empirical and normative debate).[147]

A focus on compromise would require analysts to consider the complex ways in which the terrain of human exchange is not fully captured by an oscillation among interests, reason, and rights. Analysts of compromise must observe how interests, reasons, rights—and problems themselves—are defined by status quo hierarchies and inequalities. As such, problems may require multiple forms of political and social contestation so that people can reconceptualize their interests and rights before reaching consensus—or, rather, before they engage in compromises that are irremediably shaped by social and structural constraints. Likewise, analysts of compromise must consider how people are motivated to act for and through a range of higher order, and potentially tacit, justifications and values.[148] At times, such alternative forms of human coordination may create the experiential conditions for collaboration—including for principled acts of compromise— more effectively than formalized processes of reason-giving and rational debate.[149] Of course, compromise is not the only way to draw attention to how consensual processes of allocating symbolic and material surplus can follow social and moral logics other than growth and distribution or legal reason and rights. But it is both a common way that people actually encounter principle and power in human exchange, and one that remains largely unelaborated in alternative movements in law.

Notes

1. Robert H. Mnookin & Lewis Kornhauser, *Bargaining in the Shadow of the Law: The Case of Divorce*, 88 Yale L. J. 950 (1979).

2. This, of course, is a stylized account of adjudication. As Martha Minow rightly notes, "in a sophisticated view of judging, the decision need not always result in an all-or-nothing result but instead can apportion ownership, or blame, or liability across multiple parties." Martha Minow, *Is Pluralism an Ideal or a Compromise? An Essay for Carol Weisbrod*, 40 Conn. L. Rev. 1287, 1298 (2008). Still, as Minow suggests, on most views of adjudication, compromise "connotes abandonment of the required craft and devotion to principle." Martha Minow, *Affordable Convergence: "Reasonable Interpretation" and the Affordable Care Act*, 126 Harv. L. Rev. 117, 147–48 (2012). Other scholars, in turn, have observed the various kinds of "compromises" that judges may, in fact, pursue. *See, e.g.*, Duncan Kennedy, *Strategizing Strategic Behavior in Legal Interpretation*, 1996 Utah L. Rev. 785, 795–96 (arguing that as a strategy to maintain neutrality, judges split "the difference between other people's ideological positions"); Cass R. Sunstein, *Trimming*, 122 Harv. L. Rev. 1049, 1065–1067 (2009) (likewise suggesting that judges may articulate a middle position between extreme or controversial constitutional issues); Lee Epstein & Jack Knight, *The Choices Justices Make* 58–79 (Washington, DC: CQ Press 1998) (arguing, based on an empirical analysis, that US Supreme Court Justices at times strategically modify how they reason about the merits of a case in order to accommodate the views of other Justices necessary to secure coalitions).

3. Martin Shapiro, in fact, argues that it is precisely because the vast majority of people who file cases in court settle via mediation and negotiation, that judges can act as if they interpret formal legal rules to reach all-or-nothing outcomes rather than also apply equitable discretion to achieve more flexible solutions: "When the legal system shifts a high proportion of outcomes from trial to the mediation or negotiation preceding possible trial, it encourages mediate solutions without unmasking judicial discretion." Martin Shapiro, Compromise and Litigation, in *NOMOS XXI: Compromise in Ethics, Law, and Politics* 163, 173 (ed. J. Roland Pennock and John W. Chapman) (New York: New York University Press, 1979).

4. *See* notes 91–92, 107 and surrounding text. Carrie Menkel-Meadow's recent work on compromise is an important exception. It describes compromise as a moral practice subject to contextual standards of evaluation. *See, e.g.*, Carrie Menkel-Meadow, *Ethics of Compromise*, in Global Encyclopedia of Public Administration, Public Policy, and Governance (ed. A. Farazmand, 2016); Carrie Menkel-Meadow, *The Variable Morality of Constitutional (and Other) Compromises: A Comment on Sanford Levinson's Compromise and*

Constitutionalism, 38 Pepp. L. Rev. 5 (2011); Carrie Menkel-Meadow, The Ethics of Compromise, in *The Negotiator's Fieldbook* 155 (ed. Christopher Honeyman and Andrea Kupfer Scheider, 2006); Carrie Menkel-Meadow, *Compromise, Negotiation, and Morality,* 26 Negotiation J. 483 (2010).

5. *See* Duncan Kennedy, *Form and Substance in Private Law Adjudication,* 89 Harv. L. Rev. 1685, 1717–1718 (1976).

6. *See id.* at 1732.

7. As Mnookin and Kornhauser put it: "a bargaining theory must take note of possible altruism or spite." Mnookin & Kornhauser, note 1, at 968.

8. One could therefore of course argue that compromise is something that existing models of negotiation can assimilate without any change in either practice or theory. As Simon Căbulea May (this volume) reasons, even though mainstream negotiation theorists do not attend to compromises in the various ways I describe, they need not "deny the existence" of such compromises or deny that there are valid reasons to engage in them "any more than financial advisors must deny the existence of irreducibly altruistic reasons for charitable donations." But observing the absence of conceptual conflict between negotiation theory and compromise does not itself, I argue, capture how the field of negotiation has evolved on the ground. A telling example of the field's contemporary cultural logics, May submits that "making concessions is not, in and of itself, particularly difficult—negotiators do not need much practical advice about how to be less successful in the pursuit of their ends," and hence that engaging with particular kinds of moral compromise "seems to be quite beyond the scope of [negotiation] theory" as its own prominent authors define it. If only concessions were easy to make and negotiators needed no practical reflection or skill to advance them. Indeed, it is precisely this conclusion—that managing or even advancing and emphasizing loss is beyond the scope of negotiation theory properly understood—that my chapter aims to open up for analysis and exploration.

9. I should add: there is a good deal of work defining compromise. Scholars provisionally distinguish between compromise as a process— that is, a way of reaching a solution through unilateral or mutual concessions—and as an outcome—a solution in which one or all negotiators gain and lose some of their ends. *See, e.g.,* Martin P. Golding, The Nature of Compromise: A Preliminary Inquiry, in *NOMOS XXI,* note 3, at 3, 7–8; Arthur Kuflik, Morality and Compromise, in *NOMOS XXI,* note 3, at 39–41; Mohamed Nachi, *The Morality in/of Compromise: Some Theoretical Reflections,* 43 Social Science Information 291 (2004), 293–296. Scholars also distinguish analysis of compromise within negotiations from meta-questions such as whether one's rival is a legitimate negotiation partner; see Robert Mnookin, *Bargaining with the Devil: When to Negotiate and When*

to Fight (New York: Simon & Schuster, 2010), or whether it is morally defensible to resolve a particular substantive controversy through mutual concessions. *See, e.g.,* Golding, at 5–6; Nachi, at 298–300; Avishai Margalit, *On Compromise and Rotten Compromises* (Princeton, NJ: Princeton University Press, 2010). In this chapter, I take up only compromise *in* negotiations.

10. *See, e.g.,* J. Patrick Dobel, *Compromise and Political Action: Political Morality in Liberal and Democratic Life* 59 (Savage, MD: Rowman & Littlefield, 1990) ("The compromises I am concerned with differ from a bargain, deal, or simple exchange relation"); Margalit, note 8, at 40 (distinguishing an agreement reached via mutual trade within a fixed bargaining range from "sanguine compromise" that also involves moral questions of human recognition); Richard Bellamy, *Liberalism and Pluralism: Towards a Politics of Compromise* 93–102 (London: Routledge 1999) (defining compromise as a practice of reciprocal accommodation that includes the adoption of a "moral standpoint" and a "communitarian-minded understanding of liberalism" and thus one that is distinct from trading for mutual advantage); John E. Coons, Compromise as Precise Justice, in *NOMOS XXI*, note 3, at 190, 191 (distinguishing compromise from "a common higgle, the maximizing of utilities under conditions of relative freedom"); Chiara Lepora, *On Compromise and Being Compromised*, 20 J Political Philosophy 1, 4 (2012) (defining compromise as a resolution of a matter of principled concern that is distinct from reaching a "deal" or "bargain").

11. *See* Frances M. Kamm, *The Philosopher as Insider and Outsider*, 15 J. of Medicine and Philosophy 347, 360 (1990) (describing a morally appropriate compromise as one "that is [not] influenced by the relative position of the disputing parties, their ability to bluff . . . the ability of a party to hold out longer, and differences in who needs agreement more"); Golding, note 2, at 15 (Compromise "should not be a plain function of the relative bargaining strengths of the parties"); Margalit, note 8, at 53 ("clear cases [of compromise] are cases of agreements free from coercion").

12. Golding, note 2, at 15–17.

13. Theodore M. Benditt, Compromising Interests and Principles, in *NOMOS XXI*, note 3, at 26–27.

14. Kuflik, note 8, at 38, 43, 49–51. Kuflik thus argues further that compromise processes require first-order constitutional rights and liberties that are not subject to compromise. *Id.* at 43. For a similar argument, see Henry S. Richardson, *The Stupidity of the Cost Benefit Standard*, 29 J. Legal Stud. 971, 996–7 (2000).

15. Kuflik, note 8, at 64.

16. Henry S. Richardson, *Democratic Autonomy: Public Reasoning about the Ends of Policy* 148 (New York: Oxford University Press, 2002) ("Compromise . . . is different from simply coming to appreciate the other's argu-

ments and modifying one's view accordingly"); Lepora, note 9, at 4 (distinguishing a case of compromise from one of correction); Simon Căbulea May, *Moral Compromise, Civic Friendship, and Political Reconciliation*, 14 Critical Rev. Int'l Social & Political Philosophy 581, 583–84 (2011) (likewise arguing that "compromise differs from consensus about the merits of the various options" and "involves support for an inferior position").

17. *Id.*

18. Sophocles, *Antigone* (David Mulroy, trans., 2013).

19. *Id.* at 12–14, 35–36.

20. *Id.* at 25.

21. Georg W. F. Hegel, Lectures on the Philosophy of Religion II.3.a (1895), *quoted in* George Steiner, *Antigones* 37 (New Haven, CT: Yale University Press, 1984) (describing this passage as Hegel's "canonic text" on *Antigone*).

22. *See, e.g.,* Philip A. Glotzbach in Conflict and Compromise, Commencement Remarks, May 16, 2009.

23. Richardson, note 15, at 148.

24. Margalit, note 8, at 40.

25. *Id.* at 41, 43.

26. Dobel, note 9, at 80.

27. *See* Sophocles, note, at 57.

28. Amy Gutmann & Dennis Thompson, *The Spirit of Compromise: Why Governing Demands It and Campaigning Undermines It* 9–10 (Princeton, NJ: Princeton University Press, 2012).

29. *Id.*

30. *See, e.g., id.* at 9. Gutmann and Thompson leave open the possibility that lawmakers may justify their concessions in the name of higher-order principles such as democracy or even progress and justice. *Id.* at 101–109 (describing "principled prudence"). They would also evaluate compromises normatively based upon how they include the "welfare, rights, respect, and other relationships among the parties." *Id.* at 77.

31. Michael Alberstein, *Pragmatism and Law: From Philosophy to Dispute Resolution* 254 (Burlington: Ashgate, 2002) (citing a PON brochure). I should add: the term "problem-solving negotiation" was first coined in 1984 by Carrie Menkel-Meadow, another pioneering scholar in the field and also among the few whose later work explicitly engages with compromise. *See* Carrie Menkel-Meadow, *Toward Another View of Legal Negotiation: The Structure of Problem Solving*, 31 UCLA L. Rev. 754 (1984).

32. Gabriella Blum & Robert H. Mnookin, When *Not* to Negotiate, in *The Negotiator's Fieldbook: The Reference for the Experienced Negotiator* 101, 110 (ed. Andrea Kupfer Schneider & Christopher Honeyman) (Washington, DC: American Bar Association, 2006).

33. *See, e.g.*, Robert H. Mnookin, *Why Negotiations Fail: An Exploration of Barriers to the Resolution of Conflict*, 8 Ohio St. J. Disp. Resol. 235, 245 (1993) (describing loss aversion).

34. *Id.* at 249. *See also* Russell Korobkin, *Inertia and Preference in Contract Negotiation: The Psychological Power of Default Rules and Form Terms*, 51 Vand. L. Rev. 1583, 1627 (1998).

35. For example, Robert Bush and Joseph Folger promote a model of mediation dedicated to fostering individual empowerment and the moral recognition of one's rivals. *See, e.g.*, Robert A. Baruch Bush & Joseph P. Folger, *The Promise of Mediation: The Transformative Approach to Conflict* (San Francisco: Jossey-Bass, 2005). Scholars outside of law have developed a field of narrative mediation drawing on post-modern theories of conflict as discursive practice. *See, e.g.*, John Winslade & Gerald Monk, *Narrative Mediation: A New Approach to Conflict Resolution* (San Francisco: Jossey-Bass, 2000); Sara Cobb, *Empowerment and Mediation: A Narrative Perspective*, 9 Negot. J. 245 (1993).

36. Melvin Aron Eisenberg, *Private Ordering Through Negotiation: Dispute-Settlement and Rulemaking*, 89 Harv. L. Rev. 637 (1976).

37. *Id.* at 638–639.

38. *Id.* at 639.

39. *See* Mnookin & Kornhauser, note 1, at 997 (referencing Eisenberg's argument to illustrate the "the continuity between the social processes of negotiation and adjudication"); *see also* Shapiro, note 3, at 172 ("It is necessary to emphasize, as Eisenberg has done, that . . . where [l]itigation is potentially present, negotiated outcomes will reflect the values expressed by the law").

40. Mnookin & Kornhauser, note 38, at 75–80.

41. Eisenberg, note 35, at 640.

42. *Id.* at 640–642. According to Eisenberg, the local magistrate made clear that in court he would have applied inheritance law to award all the land to the son. *Id.* at 656.

43. *Id.* at 642.

44. Eisenberg, note 35, at 645.

45. *Id.* at 645–646.

46. *Id.* at 647–648.

47. *Id.* at 648–649.

48. Roger Fisher, *Do We Want to "Win" the Cold War?*, Bulletin of the Atomic Sciences, January 1962, 33.

49. *Id.*

50. *Id.* at 34.

51. *See, e.g.*, Roger Fisher, *International Law: A Toolbox for the Statesman*, 9 Cal. W. Int'l L.J. 469, 475 (1979); Roger Fisher, *Fractionating Conflict, in*

International Conflict and Behavioral Science 91, 94 (ed. Roger Fisher, 1964).

52. Fisher, *Fractionating Conflict*, note 50, at 103.

53. *Id.* at 91.

54. *Id.* at 92.

55. Roger Fisher, *Points of Choice: International Crises and the Role of Law* 37 (New York: Oxford University Press, 1978).

56. *Id.* at 26; *See also* Fisher, *International Law*, note 50, at 478 ("As international lawyers, we have to convince our clients that . . . what they really want is a system that can handle problems and make little disputes out of what might be big disputes. We want to keep the hands small so that when we lose some we lose small ones and so that there is no crisis over what is going on").

57. Fisher, *Points of Choice*, note 54, at 25–26 (emphasis added).

58. Fisher, *International Law*, note 50, at 474–75.

59. Roger Fisher, *International Conflict for Beginners* 129, 158 (New York: Harper & Row, 1969) (emphasis added).

60. Larry D. Kramer, *The People Themselves: Popular Constitutionalism and Judicial Review* 963–66 (New York: Oxford University Press, 2004).

61. *See generally* Amy J. Cohen, *Revisiting* Against Settlement: *Some Thoughts on Dispute Resolution and Public Values*, 78 Ford. L. Rev. 1143, 1150–57, 1161 (2009).

62. Owen M. Fiss, *The Law Regained*, 74 Cornell L. Rev. 245, 249 (1989). *See also* Owen M. Fiss, *Comment: Against Settlement*, 93 Yale L.J. 1073 (1984); Owen M. Fiss, *The Social and Political Foundations of Adjudication*, 6 Law & Hum. Behav. 121 (1982); Owen M. Fiss, *Forward: The Forms of Justice*, 93 Harv. L. Rev. 1 (1979).

63. Richard A. Posner, *The Law and Economics Movement*, 77 Am. Economic Rev. 1, 5 (1987); Herbert Hovenkamp, *The First Great Law & Economics Movement*, 42 Stan. L. Rev. 993, 994 (1990).

64. *See, e.g.*, Warren E. Burger, *Agenda for 2000 A.D.—A Need for Systematic Anticipation*, in The Pound Conference: Perspectives on Justice in the Future 23, 31–34 (1979) ("It is no longer economically feasible to employ lawyers and conventional litigation processes for many 'minor' or small claims"). Of course, as Marc Galanter has shown, the "litigation explosion" was more rhetorical than real. *See, e.g.*, Marc Galanter, *The Day After the Litigation Explosion*, 46 Md. L. Rev. 3 (1986); Marc Galanter, *Reading the Landscape of Disputes: What We Know and Don't Know (and Think We Know) About Our Allegedly Contentious and Litigious Society*, 31 UCLA L. Rev. 4, 10–11, 36–69 (1983). Left critics therefore suspected that the legal establishment's support for ADR in fact reflected conservative backlash against progressive victories won in courts. For a description of some these criti-

cisms, as well as for historical analysis of a competing progressive narrative of ADR associated with the community mediation movement, see Amy J. Cohen & Michael Alberstein, *Progressive Constitutionalism and Alternative Movements in Law*, 72 Ohio St. L. J. 1083 (2011).

65. Mnookin & Kornhauser, note 1, at 973.

66. *See, e.g.*, William L. Ury, Jeanne M. Brett, & Stephan B. Goldberg, *Getting Disputes Resolved: Designing Systems to Cut the Costs of Conflict* 17 (San Francisco: Jossey-Bass, 1988) ("Although reconciling interests is generally less costly than determining rights, only adjudication can authoritatively resolve questions of public importance."); Lawrence Susskind & Jeffrey Cruikshank, *Breaking the Impasse: Consensual Approaches to Resolving Public Disputes* 17 (New York: Basic Books, 1987) ("When fundamental constitutional rights are at stake, we properly turn to our judicial system").

67. *See, e.g.*, Herbert Hovencamp, *Coase, Institutionalism, and the Origins of Law and Economics*, 86 Indiana L.J. 499, 515, 518 (2011).

68. *See* Lionel Robbins, *An Essay on the Scope and Nature of Economic Science* (London: Macmillan & Co., 1935). In the 1930s, Lionel Robbins transformed marginalist and welfarist economics by insisting upon "ordinalism," that is, the impossibility of interpersonal comparisons of utilities among individuals or groups (and thus challenged the "economic" basis for transferring welfare among classes). *Id.* at 120–121; *see also* Hovencamp, note 62, at 1033–1037; Hovencamp, note 66, at 502–515, 518, 521.

69. Hovencamp, note 66, at 499. Hovencamp further describes Coase as "completely ordinalist in this thinking" and notes that "by the time *The Problem of Social Cost* was written the ordinalist victory in neoclassical economics was complete." *Id.* at 515, 529–530, 541. *See also* Richard A. Posner, Values and Consequences: An Introduction to Economic Analysis of Law, in *Chicago Lectures in Law and Economics* 189–190 (ed. Eric A. Posner) (St. Paul, MN: Foundation Press, 2000) (dating the contemporary American field of law and economics with *The Problem of Social Costs* as well as other work in the 1960s by Guido Calabresi and Gary Becker).

70. R. H. Coase, *The Problem of Social Cost*, 3 J.L. & Econ. 1 (1960).

71. *Id.* at 1–8.

72. Douglas Stone, Bruce Patton, & Sheila Heen, *Difficult Conversations: How to Discuss What Matters Most*, ch. 4 (New York: Penguin Books, 1999).

73. *See* Neil Duxbury, *Patterns of American Jurisprudence* 395 (New York: Oxford University Press 1995).

74. *See, e.g.*, Richard. A. Posner, *The Ethical and Political Basis of the Efficiency Norm in Common Law Adjudication*, 8 Hofstra L. Rev. 487, 488–89 (1980) ("Because of the impossibility of measuring utility directly, the only way to demonstrate that a change in the allocation of resources is Pareto superior is to show that everyone effected by the change consented to it").

75. *Id.*, note 73, at 492.

76. *Id.* Jules Coleman, *Efficiency, Utility, and Wealth Maximization*, 8 Hofstra L. Rev. 509, 534–535 (1980) (using the lottery example to distinguish consent to risk of loss from consent to loss, irrespective of whether it is fair for a particular contracting party to bear a loss).

77. Robin West, *Authority, Autonomy, and Choice: The Role of Consent in the Moral and Political Visions of Franz Kafka and Richard Posner*, 99 Harv. L. Rev. 384, 385–386 (1985).

78. Richard Epstein, *Discussion: The Classical Theory of Law*, 73 Cornell L. Rev. 310, 312 (1988).

79. Richard A. Posner, *Reflections on Consumerism*, 20 U. Chicago L. School Record 19, 24 (1973).

80. For an important early example, see Robert Cooter, Stephen Marks, & Robert Mnookin, *Bargaining in the Shadow of the Law: A Testable Model of Strategic Behavior*, 11 J. Legal Stud. 225, 226 (1982). The authors explain that bargaining in the shadow of the law is a game where players act optimally in order to maximize their expected utility when they form rational predictions that they, in turn, use to shape their decisions. *Id.* at 226, 228–229, 233.

81. Owen Fiss, *The Social and Political Foundations of Adjudication*, 6 Law & Hum. Behav. 121,122–123 (1982).

82. As Frank Sander, another important ADR scholar at Harvard Law School, put it in 1994: "An important by-product of the recent interest in alternative dispute resolution has been to refocus our attention on negotiation as a vital and persuasive process that can be taught." Frank E. A. Sander, *Dispute Resolution Within and Outside the Courts—An Overview of the US Experience* (unpublished manuscript cited in *Alberstein*, note 30, at 263 n. 48). A classic example is Roger Fisher's 1983 oil pricing exercise, which teaches students, through a simulated prisoner's dilemma, when and why collaboration is more rational than competition. The exercise is available for purchase at PON's Teaching Negotiation Resource Center, www.pon. harvard.edu. According to available sales data, between 2004 and 2013 the exercise was distributed to 83,321 people. Personal email from Luke Adolph, Manager, Clearinghouse Operations, Teaching Negotiation Resource Center, Waltham, MA, March 19, 2014.

83. Roger Fisher & William Ury, *Getting to Yes: Negotiating Agreement without Giving In* (ed., Bruce Patton) (New York: Penguin Books, 1981).

84. *Id.* at vi.

85. *Id.* at 55.

86. Mnookin & Kornhauser, note 1, at 975.

87. Roger Fisher, *Reply to the Pros and Cons of Getting to Yes*, 34 J. Legal. Educ. 115, 120–121 (1984).

88. *Id.* at ch. 3: "Focus on Interests Not Positions" and ch. 4: "Invent Options for Mutual Gain."

89. *See* Mary Parker Follett, *Dynamic Administration: The Collected Papers of Mary Parker Follett* (ed. H. C. Metcalf & L. Urwick) (New York: Harper and Brothers Publishers, 1942). This idea was introduced into labor negotiation theory in 1965 by Richard Walton and Robert McKersie who, drawing on Follett, distinguish integrative from distributive bargaining, but it had no perceptible effect that I have discovered on Fisher's early writing. Richard E. Walton & Robert B. McKersie, *A Behavioral Theory of Labor Negotiations: An Analysis of a Social Interaction System* 5, 7 (Ithaca, NY: ILR Press, 1965).

90. Fisher & Ury, note 82, at 59.

91. *Id.* at 59, 61.

92. *Id.* at 11. *See also* Walton & McKersie, note 88, at 129 (similarly describing compromise as a non-integrative approach to conflict resolution).

93. Fisher & Ury, note 82, at 76–79.

94. R. H. Mnookin, Instructions and Discussion Questions for the Thomas-Kilmann Conflict Mode Instrument (1996). *See also* Menkel-Meadow, note 30, at 768–775 (describing compromise in a similar fashion).

95. Richard A. Posner, *The Ethical Significance of Free Choice: A Reply to Professor West*, 99 Harv. L. Rev. 1431, 1439 (1986).

96. *See* Cohen & Alberstein, note 63, at 1101–1102; *see also* Fisher & Ury, note 82, at 30–33, 56; Roger Fisher & Daniel Shapiro, *Beyond Reason: Using Emotions as You Negotiate* 15 (New York: Penguin Books, 2005); Stone, Patton, & Heen, *Difficult Conversations*, supra note 71 at 85–108; Daniel L. Shapiro, *Emotions in Negotiation: Peril or Promise?* 87 Marq. L. Rev. 737 (2004).

97. *See, e.g.*, Robert H. Mnookin, Scott R. Peppett, & Andrew S. Tulumello, *Beyond Winning: Negotiating to Create Value in Deals and Disputes* 14–17 (Cambridge, MA: Belknap Press, 2000) (ch. 6: Psychological and Cultural Barriers).

98. *Id.* at 646 (emphasis partially added).

99. David A. Lax & James K. Sebenius, *The Manager as Negotiator: Bargaining for Cooperation and Competitive Gain* 114 (New York: Free Press, 1986). Their model, borrowed from game theorists and economists, they explain, "fully characterize[s] negotiators according to (1) their values and attitudes toward risk and time (represented by 'utility functions'); (2) their beliefs and forecasts (represented by probability distributions); (3) what they originally possess (called initial endowments); and (4) their capabilities to produce (represented by 'production functions')." For an-

other universalizing trade-based model, see Russell B. Korobkin, *A Positive Theory of Legal Negotiation*, 88 Georgetown L. J. 1789, 1791 (2000) (arguing that a dichotomy between defining a bargaining zone and allocating surplus value "provides a complete description of the negotiation process"). *Id.*

100. Lax & Sebenius, note 98, at 68.

101. *Id.* at 75.

102. Mnookin et al., note 96, at 14–17.

103. Lax & Sebenius, note 99, at 33. *See also* Mnookin et al., note 96, at 9 ("a skillful negotiator moves nimbly between imaginative strategies to enlarge the pie and conservative strategies to secure an ample slice").

104. Fisher & Ury, note 82, at 85–98, 89, 92.

105. *Id.* at 89. Mnookin, Peppet, and Tulumello second this approach, adding ideas to minimize risks of exploitation in distribution, such as recognizing hard tactics, changing the players, and, if necessary, walking away from a deal. Mnookin et al., note 101, at 267–270, 211–221.

106. Fisher & Ury, note 82, at 89.

107. *Id.* at 93.

108. *Id.*

109. I should add: from within this model of interest-based dispute resolution, a recent strand of scholarship and practice offers strategies for addressing value-based disputes, which are defined as "disputes in which the parties' values and identities are so important to the dispute that they interfere with the parties' ability to settle interest-based issues" through trade and distribution. *See generally* Teaching about the Mediation of Values-Based and Identity-Based Disputes: Teaching Notes to Accompany Three Role-Play Simulations, available from the Clearinghouse, Program on Negotiation, Harvard Law School (2010). This teaching note, which summarizes work spearheaded by Larry Susskind and Jennifer Brown, offers the following five options: (1) withdraw from the conflict; (2) negotiate interests separate from values; (3) facilitate discussion of values apart from trying to reach a settlement; (4) appeal to shared or "universal" values to forge common ground; and (5) most "risky," encourage parties to revise and change their values. *Id.* at 6–11. Option five approaches (but is not the same as) compromise shaped by principle where parties decide to sacrifice some of the interests or values driving the dispute because of other extrinsic values they hold.

110. Minow, *Is Pluralism an Ideal or a Compromise*, note 2, at 1298.

111. *See, e.g.*, Delfina Vannucci & Richard Singer, *Come Hell or High Water: A Handbook on Collective Process Gone Awry* (Oakland: AK Press, 2010); Peter Gelderloos, *Consensus: A New Handbook for Grassroots Social, Political, and Environmental Groups* (Tucson, AZ: See Sharp Press, 2006).

112. *See generally*, Amy J. Cohen, *On Being Anti-Imperial: Consensus-Building, Anarchism, and ADR*, 9 Law, Culture, and the Humanities 233 (2013) (including for a discussion of anarchist writers that support modified (majoritarian) forms of consensus in particular decision-making contexts); David Graeber, *Direct Action: An Ethnography* (Oakland: AK Press, 2009) (especially ch. 7: "Meetings"). For broader overviews and critiques of consensus-building in American social movements, see Francesca Polletta, *Freedom Is an Endless Meeting: Democracy in American Social Movements* (Chicago: University of Chicago Press, 2002); Paul Lichterman, *The Search for Political Community: American Activists Reinventing Commitment* (Cambridge: Cambridge University Press, 1996); Barbara Epstein, *Political Protest & Cultural Revolution: Nonviolent Direct Action in the 1970s and 1980s* (Berkeley: University of California Press, 1991).

113. For a more detailed examination of these practices, see Cohen, note 111, at 253–255.

114. Graeber, note 111, at 305; *see also* Consensus (Direct Democracy @ Occupy Wall Street), www.youtube.com/watch?v=6dtD8RnGaRQ.

115. *See* Cohen, note 111, at 250–252.

116. For examples, see Graeber, note 111, at 119, 94; for more discussion see Cohen, note 111, at 253–255.

117. Or, as Margalit argues, compromise can operate "to confer recognition on one's rival and to dispel an image of domination." Margalit, On Compromise, note 8, at 41.

118. Amalia Kessler, *Inventing American Exceptionalism: The Origins of American Adversarial Legal Culture, 1800–1877* (New Haven, CT: Yale University Press, 2017) (see ch. 5: "Market Freedom and Adversarial Adjudication: The Nineteenth-Century American Debates over (European) Conciliation Courts and the Problem of Procedural Ordering").

119. *Id.* at at 200–202.

120. *See id.* at 218–220.

121. *Id.* at 201–202.

122. *See id.* at 215.

123. J. K. Gibson-Graham, *Enabling Ethical Economies: Cooperativism and Class*, 29 Critical Sociology 123, 138 (2003).

124. *Id.* at 10, 94–95. *See also* David Luban, *Bargaining and Compromise: Recent Work on Negotiation and Informal Justice*, 14 Philosophy and Public Affairs 397, 414 (1985) (describing the paradox of compromise: "commitment to principle means commitment to seeing it realized. But in practice this means compromising the principle"); Fisher, International Conflict, note 50, at 90–91 (arguing similarly that "adopting a more limited objective [can] increase the chance of obtaining it" and illustrating the point with what he described as the US federal government's incremental ap-

proach to ending racial discrimination as it was condoned by various state governments).

125. Gutmann & Thompson, note 27, 14–15.

126. Michael Moffitt, *Three Things to Be Against ("Settlement" Not Included)*, 78 Fordham L. Rev. 1203, 1213 (2009).

127. Fisher & Ury, note 82, at 42–43. *See also* Lax & Sebenius, note 98, at 31 (describing how this agreement depended "upon probing the real interests of the two sides"). *See also* Jane Mansbridge, *Deliberative and Non-deliberative Negotiations*, Harvard Kennedy School Working Paper RWP09–010 at 16 (2009) (referencing this example to describe integration).

128. Statement to the Knesset by President Sadat, November 20, 1977, reproduced in the *Jerusalem Post*, November 21, 1977, at 5.

129. Steven A. Cook, *The Struggle for Egypt: From Nasser to Tahrir Square* 147–148 (New York: Oxford University Press, 2012). As Cook writes, the peace treaty "produced precisely the results Sadat had so intently hoped to avoid, a separate peace." *Id.* at 150.

130. *See, e.g., id.* at 142–143, 145–147 (suggesting that Sadat's address to the Israeli Parliament was itself perceived as an act of recognition against the advice of many of his allies).

131. *See generally* Jon Elster, *Sour Grapes: Studies in the Subversion of Rationality* 118 (New York: Cambridge University Press, 1983) (discussing adaptive preferences); Amartya Sen, *Commodities and Capabilities* (New Delhi: Oxford University Press, 1999).

132. *See* Duncan Kennedy, *Disenchantment of Logically Formal Legal Rationality, or Max Weber's Sociology in the Genealogy of the Contemporary Mode of Western Legal Thought*, 55 Hastings L.J. 1031, 1049 (2004) (describing Weber on freedom of contract); *see also* Robert Hale, *Coercion and Distribution in a Supposedly Non-Coercive State*, 38 Political Science Quarterly 470 (1923).

133. David Szablowski, *Transnational Law and Local Struggles: Mining, Communities and the World Bank* 45–46, 205 (Portland: Hart Publishing, 2007).

134. *Id.* at 209.

135. Szablowski, note 132, at 215–216.

136. Minow puts the point well when she observes that "it is not always easy to distinguish compromise from convergence." Minow, *Is Pluralism an Ideal or a Compromise*, note 2, at 1303. Indeed, Minow's example of convergence (finding "common ground without sacrificing principle") is a potential illustration of the point. Briefly summarized, proponents and opponents of marriage equality agreed on an employment regime where a worker could receive health benefits for a legally domiciled member of his or her household. *Id.* at 1301–1303. On one interpretation, both sides

converged on the shared principle of expanding health coverage while staying faithful to their views for or against marriage equality. On another interpretation, to advance the principle of healthcare for all, proponents of marriage equality relinquished some symbolic and dignitary capital in a struggle for gay marriage while opponents conceded to participate in a regime of de facto recognition.

137. Duxbury, for example, describes the economist Gary Becker's efforts to show that altruism and love among other values are "susceptible to neo-classical economic explanation." Duxbury, note 72, at 378.

138. J. Roland Pennock & John W. Chapman, Preface in *XXI NOMOS*, note 3, at vii.

139. *Id.*

140. *Id.*

141. *See* Charles F. Sabel & William H. Simon, *Destabilization Rights: How Public Law Litigation Succeeds*, 117 Harv. L. Rev. 1015 (2004); *see also* Joanne Scott & Susan Sturm, *Courts as Catalysts: Rethinking the Judicial Role in New Governance*, 13 Colum. J. European L. 565 (2006).

142. Fisher, *Points of Choice*, note 54, at 37.

143. For a description of the negotiation process that democratic experimentalists envision, see Sabel & Simon, note 140, at 1067–1070.

144. For elaboration, see *id.* at 1054–1056, 1067, 1073–1082.

145. *Id.* at 1099 and n. 234.

146. *Id.* at 1099.

147. For a summary of criticisms, see Amy J. Cohen, *Governance Legalism: Hayek and Sabel on Reason and Rules, Organization and Law*, 2010 Wis. L. Rev. 357, 358–359 notes 2, 3, & 4.

148. *See also* Carrie Menkel-Meadow, *The Lawyer's Role(s) in Deliberative Democracy*, 5 Nev. L.J. 347 (2004).

149. *See also* Amy J. Cohen, *Producing Publics: Dewey, Democratic Experimentalism, and the Idea of Communication*, 9 Contemporary Pragmatism 143 (2012).

5

COMPROMISE IN NEGOTIATION

SIMON CĂBULEA MAY

Negotiation is both an adversarial and a cooperative activity. It is adversarial because the parties have conflicting aims and it is cooperative because they have aims in common. The parties are at odds, but, if the negotiation process is to work, they cannot be entirely at odds. Compromise in negotiation typically reflects both aspects. Compromise is adversarial insofar as the parties usually try to concede as little as possible to each other, but it is cooperative insofar as the parties must nevertheless work together to reach an agreement that advances their goals, albeit imperfectly.

Since compromise is the paradigmatic feature of negotiation, we should expect contemporary negotiation theory to be able to explain its place in dispute resolution. In her contribution to this volume, Amy Cohen argues that orthodox accounts of negotiation—in particular, the model of "principled negotiation" developed by Roger Fisher and William Ury—fail in this task.[1] This is because these accounts incorporate two distinct logics—the economic logic of growth and the legal logic of distribution on the basis of objective criteria—that do not account for what happens in compromise. Her argument focuses on what she terms *compromise shaped by principles* and *compromise shaped by constraints*. The former involves the concessions a party makes on the basis of independent values, rather than on the basis of instrumental calculations. The latter involves the concessions a party is forced to make in representing its positions as negotiable interests.

I argue here that the principled negotiation model can accommodate the forms of compromise Cohen identifies. However, two types of error must be avoided. The first type of error is to combine the model with an impoverished account of practical rationality. The second type of error is to extend the model from its original role as a set of practical maxims for negotiators and advance it as a generic conception of the ethics of negotiation as a cooperative activity. In section I, I set out a basic schema of compromise and briefly discuss how it coheres with the principled negotiation model. In section II, I discuss how the model can accommodate Cohen's two types of compromise if it avoids crude assumptions about practical rationality. In section III, I argue against the tendency to understand principled negotiation as a generic conception of negotiation ethics.

I.

Suppose that *A* and *B* are parties to a collective decision and that *X*, *Y*, and *Z* are the various options they could select.[2] *A* and *B* compromise with one another when:

(1) (a)   *A* prefers $X > Y > Z$,
     (b)   *B* prefers $Z > Y > X$,
(2) (a)   *A* accepts *Y* instead of *X*,
     (b)   *B* accepts *Y* instead of *Z*,
(3) (a)   *A* accepts *Y* because of (1) and (2)(b), and
     (b)   *B* accepts *Y* because of (1) and (2)(a).

This basic schema captures three central elements of compromise: (i) reciprocal concession on the basis of (ii) enduring disagreement or conflict within (iii) a collective decision-making procedure. Although *A* and *B* both accept *Y*, they do not reach a consensus about what the collective decision should be—each continues to prefer a different option. The fact of this enduring disagreement leads each party to depart from its initial preference but not to reject it as mistaken. Thus, we can distinguish between two kinds of reason that a party may have to modify its position. First-order *reasons for correction* concern what the party should prefer the collective decision to be, assuming the other parties could be brought to agree. Second-order *reasons for compromise*, in contrast, concern how firmly the party should hold to its (presumptively correct) first-order position, once the fact of disagreement between the parties is taken as given. Reasons for compromise are therefore essentially dependent on the presence of disagreement or conflict between the parties about the collective decision; they are not (also) reasons to regard an initial preference as mistaken. The difference between accepting an option on the basis of a reason for compromise rather than a reason for correction can be illustrated by the following test. Suppose A shifts its support from X to Y in response to the disagreement between the parties. If A would continue to prefer to persuade B to accept X, if only it could, then it supports Y as a compromise. In contrast, if A would no longer prefer to persuade B to accept X, then, other things being equal, it has corrected its initial preference ordering.

Reasons for compromise differ from *reasons for deference*, although these too can involve acceptance of a suboptimal decision. To illustrate, a minority party does not (typically) compromise when it accepts that it has been outvoted by a majority. Its acceptance of the majority's inferior choice is not the ex ante acceptance of an option within deliberation about a collective decision, but rather the ex post acceptance of the outcome of the decision procedure. The minority party defers to the majority's authority to determine this outcome, in a manner not entirely unlike how liberal individuals defer to the right of their neighbors to make suboptimal personal choices. In more unusual cases, the minority may only first accept a majoritarian procedure as a compromise, perhaps if it believes that the collective decision should be made unanimously. Such cases involve both compromise and deference, but at different points: the minority party first compromises by accepting the majoritarian rule and then defers to the majority's authority on the basis of the rule.[3]

The schema I have presented is basic in two ways. First, it presents a very simple model of compromise. Actual cases are often far more complicated than just two agents making a single choice between three options. The number of parties may be greater, there may be an indefinite number of options to consider, and the choice they have to make may be only one in an ongoing series of decisions (including decisions about decisions, etc.). A process of compromise may also be incomplete if the parties narrow their differences through mutual concession but fail to reach a final agreement on a specific proposal. Despite their failure, it can be very important to acknowledge their concessions as a form of compromise. Complexities such as these can be added to the model as necessary.

Second, the schema presents a generic model of compromise, one that applies across different social contexts. *A* and *B* might be members of a hiring committee deciding which candidate to interview, traders haggling over the price of a commodity, judges choosing which novelist to award a prize, political parties deliberating about foreign policy, or friends wondering what film to see. The schema says nothing about how the two agents are related or how they regard each other. It leaves open whether their preference orderings reflect different values, beliefs, judgments, tastes, or benefits, and hence why these preferences should conflict. As far as it goes, the schema does not distinguish between strategic bargains and any other kind of interpersonal compromise. As a consequence, it makes no assumption that cannot be accommodated within contemporary negotiation theory.

Consider Fisher and Ury's model of principled negotiation, which they recommend in preference to simple positional bargaining. The model comprises four key maxims:

(i)   Separate the people from the problem.
(ii) Focus on interests, not positions.
(iii) Invent options for mutual gain.
(iv) Insist on using objective criteria.

In principled negotiation, compromise is unfortunate. The parties should not simply split the difference between their positions or let counterproductive bargaining practices impede the creation of mutually satisfactory solutions. Instead, they ought to explore creative ways to integrate their underlying interests. Thus, if *A* and *B* are willing to move past any mutual suspicion or antipathy they might feel, they might develop a new possibility, *W*, such that:

(1*) (a) *A* prefers $W \geq X > Y > Z$
      (b) *B* prefers $W \geq Z > Y > Z$

In this happy circumstance, the parties can reach consensus on *W* without any need for compromise, since each regards it as at least as good as their initial preference. The canonical story about two sisters quarreling over an orange illustrates this situation.[4] Since the one sister wants only the pulp and the other sister only the peel, they can each get all that they want if they approach their conflict constructively. Nevertheless, such cases of fully integrative negotiation are the exception rather than the rule. Once the Pareto frontier has been reached, some measure of compromise is usually inevitable. These more typical cases have the following structure:

(1**) (a) A prefers $X > V > Y > Z$
      (b) B prefers $Z > V > Y > Z$

Some progress has been made, since each party prefers V to Y, but V remains a compromise from both their perspectives.

II.

A.

Cohen uses the example of compromise shaped by principles to argue that the negotiation theory's focus on interests ignores the important role of norms in dispute resolution. The main elements of this argument can be set out in three points. For the sake of simplicity, I discuss moral norms, although other types of normative commitments can be included as necessary.

1. Moral Reasons for Compromise
Negotiators do not only decide disputes by appeal to their self-interest. Instead, it is not at all uncommon for the parties to appeal to various moral norms in support of their positions, and to resolve disputes by working out a reasonable accommodation that reflects the strengths of the moral values at stake. In his example of a Tanzanian inheritance dispute, Melvin Eisenberg identifies three relevant norms: the right of the son to inherit his father's land, the responsibility of a well-off person to assist relatives in need, and the right of caregivers to some share in a deceased relative's estate.[5] He claims that the division of the land between the two relatives "accommodated all of the relevant norms by tacitly

recognizing that as a matter of principle Kadume [the son] and Soine [the uncle] each had a right to the land."[6] Cohen claims that Fisher and Ury's model would recommend that the two relatives resolve the inheritance dispute in a very different way:

> The son and the relative would be encouraged to move away from a debate about abstract principle . . . Instead, they would be asked to explain *why* they want the land and to represent their interests and needs in multiple ways. Perhaps the relative would answer that he desires compensation for some of his labor caring for the father as the father aged. And perhaps if pressed by the facilitator to dig a bit deeper, the relative might add that he also wants some recognition and appreciation from the son. Perhaps the son would assert that in addition to the land he desires a connection with his father as well as status in the community as his father's rightful heir. . . . Could the parties work out a long-term sharecropping arrangement that gives the son the right to own the land with the accordant status in the community, and that gives the relative the right to use the machinery and to farm and profit from the land and thus some compensation and recognition from the son? Wouldn't that leave them both "better off" according to their own standards of value than dividing the land into separate parts?[7]

Two points can be raised in response. First, the model would not necessarily recommend the relatives resolve the dispute in a different manner. As Cohen notes, negotiation theory is formally agnostic about the goals the parties pursue. Fisher and Ury do not define a person's interests narrowly as those things that make her better off, that is, her self-interest. Instead, interests are defined broadly as the "desires and concerns [that] motivate people; they are the silent movers behind the hubbub of positions."[8] A person's interests are, in essence, the *purposes* or *ends* which she intends her positions to promote. Fisher and Ury's claim, therefore, is that disputes can be more efficiently resolved by attending to these underlying purposes, not (simply) that they can be more efficiently resolved by considering how each party can be made better off. Insofar as Kadume and Soine are genuinely committed to the three moral norms Eisenberg mentions, there is nothing in the model's second maxim that could tell against the way they resolved their dispute.

Second, Eisenberg's description of the case leaves it somewhat unclear whether the two relatives agree that the division of land between them is equitable. Kadume might come to believe that although he has a strong moral right to inherit the land, he is also under an obligation toward his uncle to acknowledge and accommodate his interests. Similarly, Soine need not believe that justice requires he receive all the land. If so, then the division they reach is a compromise only in a limited or provisional sense, that is, relative to their conflicting interests narrowly defined. Once the two relatives' moral commitments are taken into account, the resolution of their dispute is better understood as a consensus (albeit a consensus that perhaps emerges only through the broader community's deliberative efforts). The moral norms here act as reasons to correct the initial preferences. The two relatives can only be said to compromise *tout court* if they continue to disagree about what outcome would have been preferable relative to all their underlying desires and concerns, both moral and non-moral.

2. Moral Reasons for Moral Compromise
Parties in dispute typically continue to have different beliefs about which collective decision would be morally preferable. In Fisher's discussion of the transnational legal system, different states can be presumed to have different evaluations of the justice of their claims.[9] If it is true that a powerful state must be prepared to lose some issues for the sake of the system's viability, and that this system has independent moral weight, then the state has, to that extent, moral reason to accept moral compromises. It would be preferable if it could persuade its opponents of the justice of its claims, but, failing that, it is morally best not to force every issue. The second point, then, is that there can be moral reasons for moral compromise in negotiation.

It is unclear, however, why the example of compromise in the transnational legal system poses a challenge to contemporary negotiation theory. First, if the theory is agnostic about the kind of ends that agents in conflict might pursue, as it should be, then there is no formal impediment to the idea that states can have irreducibly moral reasons for action. Second, there can clearly be (moral or non-moral) instrumental reasons for concessions that are not grounded in an assessment of a party's bargaining strength in the immediate context. *A* might accept *Y* as a compromise, since it would prefer to *persuade B* to accept *X* instead. But it does not follow that *A* should prefer to use its bargaining power to *force B* to accept *X*, if it could. The manner in which a collective decision is reached often affects the reasons to prefer one outcome over another.

3. Non-Instrumental Moral Reasons for Moral Compromise

A third point is raised by Cohen's reference to the distinctive phenomenology of compromise shaped by principles. In such cases, the parties make concessions to each other, not in proportion to the strength of their bargaining position or for separate instrumental reasons, but because of independent values they wish to express. Compromise shaped by principle is a "performative act: an expression of higher-order values such as respect, recognition, paternalism, solidarity, or community."

In the example of the transnational legal system, the moral reason for compromise is instrumental (or *pragmatic*): if the powerful state were to exploit its bargaining strength to the utmost in each dispute, the long-term consequences would be severe. In contrast, the values of respect and solidarity (etc.) provide non-instrumental (or *principled*) reasons for action. If it is true that an individual's intransigence on some matter in itself expresses disrespect for her opponents in negotiation, then she has a moral reason to compromise that is not grounded in the valuable causal consequences of concession. We can accordingly distinguish between four types of potential moral reasons in negotiation, as shown in table 5.1.

TABLE 5.1. MORAL REASONS IN NEGOTIATIONS		
	Non-instrumental	Instrumental
First-order reasons for correction	E.g., fairness requires *X* distribution of land	E.g., *Y* distribution of land would benefit the community most
Second-order reasons for compromise	E.g., respect for other parties requires that intransigence be avoided	E.g., the viability of a dispute resolution system requires sacrifice on some issues

As it happens, I do not think that the value of respect provides a very good moral reason for moral compromise, but that is neither here nor there.[10] In at least some social domains, agents can have non-instrumental moral reasons of some kind to forge moral compromise agreements with their fellows.[11] Certainly, agents can take themselves (whether correctly or not) to have such reasons in any domain they like. The present question is whether there is anything in the notion of a non-instrumental moral reason for moral compromise that is at odds with the presuppositions of negotiation theory. Two points suggest that there is not.

First, Fisher and Ury's model is clearly compatible with (first-order) non-instrumental moral reasons for correction. Insofar as they accept that agents can adopt any kind of end, they accept that agents can adopt the values of justice and fairness as ends. If justice and fairness require a certain resolution of a dispute, then the agents have a non-instrumental moral reason to prefer that option. But if the model does not preclude first-order non-instrumental moral reasons, then it need not preclude second-order non-instrumental moral reasons.

Second, Fisher and Ury advocate their model on instrumental grounds—they describe its maxims as practical (rather than moral) advice for people who "fear getting less than they should in a negotiation."[12] It may be the case that such people also accept (or should accept) that they have good moral reason to compromise in negotiation. But this seems to be quite beyond the scope of the theory. Making concessions is not, in and of itself, particularly difficult—negotiators do not need much practical advice about how to be less successful in the pursuit of their ends. That Fisher and Ury ignore non-instrumental moral reasons for compromise does not mean that they must deny the existence of such reasons, any more than financial advisors must deny the existence of irreducibly altruistic reasons for charitable donations.

B.

Cohen also argues that negotiation theory has difficulty accommodating compromise shaped by constraint. The problem she raises concerns how parties are advised to move beyond their initial positions and represent their interests in a manner conducive to the development of mutually preferable options and the distribution of goods on the basis of objective criteria. This process can itself involve loss: "agreeing to an outcome at odds with one's position and compromising one's interests can appear more similar than distinct." In her example, Peruvian villagers find that money is not an adequate substitute for the various goods they lose when they are pressured to sell their land. Not all goods are interchangeable.

It is unclear, though, why such incommensurability or pluralism cannot be recognized within negotiation theory. If the theory does not presume to stipulate the content of each party's desires and concerns, then it cannot stipulate that these desires and concerns can all be given a dollar value, as it were, at the end of the day. The advice to negotiators to explore avenues for trade and substitution can be seen as good advice, as far as it goes. There need not (and should not) be any presumption that this is always possible, or that uncompensated loss is always avoidable. Moreover, although market value might provide an objective criterion for the distribution of gains in some contexts, there is no reason why it can be an objective criterion in all disputes. Fisher and Ury understand objective criteria as standards that are independent of the will of the parties, not as just any formally neutral standards.[13] For instance, an objective criterion in a divorce proceeding could be developed by asking the parents to decide on child visitation rights before determining which parent should enjoy custody.[14] There is no suggestion that the parents would do well to treat access to their children as a commodity to be assigned a cash value.

In cases where a low-power group has no option but to accept financial compensation for a non-fungible good, we can distinguish between two agreements between the parties: first, to negotiate some or other price for the good, and second, to a particular price. Both agreements can be seen as compromises if the low-power group would prefer not to sell the good for any dollar amount. No doubt there can be good reasons for it to make these concessions. But there is no reason why negotiation theory must suppose that using market value as the criterion to settle the price cannot itself be a type of compromise.

I have argued that negotiation theory—and the principled negotiation model in particular—is not challenged by the two types of compromise Cohen identifies, as long as certain crude assumptions about practical rationality are avoided: (i) that a party's rational preferences represent its self-interest narrowly construed, (ii) that a party only ever has instrumental reasons to accept one option rather than another, and (iii) that a party's various interests are always commensurable and therefore conducive to trade and substitution. No doubt, some negotiation theorists may implicitly or explicitly make one or another of these errors. But if this tendency is anything more than just a convenient shorthand, then a deeper worry looms: the problem is not that they fail to understand the role of compromise in dispute resolution, but rather that they fail to understand the place of value in human life.

III.

A second way to misuse the model of principled negotiation is to advance it as a generic account of the ethics of negotiation as a cooperative activity. On this view, the four maxims are to be understood, not as useful practical advice for negotiators, but as moral principles that govern how parties should resolve their disputes, whatever those disputes may be about (including disputes about moral principles).

I claimed at the outset that despite its adversarial features, negotiation is a cooperative activity. The parties accordingly have two kinds of reasons that govern their conduct within the process. *Cooperative reasons* are grounded in the norms that define the fair terms of cooperation between the participants. Each party has, as a participant in the activity, standing to demand that the other parties comply with these norms. They are the moral "rules of the game," and failure to respect them constitutes a kind of foul play. *Independent reasons*, in contrast, are those that other parties do not have the standing to enforce *qua* participants in the activity. Failure to act on the basis of an independent reason may be a serious failing—one that other participants are free to criticize—but · it does not constitute a violation of the fair terms of cooperation between the parties.

The distinction between cooperative and independent reasons is simply a distinction between reasons with different functional roles. Independent reasons can be moral reasons, whether instrumental or (like cooperative reasons) non-instrumental in form. In some contexts, they can be weightier than cooperative reasons. Instrumental reasons can be specific to a single party or common to all parties, if they happen to share certain goals, and cooperative reasons can be controversial if the parties disagree about the proper rules of their joint activity. In extreme cases of disagreement—those concerning the constitutive rules of a practice—the parties cannot participate in the activity together unless some resolution is reached. For instance, two chess players cannot play chess unless they both accept the *en passant* rule since that rule is part of what defines the game. But not all cooperative reasons are grounded in such constitutive rules. The Spanish priest Ruy López de Segura advised chess players to seat their opponents with the sun in their eyes. Underhanded tricks like this represent a failure to cooperate fairly with one's opponent in playing chess, but do not, for all that, entail any failure to play chess.

There are a number of plausible candidate norms of cooperative negotiation. For instance, we might think of the following maxims as defining some of the fair terms of negotiation:

(i)   Listen to what the other party has to say.
(ii) Do not lie about your concerns and interests.
(iii) Do not threaten violence if you cannot have your way.
(iv) Do not accept agreements that you do not intend to honor.

Since the principled negotiation model advises parties to explore avenues for mutual gain, it is a natural candidate for a conception of the ethics of fair negotiation. On this approach, the maxims of the model provide cooperative reasons: each party has moral standing to demand that the other parties seek integrative solutions to their conflict in preference to positional bargaining. When the conflict between the parties concerns their self-interest, that is, their interests narrowly defined, there is a great deal of merit in this proposal. Other things being equal, a substantively fair bargain is one that advances each party's interests. A reasonable party does not exploit its bargaining strength to advance its own interests as ruthlessly as possible or to squeeze as many concessions from its adversaries as it can. Instead, it cooperates properly when it is willing to accept less than it can get from the negotiation for the sake of fairness.

I argued above that the principled negotiation model cannot capture the important place of normative commitments in dispute resolution unless a party's interests are defined broadly, as concerns or purposes that need not represent its narrow self-interest. But it is precisely this formal agnosticism about ends that defeats any proposal to treat the model as a generic conception of negotiation ethics. Whether the four maxims can be sustained as principles defining the fair terms of cooperation in negotiation depends entirely on the context and nature of the dispute. Consider the second maxim: parties should invent options for mutual gain. If this is treated as a norm of cooperative negotiation, and not just as an independent reason, then each party must take on some responsibility for the other parties' successful realization of their goals. This cooperative interpretation of the second maxim means that *A* has a principled moral reason to work with *B* to find a resolution that accommodates both parties' concerns, even if it has no independent (pragmatic or principled) reason to offer concessions. But whether *A* has any moral reason to value *B*'s goals in this way depends entirely on what those goals are and what type of relationship exists between the parties.

To illustrate, suppose two political parties disagree about the moral justifiability of competing legislative proposals. I argue elsewhere that political leaders only ever have pragmatic moral reasons to accept moral compromise agreements, that is, reasons grounded in the valuable causal consequences of the concessions.[15] On my view, it is no part of a cooperative conception of political negotiation concerning matters of moral importance that parties place any value on accommodating their opponents' aims—assuming, that is, that they have no first-order reasons for correction to integrate these aims into their own positions. Political leaders have a moral responsibility to promote justice and the public good through democratic means as efficiently as possible, and no cogent consideration, I argue, justifies tempering this responsibility with principled reasons for moral compromise.

In his contribution to this volume, Eric Beerbohm advances a view that agrees with the cooperative interpretation of the second maxim of principled negotiation.[16] Beerbohm claims that to participate genuinely in the practice of legislative compromise, legislators must observe certain constitutive rules: they must share a commitment to "place weight on accommodating other participants' positions" and should therefore, "barring defeaters . . . offer non-strategic concessions that make the package acceptable to the other party." Whereas the "practitioner" can wholeheartedly accept these rules, the "strategist," who accepts only pragmatic reasons for moral compromise, cannot.

However, Beerbohm's argument includes a caricature of the strategist's position. He claims, *inter alia*, that the strategist does not accept the process of compromise in legislative negotiation as a cooperative activity; that she is ruthless and demands capitulation from her co-legislators, whom she regards as obstacles; that she countenances deceit in negotiation whenever it is useful; that she places no value on jointly enacting laws with the representatives of other citizens; that she values only legislative output and ignores the procedural side of justice; that her only reason to reject a proposal is its failure to advance her substantive principles of justice; and that she fails to recognize legislative negotiation as a morally distinctive activity, differing in kind from negotiation in other social spheres. All of these positions are, I believe, objectionable, but none of them follows from the claim that there are only pragmatic reasons for moral compromise in politics.[17]

Since democratic procedures are required by a conception of citizens as free and equal, political leaders have principled moral reason to value the activity of democratic co-legislation with all freely and fairly elected representatives of the people, quite apart from its substantive output. Within these procedures of deliberation and negotiation, political leaders also share a moral responsibility to cooperate with each other in reaching substantively correct decisions, that is, decisions that best promote justice and the common good. This leaves it entirely open, however, just what the terms of cooperation in democratic legislative negotiation should be. On my view, one moral rule of the political game is a commitment to the equality of all citizens—racist political proposals are not simply manifestos of substantive injustice, but also profound violations of democratic procedure.[18] A second moral rule of the political game is that legislators must avoid lying about the philosophical justifications they accept for their positions. Far from being a context where the usual norms against deceit are suspended, political discussion about matters of principle must be honest if the public interest in open and democratic government is to be vindicated.

Legislative negotiation is therefore a morally distinctive activity: legislators must have higher moral standards than poker players or, for that matter, mafia dons. But legislative negotiation is also morally distinctive in being less demanding in its governing norms than dispute resolution in some other social spheres. Political leaders share a moral responsibility to reach correct decisions, as best they can, not decisions that distribute success in the realization of goals as broadly as possible. The fact of this shared responsibility implies nothing about whether it is valuable for legislators to share liability for the outcome of the process and, on that basis, to offer concessions to each other on non-instrumental grounds. Instead, it is precisely because citizens share ultimate authority over the law, that legislators cooperate best, other things being equal, when they deliberate and negotiate in a manner that is most conducive to a relationship of democratic accountability between citizen and representative. Since shared liability dulls this relationship of accountability, as Beerbohm notes, there are both substantive and procedural grounds to be skeptical of non-instrumental reasons for moral compromise in politics.

IV.

Parties to a collective decision compromise with each other when they accept mutual concessions in response to the fact of enduring disagreement about which decision would be preferable. Using Fisher and Ury's model of principled negotiation as an example, I have argued that negotiation theory is not challenged by the various types of moral reasons that parties often have to forge compromise agreements in the resolution of their disputes, as long as certain crude assumptions about practical rationality are avoided. But it is precisely this step that precludes using the model as a generic conception of negotiation ethics and hence as a source of cooperative reasons for moral compromise. What counts as genuine cooperation in negotiation differs from one social context to another.

NOTES

1. Amy Cohen, "On Compromise, Negotiation, and Loss," chapter 4 in this volume. Roger Fisher and William Ury, *Getting to Yes: Negotiating Agreement Without Giving In*, 2nd edition. New York: Penguin Books, 1991.

2. The following discussion draws on Simon Căbulea May, "Principled Compromise and the Abortion Controversy," *Philosophy and Public Affairs*, 33 (4), 2005: 317–48. Simon Căbulea May, "Moral Compromise, Civic Friendship, and Political Reconciliation," *Critical Review of International Social and Political Philosophy*, 14 (5), 2011: 581–602. Simon Căbulea May, "Compromise," *International Encyclopedia of Ethics*, ed. H. LaFollette. Hoboken, NJ: Blackwell, 2013, pp. 959–68.

3. This distinction between compromise and deference suggests that Cohen's example of "standing aside" in anarchist collectives may not in fact be best understood as an example of compromise at all (38–41). What matters is whether the anarchists (implicitly) accept a decision rule granting the majority defeasible decision-making authority, subject only to an individual veto power properly exercised in some limited range of circumstances. If so, then the minority group merely defers to the majority, for all that has been said, and does not also *ipso facto* compromise with them.

4. Fisher and Ury, *Getting to Yes*, pp. 56–57; on the origin of this story, see also Deborah Kolb, "The Love for Three Oranges Or: What Did We Miss About Ms. Follett in the Library?" *Negotiation Journal*, 11 (4), 1995: 339–48.

5. Melvin Aron Eisenberg, "Private Ordering Through Negotiation: Dispute-Settlement and Rulemaking," *Harvard Law Review*, 89 (4), 1976: 637–81.

6. Eisenberg, "Private Ordering," p. 646.

7. Cohen, "On Compromise."

8. Fisher and Ury, *Getting to Yes*, p. 41.

9. Roger Fisher, "Do We Want to 'Win' the Cold War?" *Bulletin of the Atomic Scientists*, 18 (1), 1961: 33–35.

10. For critical discussion of the claim that respect gives political leaders principled reasons to forge moral compromise agreements, see May, "Principled Compromise," pp. 340–42.

11. In May, "Moral Compromise, Civic Friendship," I argue that spouses (and other close personal friends) who share responsibility for each other's successful pursuit of their ends have non-instrumental moral reasons for moral compromise.

12. Fisher and Ury, *Getting to Yes*, p. 155.

13. Fisher and Ury, *Getting to Yes*, p. 82.

14. Fisher and Ury, *Getting to Yes*, p. 87.

15. May, "Principled Compromise"; May, "Moral Compromise, Civic Friendship."

16. Eric Beerbohm, "The Problem of Cleans Hands: Negotiated Compromise in Lawmaking," chapter 1 of this volume.

17. Since Beerbohm attributes the strategist's position to me, he is clearly not free to define it as including these various features.

18. I argue elsewhere that this commitment sets limits on morally permissible political compromises independently of instrumental considerations. Simon Căbulea May, "No Compromise on Racial Equality," *Compromise and Disagreement in Contemporary Political Theory*, ed. C. Rostbøll and T. Scavenius. New York: Routledge, 2017.

6

UNCOMPROMISING DEMOCRACY

MELISSA SCHWARTZBERG

Citizens in the United States are overwhelmingly frustrated with Congress. The 115th US Congress began its term in January 2017 with a 19% job approval rating, according to Gallup polls. In recent years, a main cause of popular dissatisfaction with Congress has been congressional gridlock, "bickering," and "not compromising."[1] In response, calls for a renewed commitment to political compromise are understandable. Amy Gutmann and Dennis Thompson, most notably, have decried the loss of a "compromising mindset," and argue that recovery of this attitude must anticipate any institutional change designed to reduce sclerosis.[2] The urgent need for action constitutes one major argument on behalf of compromise; the second argument, offered by Amy Cohen and Michele Moody-Adams in their chapters for this volume, is that compromise is the soul of democratic solidarity, an expression of a shared ethos.[3]

The problem of legislative gridlock is indeed grave, and the diagnosis—failure to compromise—seems self-evident. Given that our communities face critical problems requiring redress, and given disagreement among citizens and their representatives over appropriate remedies, compromise appears to be the only practical solution. From a more abstract perspective, willingness to compromise is in many ways a signal trait of the admirable democratic citizen. As she confronts the disagreement of her peers, she should listen and deliberate from a perspective of epistemic humility; she should adjust her preferences to accommodate their viewpoints and should ultimately vote for a policy that she believes will best realize the common good, or at least accommodate as many disparate interests as possible. The problem, many argue, is one of motivation: the "uncompromising mindset" of politicians, or their blinkered attention to pure power politics. If only we could foster trust and mutual respect across the aisle, we could begin to solve the problems facing our society. The motivation to compromise is the grease that will enable the wheels of legislation to begin to move.

Here I wish to affirm, against new challenges, the standard argument that the motivations of legislators derive from the institutions in which they are embedded. For instance, if reelection demands constant appeal to special-interest groups for fund-raising, the incentive to compromise will diminish; enact campaign finance reform, and perhaps the political consequences of moderating policy will become less dire. Similarly, the problem of gridlock in Congress is insoluble under institutional rules specifically operating to promote it, notably but not exclusively the cloture rule governing the filibuster. It is not the case, as Gutmann and others have argued, that a shift in mindset must precede institutional reform, and that a compromising or solidaristic ethos is necessary to generate compromise-promoting institutions. Instead, implementing reforms designed to promote compromise may require the "nuclear option"—the hallmark of an uncompromising mindset.

Moreover, reforms aimed at eliciting compromise need not, and probably should not, take the form of compromise-promoting institutions as such. Compromise should in general arise as a secondary by-product of other institutional features: most centrally, majority rule and the policy flexibility associated with relatively easy institutional change. Institutions such as the filibuster and "consensual decision-making" may well reproduce sclerosis and existing hierarchies of power. Majoritarian decision-making, admittedly, introduces a risk of policy instability. Yet in reducing the decisional costs of legislation and by lowering the stakes of legislation through the prospect of revision, majority rule may, paradoxically, induce compromise more readily than would consensus-seeking institutions.

On Mindsets and Motivations

In their writings on political compromise, Gutmann and Thompson argue that the "permanent campaign" is the major barrier to the development of the compromising mindset; it encourages the adoption of principled stands and an effort to distinguish oneself from competing candidates, both within and outside of one's own party. Though one might expect that the desire to capture the median voter would encourage compromise, Gutmann and Thompson imply that the modification of positions to capture independent voters is in essence perfunctory, and even that is seen as "suspect in the eyes of their more ardent supporters."[4] Yet a shift in mindset could mitigate the effects of polarization, they argue. Politicians ought to adopt "principled prudence" (the recognition that an outcome, even if far from ideal, is superior to the status quo) and an attitude of mutual respect, rather than cynicism and distrust; this constitutes "economizing on disagreement." Compromise is important for Gutmann and Thompson because of the conservatism that results from its absence: the "greater the resistance to compromise, the greater the bias in favor of the status quo."[5]

Similarly, Amy Cohen and Michele Moody-Adams reflect upon how the failure to compromise may lead to tragic outcomes. Each invokes *Antigone*, featuring a conflict between individual convictions, particularly those relating to religious obligations, and political authority. Moody-Adams begins her chapter with a more traditional retelling, whereas Cohen imagines a "deep compromise" forged between Antigone and Creon. *Antigone* is famously a conflict over principles. The motivational failure that Moody-Adams diagnoses, and that Cohen reimagines, is one of respect: both Antigone and Creon fail to respect the others' commitments, fail to embrace their shared ties of kinship and polis, fail to acknowledge the fallibility and partiality of their own judgments. In Cohen's non-tragic *Antigone*, they transcend these failures and agree to bury Polynices in a remote location outside of the city. They are motivated to compromise by recognizing the higher principle of solidarity and kinship, not through coercion or purely as a function of power disparities, and they come to a resolution that is marked by the revision of their ends.

Cohen's non-tragic version of *Antigone* displays what Cohen and others refer to as a principled compromise. But note that there is a difference between actors compromising their principles, and actors who reach a compromise *because* of a deeper commitment to principle. Non-tragic *Antigone* is both, since each trims a commitment to principle: Antigone to burying her brother inside the city on grounds of kinship and reverence for the gods, and Creon to state authority. Motivated by a shared set of familial commitments, Antigone to her prospective father-in-law (and uncle)'s rule, Creon to his son's bride, a principled compromise emerges. But one can compromise over principle because of a commitment to a deeper principle, just as one can compromise over principle for the sake of material interests. Or one can compromise over interests for the sake of principle, as one might readily gloss non-tragic *Antigone*: Antigone fears punishment for impiety, and Creon wishes to consolidate his rule, but they compromise because of a shared principled commitment to kinship.

Cohen and Moody-Adams each defend an account of principled compromise, one they distinguish from bargaining on motivational grounds. Compromises over either principles or interests are typically rooted in an "extrinsic or higher-order end," in her examples, respect, solidarity, community, obligation, or love. The model of compromise borne out of constraint, whether the object of compromise is either principle or interest, is rooted in cost-benefit analysis and instrumental rationality. The model of compromise borne out of principle, again whether the object of compromise is either principle or interest, is of expressive, altruistic action.

Yet principles and interests are likely co-constitutive. That is, principles invariably shape our conceptions of our interests, and our interests may guide our selection of principles. If we focus on motivations rather than mechanisms—or suggest, as Cohen and others do, that the presence of particular motivations ought to guide our choice of institutions—we leave ourselves open to strategic misrepresentation, as actors may shop for a venue or set of institutional mechanisms in which they believe they may prevail. As such, in designing institutions, whether for dispute resolution or for legislation or other conflict-ridden circumstances, one goal should be to minimize the extent to which their healthy functioning relies upon the adoption of a particular mindset. To paraphrase James Madison, if men were angels, no dispute-resolution mechanism would be necessary. This is not to suggest that institutions ought necessarily to be designed for knaves, nor that altruistic motivations do not often shape the contours of the compromises that emerge. But since we cannot depend on such motivations, and since disputants have strategic incentives to misrepresent their motives—particularly if institutional choice rests on their avowals—our primary aim should be to design institutions that will help to encourage compromise even in the context of purely self-interested behavior.

Compromises emerge because people recognize that they are engaged in a long-term endeavor: this holds whether we negotiate over principles or interests, or whether the aim is a long-term realization of each party's entwined interests or to agreement on a norm or principle, or some combination thereof. If we had no expectation of future interactions, and no shared goal apart from the gains to be had from a single trade, then we would have minimal incentives to compromise rather than simply to bargain as one would in a one-shot game. If we are buying a rug from a street vendor, we have no incentive to reflect upon what this bargain will imply for future interactions. In contrast, legislators must play a long game, establishing compromises over policy and their own institutions that would maximize their gains when their party is in power while minimizing their losses when they are in the minority. Marital compromises, similarly, must entail the view of a long game, and that bargaining strategy should be shaped by the recognition that there will be countless iterations and various loci, perhaps even later that same day. So if we can discern a motivation for compromise, it may merely be to establish durable institutions or relationships in the face of competing preferences, whether over interests or principles.

This claim in fact lurks beneath the "permanent campaign" logic developed by Gutmann and Thompson; the permanent campaign prioritizes maintaining durable relationships between legislators and interest groups over fostering those across the aisle. As they suggest, ideological polarization inhibits the development of a compromising mindset, since there is little common ground, and few integrative solutions seem available. Given ideological polarization and the permanent campaign, instead of exhorting legislators to adjust their mindsets, first we must recognize that the institutional context creates a prisoner's dilemma: adjusting one's mindset unilaterally in a strategic environment that rewards uncompromising behavior is likely to lead to abject defeat of the legislator's agenda. If the structure of campaign finance requires a permanent campaign, with appeal to special-interest groups, adopting an uncompromising mindset is necessary for there to be any probability of legislative success.

Although Gutmann and Thompson acknowledge that the institutional structure of elections does constitute a major barrier even for those who possess "appropriate mindsets," they suggest that institutional reforms are possible only subsequent to a dispositional shift. This argument has some prima facie validity, since we can presume that volition precedes political action. In their view, there must be a will to create compromise-fostering institutions before the work of compromising-fostering reform can begin. Cohen argues similarly: actors motivated by the principles of mutual respect and group solidarity—"volitional acts of self-expression"[6]—will work to achieve the performative act of consensus. It is, of course, possible that consensus institutions, such as the General Assembly in the Occupy movement, may attract individuals who are motivated to compromise on the basis of the principle of compromise. So compromise-promoting institutions might do a good job of reaching compromise among actors motivated by the principle of compromise.

Or perhaps it might not. My objection to all of this, if it is not yet clear, is that if institutional reform requires political actors to adopt a mindset that would leave them strategically vulnerable, the effort is doomed. Fortunately, in my view, it does not: in fact, institutions designed to promote a compromising mindset have in fact been a latent cause of legislative gridlock and have enabled a minority to block salutary compromises. This is most clear, as I shall discuss, in the case of the filibuster, and the general failure to deploy the "nuclear option" to eliminate it for legislation. But it is latent as well in Cohen's example of Occupy, which I shall also take up shortly. Paradoxically, majority rule may be more likely to generate compromise, at least in the long run, than consensus-seeking institutions. Compromise neither depends upon a shift in mindset nor the motivation to achieve agreement as such; instead, it may result from majoritarian bargaining.

Institutions condition incentives, and so the primary obstacle to compromise is thus institutional rather than dispositional. Let me now turn to two examples to suggest why this is. The first is the filibuster, praised by legislators as the senatorial bulwark in favor of compromise, and cited by Gutmann and Thompson as an example of the sort of reform for which the compromising mindset is a necessary precondition. The second is the consensus rules underlying Occupy, returning to Amy Cohen's example.

FILIBUSTER AND ITS REFORM

Supporters of the filibuster regard it as a crucial device promoting compromise in the Senate. The three-fifths (60-vote) rule governing cloture ostensibly promotes compromise by obliging a majority party (possessing fewer than 60 votes) to seek support across the aisle. In 2010 Senate hearings on the filibuster, senators repeatedly invoked the importance of consensus-building as the primary reason for preserving the Senate. In the words of Sen. Pat Roberts (R-KS), "The filibuster is the essence of the Senate. It is not a tool of obstructionism or dysfunction. It is meant to foster greater consultation, consensus, and cooperation between the parties."[7] In Sen. Lamar Alexander's (R-TN) words, "The whole idea of the Senate is not to have majority rule. It is to force consensus. It is to force there to be a group of senators on either side who have to respect one another's views so that they work together and produce 60 votes on important issues."[8]

Defenders argue that the use of the filibuster lies in its use and abuse—again, in the attitudes or "mindset" of senators rather than in the institution itself. This argument sits on both side of the aisle: John Kerry, in his farewell address to the Senate, argued: "There are moments of great frustration, for the American people and for everybody in this place. But I don't believe they are the fault of the institution itself. It is not the rules that confound us per se. It is the choices people make about those rules. . . . [T]he problems we live through today come from individual choices of Senators themselves, not the rules."[9] Similarly, Senate Majority Leader Mitch McConnell (R-KY) suggested to the *New York Times* that "This notion that the Senate is dysfunctional is not because of the rules," he said. "It's because of behavior."[10] But the filibuster has induced obstructionist and narrowly partisan behavior since the nineteenth century, as Binder and Smith have conclusively demonstrated.[11] The invocation of cloture has certainly spiked in recent years, suggesting that legislative behavior, measured in terms of willingness to block the majority, does matter. Yet the strategic incentive to act in an obstructionist rather than compromising fashion is produced by the filibuster, in tandem with other political and institutional factors. Legislative gridlock—defined by Keith Krehbiel as "the absence of policy change in equilibrium in spite of the existence of a legislative majority that favors change"[12]—derives in large part from the supermajoritarian rule for cloture and the two-thirds majority override for a presidential veto. Krehbiel's pivotal politics model predicts that gridlock will be broken only if the status quo is extreme relative to the preferences of the president and pivotal legislators (the 60th senator or the 290th representative), or in the presence of exceptionally wide bipartisan support for policy change. Given a high level of partisan polarization, though, neither is likely to be the case. If we assume (perhaps implausibly) symmetric movement away from the center by both parties, it is difficult to imagine that there are many major policy areas in which the status quo is extreme relative to the given existing distribution of preferences. An arguably more accurate model of asymmetric polarization—in which the Republicans have moved further to the right than the Democrats have to the left—would suggest that only where the status quo policy is left of center would we be likely to observe movement. Moreover, bicameralism exacerbates the difficulty of reaching compromise, not merely because of the presence of the additional check or veto point as such, but because of policy disagreements between the two houses even under unified party control.[13]

Thus, ending the filibuster alone would not necessarily eliminate legislative gridlock—read differently, it would not eliminate the need to seek votes across the aisle, given the broader structure of Congress and veto power. But it would be an important step in the right direction, and there is little reason to believe that it would spell the death of compromise, as the models discussed above suggest. For instance, in defending his proposal to modify the filibuster to enable a decreasing majority of senators, over a period of days, to invoke cloture, former Sen. Tom Harkin (D-IA) argued that both the majority and minority would retain an incentive to compromise:

> Recently, the Minority Leader defended the abuse of the filibuster on the grounds that it forces the majority to compromise and "to resolve the great issues of the moment in the middle." I strongly disagree with him. The fact is that, right now, because of the abuse of the filibuster the minority has no incentive to compromise. They have the power to block legislation without, in many cases, even coming to the floor to explain themselves. In such a world, as we have seen over the past years, why would the minority come to the table to cut a deal? In contrast, if the minority knows that at the end of the day, a bill is subject to majority vote, they will be more willing to come to the table and negotiate seriously. Likewise, the majority will have an incentive to compromise because it will want to save considerable time, and not have to go through numerous cloture votes over a period of 16 days, plus 30 hours of debate, as allowed under my proposal.[14]

As of this writing, the Harkin plan has not succeeded: The filibuster still exists for legislation, though Senate Republicans at last eliminated the filibuster for Supreme Court appointments. Should we infer that the persistence of the filibuster derives from the failure to adopt the compromising mindset for policy, but its success for appointments? No: the end of the filibuster derived from the *uncompromising* mindset: the use of the "nuclear option." Bipartisan compromise early in 2013 had led to only modest reductions in delays. In November 2013, Democratic majority voted to reinterpret the cloture rule to require only a majority for cloture votes on executive branch nominations and lower-court nominees, over the strenuous objections of Republicans. Senate Democrats did so in full awareness of the likelihood that they would lose power, and the threat that a future Republican majority would use their new capacity to act by majority rule against them. Indeed, the Republicans argued that the Democrats would regret it once they found themselves in the minority. "Democrats won't be in power in perpetuity. This is a mistake—a big one for the long run. Maybe not for the short run. Short-term gains, but I think it changes the Senate tremendously in a bad way," said Sen. Richard C. Shelby (R-AL) to the *Washington Post*.[15] Then-Senate Minority Leader Mitch McConnell similarly remarked: "I say to my friends on the other side of the aisle, you'll regret this. And you may regret it a lot sooner than you think."[16] Indeed, in April 2017, Senate Majority Leader himself moved to change the Senate rules to permit confirmation of Supreme Court nominees with a simple-majority vote, and held that doing so would ultimately decrease partisan tensions.[17]

Thus, uncompromising behavior led to sweeping institutional change where compromising behavior had failed. And it acted to enact a majoritarian rule that would endure once they were out of the minority, anticipating—one must presume—that enabling Congress to act on nominations even when the presidency and Senate are under Republican control would be preferable to the status quo. In other words, an uncompromising mindset, given the prospect of alternation in office, may generate the changes necessary for long-term compromises.

CONSENSUS UNDER OCCUPY

When the nonmilitant atheist has to guard the door at General Assembly against the virally militant atheists who are trying to disrupt the truly harmless 'grounding meditation' that has been asked for by the vibe checker, it's just another day at the Occupation.
—This quote is from the text of a note by participant Sean McKeown[18]

Like the filibuster, consensus mechanisms frequently emerge as an alternative to the ostensibly uncompromising nature of majoritarian politics. In her chapter for this volume, for instance, Amy Cohen identifies the activity of "standing aside" in consensus decision-making, as at the General Assembly of Occupy Wall Street, as an example of compromising on principled grounds. One might regard consensual decision-making as quixotic. Yet because consensus decision rules have worked well in certain contexts, they deserve serious consideration. ACT UP (AIDS Coalition to Unleash Power), for instance, relied on consensus decision-making in its highly effective campaign to expedite access to AIDS drugs and treatment. As Cohen suggests in her chapter, consensus decision-making has been an important political institution across the globe for centuries—the Navajo Indians, hunter-gatherer societies, and village communities from sub-Saharan Africa to Scandinavia to South Vietnam all have relied on a version of consensual decision-making—as have other non-political bodies, such as the Quakers and various expert commissions.

Jane Mansbridge, in *Beyond Adversary Democracy*, described the logic of consensual institutions as deriving from commitments to fraternity, understood in the members' language as "solidarity," "community," or "sisterhood." In her view, consensus decision-making worked well in small bodies marked by common interests; "adversarial" institutions better suited larger bodies and those where interests conflicted. These common interests could—as Cohen agrees—take the form of "common adherence to principle."[19]

In the presence of common interests or a shared commitment to the principle of solidarity as marked by consensual decision-making, consensual mechanisms themselves may be otiose. Indeed, it is possible that consensus procedures do a worse job of eliciting principled compromises—and perhaps even in eliciting consensus—than do traditional majoritarian institutions. As Simon May argues in his contribution to this volume, the dissenters under consensus institutions do not compromise.[20] In fact, their status as members who "compromise motivated by principle" might be weaker than those who bargain under majoritarian institutions. The "expression and social valuation of loss" in compromise under Occupy is much weaker than those who simply lose under majoritarianism.

Why would this be? Take, for instance, a question posed to the General Assembly at Occupy Wall Street: should the community join striking Verizon workers on the picket line? At Occupy Wall Street General Assembly meetings, consensus depends upon a facilitating team to help organize deliberation. The current procedure is the following: a proposal is introduced and facilitators lead a discussion in which GA attendees take turns asking questions or making general points and the proposers respond in turn. Afterwards, the floor is opened up to friendly amendments to the proposal, which the proposers either accept or reject. The facilitator will periodically check the "temperature" of the assembly by asking participants to make hand signals signifying their agreement, ambivalence, or disagreement of the proposal. If there is widespread agreement, the proposal passes; if substantial disagreement remains, it may be tabled. Imagine that nearly everyone at the assembly immediately supports the proposal, but there are a few dissenting voices, who choose to block. There are at least four different possible scenarios. The first, happy one is that the dissenters come through a deliberative procedure to recognize the value of the proposal and change their minds. If this happens, there has been no compromise; rather, there have simply been changes of mind. The second, less sanguine outcome is that the dissenters sustain their block, and the proposal fails. There is no compromise here, as the very few have prevailed over the rest of the assembly. The third and least appealing alternative is that the dissenters are coerced into removing their block through intense psychological pressure or perhaps through ejection from the assembly: no compromise. The fourth is Cohen's scenario, in which the dissenters stand aside, effectively removing their block, because they are motivated by the desire for solidarity. Is this compromise shaped by principle?

My view is that it is not, for reasons similar to those suggested by May.[21] Compromise must, at a minimum, entail some mutual concessions. What the dissenters decided, in essence, was that they would not prevent an overwhelming majority from prevailing: in Eric Schwitzgebel's technical sense of the term, perhaps, they have chosen not to be jerks.[22] They did not alter their views—they just respected their fellow assembly-goers as epistemic peers, and out of respect, didn't use every weapon at their disposal to prevent the other side from having its way. Similarly, the overwhelming consensus did not compromise; they persuaded the dissenters to stand aside. Of course, it is possible that the deliberative process generated some mutual adjustment and thus compromise along the way—but again, the removal of the block as such was not part of this process.

Compare this decision-making procedure to a majority vote, in which the minority is outvoted. The majority has not compromised; it has won, and the minority, similarly, has lost. Is the social valuation of loss less significant here? Why? If anything, the logic of consensus is that to fail to join is, in effect, a defect of solidarity, a refusal to support the program. To join the consensus, after all, is to realize freedom and autonomy[23]: the logic of Occupy sketched here is distinctly Rousseauian. Indeed, to the extent that it is Rousseauian, then to block the consensus is to err: thus the loss possesses no value. The logic of majority rule, on the other hand, straightforwardly generates losers—their defeat is widely recognized as such, and optimally the winners are gracious in victory. But one reason for the minority to obey the outcome in a democracy is the prospect that they may have a turn at a later point to win, and so their loss is not without either consolation or social value.

The superiority of majority rule to consensus decision-making is especially acute when, as at Occupy Wall Street, a "modified-consensus" rule holds. The requirement of full consensus or unanimity proved onerous; any attendee at the General Assembly who clung to a different perspective could block a decision by the rest. As such, Occupy Wall Street operated under a "modified-consensus" rule, which is a nine-tenths supermajority rule, designed to allow for a few blocks by members who believe the decision to be fundamentally wrong, with a fall back to a "two-thirds vote."[24] This might seem reasonable: if a decision needs to be made in the presence of disagreement under time constraints, weakening the vote requirement from unanimity to supermajority seems like a sensible, pragmatic decision.

Consensualists oppose majority rule on the grounds that it seems to exclude or ignore the minority. But in fact the modified consensus rule may mean that an overwhelming majority is ignored, or that a small minority is either excluded or pressured to conform. It is also conservative: the power of these blockers may prevent proposals from passing, and thus impede the development of the movement. Though proponents of consensual decision-making are right to emphasize the problem of exclusion under majority rule, in contrast to supermajority rule, it does have the attractive feature of weighing each member's vote equally—it prevents members of a small minority from having considerably more power to affect the outcome than members of an overwhelming majority. More abstractly, it is also the case that the decision to count votes under modified consensus is at odds with the consensualists' avowed commitment to "uncoerced compromise and consent," and autonomy as a precondition to solidarity. It is very difficult to imagine why a decision is superior on consensual or compromise grounds if it is blocked against the preferences of nine-tenths minus one, or against two-thirds minus one, than under majority rule. As such, the liabilities of decision-making by consensus, in practice, are the same as those of the filibuster and other supermajoritarian decision rules: sclerosis, due largely to the power that a small—but not necessarily vulnerable—minority wields over even a very wide majority.[25]

MAJORITY RULE AND COMPROMISE

As we have seen, contemporary scholarship on compromise has emphasized its importance for democracy. In the prior NOMOS volume on compromise, Joseph Carens wrote that the collective nature of politics meant that compromise would likely be necessary to secure the cooperation of members who disagree about the best course of action; the alternative to compromise would likely be inaction.[26] The failure to compromise in the legislative setting, scholars argue, has led to gridlock, and thus to "damage to democracy as collective self-rule."[27] As Josiah Ober has argued, *demokratia* ought to be understood not merely as majority rule, but about the "capacity of a public to do things."[28]

Ober's claim is important from both a philological and philosophical perspective. Yet from a practical standpoint, the capacity for a public to do things does indeed depend upon majority rule. Majority rule may be justified on many grounds, but its most compelling justifications derive from its unique capacity to weigh individual votes, reflecting individuals' judgments, equally.[29] Peter Singer argued that because each member has equal say, majority rule constitutes the "paradigm of a fair compromise." It enables everyone in a given association "to refrain from acting on his own judgement about particular issues without giving up more than the theoretical minimum which it is essential for everyone to give up in order to achieve the benefits of a peaceful solution to dispute."[30] As Carens noted in response to Singer, the compromise rests in the fact that each individual recognizes that he will be outvoted some of the time and fail to have his preferred policy adopted; the procedure is "compromise by succession."[31] This mechanism runs strictly on alternation in office.

Yet we have reason to believe that majority rule will achieve more than mere turn-taking, with the attendant risk of policy instability. A substantial body of formal scholarship affirms that a majority party leader has incentives to secure more than a minimum winning coalition and seeks to explain the emergence of supermajority coalitions. Bargaining models suggest the incentives of majority party leaders to distribute benefits widely under certain conditions. One important result of the canonical work on legislative bargaining, by Baron and Ferejohn, is that open amendment rules generate more equal ex post distributions than do closed rules, as does urgency (impatience).[32] Under an open rule, in which an amendment can be offered to a motion on the floor of the legislature, a member has to assess the probability that the next member will either "move the previous question," concluding the amendment process, or offer a revision with a different distribution of benefits. Members' decisions are thus affected both by their evaluation of the previous policy, the risk that a future allocation will be weaker, and their patience (discount factor). So if a member wishes to ensure that her proposal will be adopted, she must ensure that whichever member is recognized next will move the previous question and support the proposal. Where there is great impatience and an open amendment rule, the distribution may be quite universalistic.

Models of coalition formation and vote buying indicate that "buying" supermajority coalitions may be cheaper in the long run than merely securing a minimum winning coalition: in other words, even under majority rule, it may be in legislators' interest to secure votes across the aisle. That is, when two vote buyers compete to secure a majority and attempt to purchase votes sequentially, supermajorities are likely to emerge. Groseclose and Snyder draw on the example of the passage of NAFTA, in which President Clinton and the Republican House leader exchanged favors for votes and created a coalition of 234 (of 434), 16 votes larger than necessary.[33] This, they suggest, was designed to ward off invasions from opponents of NAFTA, which they find to be less costly than attempting to bribe individual voters to remain with a minimal coalition after incursions. When the behavior of legislators is especially unpredictable (if turnover in a legislature is high), the incentive to secure a supermajority is especially strong.

Dynamic bargaining models yield predictions for the circumstances in which a majority may distribute spoils widely, driven by the expectation that they will lose power. Dixit et al., for instance, explore the conditions under which "Each ruling party might be willing to compromise on its actions if it could trust its successors to follow suit": if those in power recognize that they may lose it, are patient in the sense that they recognize that short-term concessions will lead to long-term gains, and recognize that they will regain power at some future time, tacit cooperation can be sustained as an equilibrium.[34] Indeed, they find that supermajority rules impede political compromise by securing gains to the party whose preferred policy is secured under that rule, giving future majorities smaller gains. In their words, "ordinary majority rule does more to protect the weak than supermajority rule, and symmetric parties would be unanimous in their preference for it if the question were put to them before each knew its political strength."[35] Instead, the expectation of losing office may encourage legislators to distribute policy concessions across the aisle. More generally, the prospect of alternation and flexibility in policy making may generate incentives to bipartisanship and compromise.

A skeptic might reply that although eliminating the filibuster would reduce legislative gridlock and reduce the status quo bias, it might generate other deleterious consequences. That is, it might move us from the dysfunction of gridlock to that of chaos: majority rule will eliminate any need to compromise, and each election would bring sweeping policy changes. Yet under supermajoritarian decision-making, the prospects of losing are dire: the probability of reaching a future supermajority to change the status quo is quite low, and so defeat is potentially permanent. Under simple majority rule, policy changes are not once-in-a-generation, and so the prospect of future revisions may both induce compromise ex ante and reduce the sense of loss ex post.

CONCLUSION

My aim here has been twofold: to defend a focus on institutions rather than on motivations, and to argue that institutions putatively designed to elicit compromise are more likely to generate sclerosis and failure to compromise than majority rule. When we focus on motivations rather than mechanisms—or suggest that the presence of some motivations ought to guide our choice of institutions—we leave ourselves open to strategic misrepresentation, as actors may shop for a venue or set of institutional mechanisms in which they believe they may prevail. Even more troubling, we may blind ourselves to the workings of power even when the agents sincerely wish to reach agreement out of solidarity. Finally, if the disputants have different motivations, and Cohen, Gutmann and Thompson, and others are right that these motivations shape institutional preferences, the challenge of compromise may migrate from the primary dispute to second-order disagreement about the mechanisms. Indeed, perhaps the powerful would advocate consensus in order to generate apparent solidaristic support for their interests, whereas the vulnerable might prefer to take their chances under majoritarian bargaining.

Political actors—perhaps people more generally—always have a mix of motives: self-interest and institutional interest; loyalty and competition; ideology and altruism. In one sense, this is unproblematic: if we measure compromise in concessions, the motivations of the agents are essentially beside the point. We cannot reliably discern people's true beliefs or motivations; beliefs and motivations may be opaque even to the parties themselves. But institutions can indeed condition mindsets: they can shape the incentives of actors and the range of acceptable solutions. As such, mechanisms that encourage members of political assemblies to adjust their claims in anticipation of multiple and repeated negotiations should have primary importance. But—as the example of the filibuster suggests—the move to these institutions may require us to keep a finger over the nuclear trigger.

Notes

1. Jeff Jones and Lydia Saad, Gallup News Service June Wave 1, June 1–4, 2013.

2. See Amy Gutmann and Dennis Thompson, "The Mindsets of Political Compromise," *Perspectives on Politics* 8, no. 4 (2010): 1125–1143; Gutmann and Thompson, *The Spirit of Compromise* (Princeton, NJ: Princeton University Press, 2012).

3. See Amy J. Cohen, "Compromise, Negotiation, and Loss," in this volume, and Michele Moody-Adams, "Democratic Conflict and the Political Morality of Compromise," also in this volume.

4. Gutmann and Thompson, "The Mindsets of Political Compromise," 1129.

5. Ibid.

6. See Amy Cohen's chapter "On Compromise, Negotiation, and Loss," in this volume.

7. *Examining the Filibuster: Hearings before the Committee on Rules and Administration*, Senate, 111th Cong. 2 (2010).

8. Ibid.

9. Senator John Kerry (D-MA) Farewell Address, US Senate. C-SPAN, Washington, DC, January 30, 2013.

10. Jonathan Weisman, "The Senate's Long Side to Gridlock," *New York Times*, November 25, 2012, p. A1.

11. See Sarah A. Binder and Steven S. Smith, *Politics or Principle? Filibustering in the United States Senate* (Washington, DC: Brookings Institution Press, 1997).

12. See Keith Krehbiel, *Pivotal Politics: A Theory of U.S. Lawmaking* (Chicago: University of Chicago Press, 1998), p. 26.

13. Sarah Binder, "The Dysfunctional Congress," *Annual Review of Political Science* (2015).

14. Congressional Record vol. 159, no. 9 (Thursday, January 24, 2013) [Senate] [pages S247–256] (statement of Sen. Tom Harkin).

15. Paul Kane, "Reid, Democrats Trigger 'Nuclear' Option; Eliminate Most Filibusters on Nominees," *Washington Post*, November 21, 2013.

16. Jeremy W. Peters, "In Landmark Vote, Senate Limits Use of the Filibuster," *New York Times*, November 22, 2013, p. A1.

17. Ed O'Keefe and Sean Sullivan, "Senate Republicans Go 'Nuclear,' Pave the Way for Gorsuch Confirmation to Supreme Court," *Washington Post*, April 6, 2017.

18. Quoted in Todd Gitlin, *Occupy Nation: The Roots, the Spirit, and the Promise of Occupy Wall Street* (New York: itbooks, 2012), p. 95.

19. Jane Mansbridge, *Beyond Adversary Democracy* (Chicago: University of Chicago Press, 1980), p. xii.

20. See Simon May's chapter in this volume, "Compromise in Negotiation."

21. Ibid.

22. Eric Schwitzgebel, "A Theory of Jerks," *Aeon Magazine*, June 4, 2014.

23. See Amy Cohen's chapter in this volume, "On Compromise, Negotiation, and Loss."

24. For the logic of these norms, see David Graeber's online account, "Some Remarks on Consensus," at www.occupywallstreet.net.

25. For historical context and a set of arguments against contemporary supermajority rules, see Melissa Schwartzberg, *Counting the Many: The Origins and Limits of Supermajority Rule* (New York: Cambridge University Press, 2014).

26. Joseph Carens, "Compromises in Politics," *NOMOS XXI: Compromises in Ethics, Law, and Politics* (New York: New York University Press, 1979), p. 126.

27. See Mark E. Warren and Jane Mansbridge et al. (including the author), "Deliberative Negotiation," *Negotiating Agreement in Politics*, American Political Science Association, Task Force Report (2013), p. 3.

28. See Josiah Ober, *Democracy and Knowledge* (Princeton, NJ: Princeton University Press, 2008), p. 5.

29. For a critical discussion of justifications for majority rule, see Schwartzberg, *Counting the Many*, ch. 5; for this particular argument, see (in a large literature) Thomas Christiano, *Rule of the Many* (Boulder, CO: Westview Press, 1996); Robert Dahl, *Democracy and Its Critics* (New Haven, CT: Yale University Press, 1989); and Jeremy Waldron, *Law and Disagreement* (Oxford: Oxford University Press, 1999).

30. See Peter Singer, *Democracy and Disobedience* (Oxford: Clarendon Press, 1973), p. 32.

31. See Carens, "Compromises in Politics," p. 134.

32. See David P. Baron and John A. Ferejohn, "Bargaining in Legislatures," *American Political Science Review*, 83, no. 4 (1989): 1181–1206.

33. Tim Groseclose and James M. Snyder, Jr., "Buying Supermajorities," *American Political Science Review*, 90, no. 2 (June 1996): 304.

34. See Avinash Dixit, Gene M. Grossman, and Faruk Gul, "The Dynamics of Political Compromise," *Journal of Political Economy*, 108, no. 3 (2000): 531–568, pp. 532–533.

35. Ibid., 554. Bowen and Zahran offer a related model of competing legislators (rather than within a two-party system) to find equilibria in which compromise—measured by a wide distribution of benefits—may emerge. The motivation to compromise, on their logic, derives from the "aversion to the possibility of being disadvantaged in the future." T. Renee Bowen and Zaki Zahran, "On Dynamic Compromise," *Games and Economic Behavior* (2012): 391–419, p. 393.

7

DEMOCRATIC CONFLICT AND THE POLITICAL MORALITY OF COMPROMISE

MICHELE M. MOODY-ADAMS

INTRODUCTION: COMPROMISE AND THE DOMAINS OF DEMOCRATIC GOVERNANCE

In his 1775 *Speech on Conciliation with America*, Edmund Burke offered a succinct account of why it is rational to be willing to compromise in politics, and indeed in almost every aspect of broader social life:

> All government, indeed every human benefit and enjoyment, every virtue, and every prudent act, is founded on compromise and barter. We balance inconveniences; we give and take; we remit some rights, that we may enjoy others; and we choose rather to be happy citizens than subtle disputants.[1]

In an era when politicians are often celebrated for unyielding commitment to "principle," even when their tenacity is little more than a campaign strategy, it may seem strange that Burke should emphasize not only the ubiquity of compromise, but also what we can gain through the sacrifices we make when we compromise. But Burke implicitly understood that when the context of negotiation is properly framed, a compromise is the most reliable means we have for responding constructively to conflict. He clearly also recognized that, given how frequently we encounter conflict, especially in political life, it is profoundly rational to be ready to seek constructive compromise in response.

Of course, the rationality of compromise must be understood in context. As Mary Parker Follett argued, in her classic essay "Constructive Conflict," compromise lies somewhere in between "domination," which involves a victory of one disputing party over the other, and "integrative consensus," where neither party has to sacrifice because the parties find a solution in which their main desires have a place.[2] As we might expect, Follett thus believed that integrative consensus is the ideally best response to conflict, primarily because it best "stabilizes" the conflicts it addresses. But she also understood that there are many "obstacles to integration," perhaps especially in political life, and that compromise is always a better alternative to integrative consensus than domination.[3] Drawing on Follett's insights about the difficulty of reaching integrative consensus in politics and taking seriously the anti-democratic dangers of trying to resolve political conflicts through domination, I contend that maintaining the willingness to compromise in democratic politics—by which I mean the varied processes and procedures of democratic governance—is clearly the rational thing to do.

In a recent contribution to the debate, Amy Guttman and Dennis Thompson agree that the "spirit of compromise" is critical to democratic governance, primarily to the work of legislators and government officials who must seek consensus on legislation and public policy despite disagreements about the fundamentals of political morality.[4] But they also contend that in contemporary democracies (especially in the United States), the spirit of compromise has been undermined by the emergence of the "permanent campaign," which encourages legislators and policy makers to hold "tenaciously" to their principles and to publicly display mistrust and suspicion of those who disagree with those principles.[5] The solution, according to Gutmann and Thompson, is to promote revisions in democratic culture and practice that would encourage political leaders to approach governing with a "compromising mindset": a blend of "principled prudence" (involving a willingness to adapt some of one's principles) and "mutual respect" (a fundamental valuing of one's opponents).[6] Their recommendations focus mainly on the means by which political journalism might be less dominated by the view that politics is inescapable, a "no-holds-barred competitive struggle in which only one side can win, and neither has any reason to cooperate with the other."[7] They also encourage schools to provide the kind of civic education that would promote understanding of compromise and its role in democracy.[8]

My aim in this chapter is to show why we should welcome this defense of the compromising mindset, and yet reject its narrow view of the domain in which the spirit of democratic compromise matters. Like many contemporary thinkers, Guttman and Thompson assume that the spirit of compromise is most important to the work of policy makers and legislators. But, as Russell Dalton and Hans-Dieter Klingemann have urged, "the wellspring of politics flows from the attitudes and behaviors of the ordinary citizen," and perhaps especially in a democracy.[9] Dalton and Klingemann also contend that taking this view seriously in the context of democratic life demands a more expansive understanding of "politics" and "political behavior" than many democratic theorists have thought.[10] In this spirit, I argue in section I that a great deal of the non-voting behavior of the ordinary citizen of a democracy not only counts as (genuinely) political behavior, but actually constitutes a realm of decision and action best understood as quotidian democracy.[11]

My argument also presumes that we need a more expansive understanding of the concept of "democratic governance" itself. On my view, the role of citizen is a political office and what democratic citizens do—when they must be taken to act primarily as citizens—is sometimes as critical to the success of democratic governance as the decisions and actions taken by legislators, executives, judges, and high-placed civil servants. It often falls to "ordinary" citizens, in the course of their daily activity, to decide whether and how to realize democratically legitimate ends, and sometimes even to ensure the successful functioning of mechanisms of democratic accountability. Thus, if the spirit of compromise is critical to democratic governance—as I follow Guttman and Thompson in believing—the spirit of compromise is also critical to what citizens do when they act as political agents in the realm of quotidian democracy. That is, the compromising mindset is a requirement of political morality at the level of quotidian democracy, just as fully as it is in the decisions and actions of the "political class." Moreover, if we fail to address the standards and principles that ought to govern quotidian democracy, we ultimately fail to provide an adequate account of democratic governance and the conditions of stable democratic institutions.

As I will show in section II, quotidian democracy is frequently shaped by tensions between the deliverances of individual conscience and demands that emanate from the sphere of public reasons and obligations. Of course, this tension is an enduring feature of political life, regardless of the mode of political organization in question. It is an important theme of Sophocles' *Antigone*, for instance, in the tragic conflict between Creon's defense of the demands of the polis and Antigone's invocation of a "higher" law, the validity of which transcends the force of those demands.[12] Equally enduring is the tendency to respond to such conflicts by trying to severely limit, or even completely disallow, the influence of (allegedly) private convictions in the public sphere. It has sometimes been claimed that this approach reflects an essentially modern, and fundamentally secular, hostility toward religious faith.[13] Yet the stance has ancient roots in a view of the world that is anything but secular. Indeed, in Sophocles' play, the Chorus chides Antigone for the "blind will" with which she asserts the superiority of divine law over human law and for her readiness to sometimes act as a law unto herself.[14]

When individual convictions are claimed to be self-evident truths that "must" be normative of collective ends, or as unimpeachable expressions of a "higher law" that automatically trumps public obligation, even the most ardent defender of democracy may be tempted by Hobbes's insistence that "the law is the public conscience" to which individual judgment must be subordinate.[15] But if we truly care about *democratic* ideals, as I'll argue in section II, we will accept that meaningful respect for the deliverances of individual conscience, along with robust tolerance of at least *some* of the political conflicts they may produce, is crucial to the persistence of stable democracies. I will also argue that meaningful respect for the deliverances of individual conscience is possible only if we reject political principles which require that we deem certain kinds of convictions (usually deliverances of conscience, including religious convictions) to be "essentially private," and inappropriate to count as justifications in the domain of public reasons.

Meaningful respect, as I defend it here, also rejects the demand for justificatory neutrality between competing conceptions of the good. It is grounded in what Charles Taylor once called "substantive liberalism" shaped by a commitment to robust toleration, yet also rooted in a *critical and fundamentally non-relativist* pluralism. This critical pluralism allows us to say—indeed sometimes requires us to say—that some convictions and ways of life are *intrinsically* too hostile to democratically legitimate purposes and institutions to merit public respect.[16] Thus, though a properly constituted democracy will display meaningful public respect for many conscientious convictions, there can be compelling grounds for substantive liberalism to justify withholding that respect from some kinds of conscientious convictions. But this is just a reminder that there are limits to the value of compromise. For instance, if the content of your conscience requires you to physically endanger another, or demands that you intentionally limit her legitimate efforts to enjoy democratically constituted rights, the political morality of a properly governed democracy requires us not only to withhold meaningful public respect from those convictions but also (within limits prescribed by democratic values) to do all that we can to reject those convictions.

Yet what do I really mean by "compromise"? In the most basic sense, a compromise is of course a way of responding to conflict by means of an agreement that involves mutual sacrifice in order to improve on existing circumstances. According to Follett, to reiterate the earlier point, compromise lies somewhere in between domination and integrative consensus, and it is the way we settle most of our controversies, whether in public life, or in semi-public and private settings.[17] But going beyond the standard discussions of compromise, I contend that we can identify a species of compromise that is closer to integrative consensus than to basic compromise. I call it *principled compromise* because it is defined by a set of principles that allow us respond to divisive political conflicts in a way that promotes continued and constructive cooperation. A principled compromise is a distinctive variant of compromise in that (1) it aspires to an agreement emerging from processes that maximize reasonable transparency; (2) it involves sacrifices that minimize harm and promote mutual respect; and (3) it seeks improvements on the status quo that are meant to promote continued cooperation.

Some theorists of deliberative democracy assume that any kind of negotiation must be incompatible with deliberative ideals. But a principled compromise inescapably *embodies* deliberative ideals such as fairness, mutual respect, and equality of opportunity to influence outcomes. Moreover, principled compromise is more deliberatively demanding than "ordinary" bargaining in two important ways. First, it requires us to consider improvements on the status quo that actually promote social cooperation, and second, it requires that we *begin* our search for agreement by attributing moral legitimacy to the "other side."[18] Since a common feature of democratic conflicts stemming from moral disagreement is the tendency to degenerate into socially destructive demonization of "the other," creating structures and promoting habits that support the spirit of principled compromise provides especially valuable resources for doctrinally and culturally complex democracies. I show in section III that protecting space for the pursuit of principled compromise helps create "deliberative" space for constructive political dissent, particularly for non-violent civil disobedience.[19] Section IV argues that protecting deliberative space for principled compromise can help us formulate reasonable responses to various forms of conscientious objection. I then argue in section V that when debates about divisive moral issues take place within deliberative space for pursuing principled compromise, the resultant deliberations can become more "authentically democratic" and may even have the potential to constructively reshape the disagreement.

My account is rooted in a larger theory of democratic citizenship and its role in protecting democratic political stability.[20] Stable democracies, on my view, are constituted not only by *vertical* relationships between citizens and the political institutions that embody their shared principles, but also by *horizontal* relationships that connect citizens with each other by means of a distinctive "civic *ethos*"—an ethos shaped, at least in part, by acceptance of shared civic virtues. This network of vertical and horizontal relationships is necessary to constitute a group of people as a "demos." That is, it is in virtue of these relationships that a people can collectively constitute a democratic sovereign, and not simply exist individually as political subjects. An essential element of the civic ethos that constitutes a democratic sovereign is widespread

willingness to seek principled compromise when integrative consensus is unavailable and when principled compromise would not
undermine other important democratic values.

The willingness to compromise is complex. For instance, it is
inextricably linked with other democratic virtues such as the willingness to sacrifice and the readiness to relinquish resentment
when our commitments fail to determine the outcome of democratic deliberation. Moreover, as I show in section VI, because we
are fallible, humility is also an important democratic virtue, and
democratic humility is sometimes best expressed in the willingness
to compromise. Taken together, these considerations about the
civic ethos that supports democratic stability mean that principled
compromise is part of the political morality that makes democracy
possible. I am to show, then, that anyone who claims the benefits
of democratic citizenship is morally required to seek constructive,
principled compromise when it emerges as a constructive possibility of democratic cooperation.

I. THE VALUE OF COMPROMISE IN THE DOMAIN OF QUOTIDIAN DEMOCRACY

I have claimed that the spirit of compromise matters as much for
what ordinary citizens do, and in a great deal of their daily activity, as it does for the work of high-placed government officials.
That is because even as private citizens much of what we do has
consequences for, and is fundamentally shaped by, reasons and
obligations emerging from the public sphere. If a feminist professor at a co-ed university in the United States decides that she
cannot "in good conscience" allow male students in her class, any
action taken on that decision has politically weighty (and democratically unacceptable) consequences for her society's efforts to
pursue democratically legitimate ends. In this case, it undermines
the national commitment to ensuring that gender is not used as
a basis for denying access to educational opportunities. Were her
decision to be taken to set an example, and become a rallying cry
for others in similar positions of responsibility, it could eventually
have ramifications that affect the persistence of democratic cooperation and even the continuity of stable democratic institutions.
What this example shows is that no citizen is a political "island,"

and that the seemingly most "private" decision to act on a personal conviction—say, "Patriarchy must be challenged whenever possible"—can have consequences that make it more than a private decision and place it in the public, political realm. This is why the dispositions and beliefs that Gutmann and Thompson identify as the compromising mindset can matter so much to some of the most "ordinary" activities of one's daily life. Principled prudence and mutual respect have a critical role to play in the ordinary actions of the private citizen—as citizen—just as fully as they do in the activity of legislators considering a measure affecting access to assault rifles.

Of course, the consequences with the greatest "political weight" typically follow from decisions and actions we take when we act in some politically "official" category—that is, in some political office. Moreover, it is tempting to think that only elected officials, political appointees, and high-level civil servants count as political officials. But virtually every day, democratic citizens who are not part of the elite "political class" make politically weighty choices and perform politically consequential actions. Our actions as "private citizens" sometimes have a profound effect on the ability of other citizens to enjoy the rights and privileges of citizenship, as well as on society's ability to realize democratically chosen ends and on the likelihood that democratic cooperation will be sustained. The role of "citizen" in a democracy is an official role that has its primary authority in the realm of quotidian democracy.

The realm of quotidian democracy is comprised of four main categories of politically weighty decisions and actions. In the first category are those politically weighty choices and actions open to us as a function of powers, privileges, and responsibilities formally associated with the role of citizen. This includes the choices one makes as a taxpayer, a voter, or a juror, for instance. In the second, and sometimes closely related, category are the sorts of choices and actions that Elizabeth Anderson has described as "participatory citizen feedback": such as signing petitions, participating in opinion polls, contributing to regulatory deliberations about exiting laws and policies, and engaging in certain kinds of public protest.[21] Anderson's view builds on Dewey's insistence in "Creative Democracy" that democracy is not "something institutional and external" but a "way of personal life."[22] She also draws on Dewey's conception of democratic decision-making as a "continuous process" in which what citizens do in the seemingly most ordinary contexts of daily life is critical to the content of democratic deliberation and to the successful functioning of democratic institutions.[23] My concept of quotidian democracy—though not entirely Deweyan in inspiration—clearly has much in common, then, with Anderson's Deweyan conception of deliberative democracy.

But there is a third category of politically weighty choices and actions which are typically open only to certain subsets of citizens: those citizens who provide the public services that Michael Lipsky describes as "street-level bureaucracies," including "schools, police and welfare departments, lower courts, legal services offices, and other agencies whose workers interact with and have wide discretion over the dispensation of benefits or the allocation of public sanctions."[24] One does not have to be elected or appointed to high political office to become a police officer, or a teacher, or a caseworker for social services. But the decision and actions one takes in these roles carry enormous political weight, as we can see from the controversies that have surrounded the use of force by police in the United States and the uses of discipline in American public schools. Moreover, the authority and power to take these decisions and actions are rightly seen as direct expressions of the authority and power of the democratic state.

In the fourth main category of politically weighty choice and action in quotidian democracy, citizens choose and act in contexts framed primarily by their private interests and purposes, but in which their choices and actions may nonetheless have profound effects on the likelihood that others will be able to enjoy the rights and privileges of citizenship. Thus, a business owner might have to decide whether to welcome someone as a customer in her place of business, despite her serious moral objections to that person's way of life. A pharmacist might have to decide whether to prescribe a medication to someone who is legally entitled to take it though he has a serious moral objection to the medication's effects.

I contend, of course, that in all the complex choices and actions that comprise quotidian democracy, the compromising mindset—that combination of principled prudence and mutual respect—is a vital component of actions and practices that protect the rights of democratic citizenship, and ultimately promote democratic cooperation and preserve stable political institutions. This claim echoes an observation contained in one of the most effective passages in Mario Cuomo's provocative address on "Religious Belief and Public Morality: A Catholic Governor's Perspective":

> to assure our freedom we must allow others the same freedom, even if occasionally it produces conduct by them which we would hold to be sinful. I protect my right to be a Catholic by preserving your right to believe as a Jew, a Protestant or non-believer or as anything else you choose. We know that the price of seeking to force our beliefs on others is that they might force theirs on us.[25]

Of course, as Cuomo's observation shows, what principled prudence and mutual respect often demand is what we can call robust tolerance of convictions and ways of life we may reject. Further, as Judith Shklar once argued, "tolerance consistently applied is more difficult and morally more demanding than repression."[26] Shklar implicitly recognizes that one of the most important virtues in the democratic civic ethos is the virtue of sacrifice and, indeed, acting in the spirit of compromise is often a way of acknowledging the political value of certain kinds of sacrifice. Still further, as Burke reminds us, protecting a shared political life that provides a secure framework for private well-being sometimes confronts us with the need to "remit some rights" (for example, a *proposed* right not to serve people whose values we reject) in order to preserve other, more important rights (the right to enjoy freedom of conscience across a wide range of activities and practices). It is possible that one reason that so many people, all along the political spectrum, have become so resistant to compromise in political life is that they have forgotten the important truth that sacrifice is an essential requirement of democratic cooperation.

Of course, some critics will object that my account of quotidian democracy, along with the expansive view of politics and political behavior which it contains, wrongly ignores the distinction between "public" and "private." But I do not see how we can avoid acknowledging that, even in a modern liberal democracy, the boundary between what is public and what is private is fundamentally permeable. One's choice to own and build a business may be individual and "private," and it may reflect important virtues of

individual initiative and industriousness. But both the choice and
its outcomes are inescapably framed by rights, privileges, and obligations that emanate from decisions and actions taken in the public sphere of democratic decision-making. Moreover, if a business
owner seeks to exclude someone from his business on the grounds
of private conscience—let's say he believes that it would be sinful
for him to sell floral arrangements for a same-sex wedding—he is
making a choice that has critical ramifications in the public sphere
of reasons and obligations. That seemingly private choice counts
as intrinsically political behavior, with weighty consequences for
the protection of democratic values such as equality before the law.
There is simply no way around the fact that the public and the private are often intertwined in this way. In my view, political thought
can fully capture the implications of this phenomenon only by recognizing the validity of the concept of quotidian democracy.

Some readers will still object to my insistence on describing the
role of citizen as a political office. But that description is just a way
of acknowledging that, particularly in a democracy, citizens can
occupy various positions in the social world that give them special
rights, privileges, and opportunities to determine the content of
laws and policies, to influence and even determine the application
of those laws and policies, and to affirm or to thwart the expression of fundamental democratic values in critical social spaces.
One may have these rights, privileges, and opportunities as a juror,
a participant in an opinion poll, a "street-level bureaucrat" such as
a police officer, or simply as an "ordinary" private citizen running
a business or working as a college professor. This suggests that in
myriad ways, and often as part of our daily lives, we all contribute
to the success or failure of democratic governance. To be sure, the
development of the Internet and, in particular, the emergence of
"social media," have created new pathways through which ordinary citizens can express political opinions and engage in the kind
of political activism that has the potential to shape public political debates and decisions. But even independent of these new
technologies, and even in the context of the modern bureaucratic
democracy, the role of "citizen" has always been best understood
as *a political office*. The public sphere in any democracy is a sphere
of reasons and obligations in which ordinary citizens make politically weighty choices every day. These choices count as political

behavior at the level of quotidian democracy, and the spirit of compromise is a vital and democratically important component of the dispositions, attitudes and beliefs which ought to shape that behavior.

II. DEMOCRATIC CONFLICT, RESPECT, AND THE SPIRIT OF COMPROMISE

Nowhere is the spirit of compromise more critical than in the various contexts in which the deliverances of individual conscience may conflict with reasons and obligations that emerge from democratic decision-making. I have claimed that if we truly care about *democratic* ideals, whenever possible the democratic public sphere ought to embody meaningful respect for the deliverances of individual conscience, along with robust tolerance of at least *some* of the political conflicts they may produce. Meaningful respect affirms a political society's commitment to fundamental liberties and encourages widespread tolerance of diversity and peaceful disagreement.[27] It also expresses that society's awareness of human fallibility (and its dangers), and recognizes the value of what might be called "conscientious citizenship": protecting social and political space in which the deliverances of individual conscience can sometimes be counted on to produce citizens who are capable of identifying, and hopefully challenging, serious injustices or "democracy deficits" that might be sanctioned by a biased, or simply unreflective, democratic majority.[28] Meaningful respect also allows us to take seriously the objection that our conscientious convictions—for instance, commitments such as religious beliefs—are not properly understood as essentially a "private" matter, since they so often give rise to what John Rawls rightly called "comprehensive conceptions" of what is of value in human life. Indeed, on my view, it is precisely *because* most religious convictions, for instance, are not essentially private, that we face so many difficult questions about the legitimate influence of religion in the realm of political decisions and actions, and in the domain of public reasons appropriate to justify those decisions and actions. The substantive liberalism defended here can allow that wherever conscientious convictions, including at least some religious values, are part of the moral consensus that shapes our *shared* political morality we do not, in Mario Cuomo's words, have to "deny them acceptability as part of this consensus."[29] But as Cuomo also observes—rightly, in my view—a democracy is not *required* to accord any conscientious convictions (including religious values) "acceptability" as part of the moral consensus.

Yet there are many obstacles to the effective realization of this strategy of treating meaningful respect for conscientious convictions as a prima facie requirement of a properly constituted democracy. First, it can be difficult to find deliberative procedures capable of giving some citizens an authentic "voice" in the political process if their deepest convictions rest on doctrines that might be challenged by fellow citizens, or rely on modes of argument not easily accessible outside of a particular tradition of belief. This difficulty is compounded by the fact that people do not simply "have" convictions. In fact, our deepest convictions are meaning-giving commitments, rooted in fundamental values, ideals, and principles which are partly constitutive of personal identity. These meaning-giving commitments frequently connect us to communities of belief and value in ways that sometimes produce a powerful sense of divided loyalties—particularly in the midst of the multicultural, doctrinally complex contexts of contemporary democracies. Most of these democracies contain many such communities of belief and value and will thus consistently confront serious challenges to any attempt to articulate a unified collective will on matters of substance, or to secure conformity to contested legislation or public policies.

In my view, the most defensible response to many of the relevant conflicts—whether the response we display as private citizens or as political leaders and high-placed agents of democratic governments—is to adopt the compromising mindset that reflects the spirit of compromise. Sometimes the best way to respond to conflict, even when it involves our deepest convictions, is to accept an agreement that involves mutual sacrifice in order to improve upon the circumstances that would exist without it. This is the attitude rightly embodied in Cuomo's observation about the price we may pay if we seek to "force our beliefs on others." But I stress that, on my account, the sacrifice made by the party whose conscientious conviction may be excluded from the shared consensus on political morality must meet important conditions. In particular, it is a condition of principled compromise that we should propose and accept only those sacrifices that minimize harm and promote mutual respect. Of course, it can be difficult to agree on what constitutes a relevant harm, what it means to "minimize" a particular harm, or on what constitutes a plausible standard for weighing the importance of various harms. But even in those situations where we find it difficult to make such evaluations, the challenge of seriously considering the full range of harms at stake in a difficult debate nonetheless has the potential to transform the conflict in profound ways, if only because it allows us to make more "audible" and accessible the "voices" of all those who might have some stake in the outcome of a decision proposed as a solution to the conflict.

To be sure, even if it is possible to make deliberation "authentically democratic," and to do so in a way that limits the number of situations in which citizens will feel torn by divided loyalties, there will inevitably be occasions on which deliberative outcomes conflict with the content of individual convictions in ways that the individual and her meaning-giving community may find difficult to accept. Doctrinally and culturally complex democracies are consistently challenged to find defensible grounds for assigning weights to the concerns of those who sincerely object to democratically agreed-upon ends and to the expectation that they should nonetheless participate in practices that promote them. The persistent possibility of such objections means that democratic societies can be stable only if they can achieve consensus on an account of the conditions under which it is appropriate to excuse dissenters from important public obligations and of the conditions in which the pursuit of collective goals can legitimately outweigh the claims of the conscientious objector.

The search for such a consensus must be informed not only by the spirit of compromise, and a special concern to approximate the standards of principled compromise, but by an understanding that the value of compromise must always be weighed in the balance against other democratic values. Even in a democracy guided by meaningful respect for conscientious convictions, we can identify legitimate constraints on the sacrifices that democratic majorities must make to express that respect, particularly when some sacrifice might limit a society's ability to promote and preserve fundamental values. Equally important, in my view, sometimes a failed search for compromise, and an ultimate refusal to sacrifice democratic values to some particular meaning-giving commitment, can fully promote the *spirit* of compromise (and the respect that substantive liberalism seeks to express) simply by attributing moral legitimacy to those with whom the democratic majority might disagree. I will discuss some examples of this process in the next section.

But a third important challenge that emerges when pursuing the strategy of meaningful respect is the difficulty of understanding how best to respond to assertive expressions of public dissent and protest. Democratic decision-making processes are fallible, and when they in fact fail, the resulting decisions and actions are bound to provoke concern and dissent. This means that in a stable democracy there must be "deliberative space" for the kind of dissent that allows us to trust in what Benjamin Barber has called the "self-correcting" character of democracy.[30] There must also be "conceptual space" in the public sphere for acknowledging the political legitimacy of conscience-driven arguments and social movements that seek to expose and rest serious injustice, or even to uncover "democracy deficits" that may not (yet) rise to the level of serious injustice. Yet, how is it possible to acknowledge the political legitimacy of dissent and protest without ultimately undermining respect for democratic institutions and for the rule of law?

Anderson convincingly argues that we can understand certain kinds of public protest as participatory feedback that has a critical role to play in the mechanisms of political accountability in a democracy.[31] But, on my view, public protest, and particularly conscience-driven protests meant to challenge injustice or expose democracy deficits by means of non-violent resistance, are virtually always far more than merely "participatory feedback." In the case of non-violent civil disobedience, we have a form of political protest that perfectly embodies the spirit of compromise. The central example I will discuss is that form of non-violent civil disobedience as embodied in the practice of the American civil rights struggles of the 1950s and 1960s. In one of the most influential characterizations of that practice, "The Letter from Birmingham Jail," Martin Luther King, Jr., claimed that the practice was fundamentally a means of opening "the door to negotiation"—in this case about how to achieve effective desegregation of public accommodations.[32] Even sympathetic critics of the Civil Rights movement eventually insisted on the political limits of this project and challenged the extent to which it could provide a long-term strategy of effective political behavior in the face of persistent socioeconomic inequality. But, as I will show in the next section, to the extent that the movement displayed the extraordinary power of the kind of "participatory citizen behavior" that is meant to invite "negotiation" (and not the confrontation with which it was too often met) it remains one of the most important pieces of evidence that promoting the spirit of compromise is critical to the well-being of democratic societies.

III. Civil Disobedience and the Value of Compromise

I have articulated a notion of principled compromise that, in my view, best expresses the spirit of compromise in a context of democratic institutions shaped by a substantive liberalism. Here I want to explore one of the most important challenges to the assumptions of that substantive liberalism: the idea that the only way to really preserve mutual respect in a culturally and doctrinally complex democracy is to place serious constraints on the kind of consideration that counts as a public reason. I contend that such constraints will ultimately have the (unintended) effect of undermining, or even prohibiting, the substantive and politically critical expression of democratically valuable dissent.

My principal concern in this discussion is John Rawls's idea of "public reason." But it must be noted that even Gutmann and Thompson's somewhat broader notion of "deliberative reciprocity," articulated in *Democracy and Disagreement*, has been thought to address the deliberative challenges I describe in section II by ultimately excluding from the deliberative forum at least some democratically valuable but *substantive* appeals to individual conviction.[33] If the criticisms I address here are apt, such views, first of all, make it difficult to understand how public deliberation could ever embody an authentic collective will and may thereby fail to provide a convincing answer to the problem of democratic legitimacy. Second, as other critics have charged, any practices shaped by these approaches will carry a serious risk of either shutting down reasonable dissent or converting it into politically dangerous resentment and resistance.[34] But, third and perhaps most important, these views make it difficult to understand how a democratic society can *really* create deliberative space for the kinds of dissent that are most likely to challenge us to confront the serious mistakes—democracy deficits and especially serious injustice—that democratic decision-making sometimes produces.

Turning, now, to the primary task of exploring the Rawlsian approach, I begin by acknowledging that, over the course of his philosophical career, Rawls gradually revised his notion of public reason out of concern to more explicitly protect the kind of deliberative space that I have described. He was particularly interested in the path of the evangelism of nineteenth-century abolitionists and in the religious commitments of twentieth-century leaders of the American Civil Rights movement. This interest was, no doubt, a function of Rawls's awareness that these religious convictions were powerful catalysts of politically constructive struggles against injustice. Indeed, on Rawls's eventual revised view, conscience-driven considerations are legitimate contributions to democratic debate "provided that in due course public reasons . . . are presented sufficient to support" whatever conclusions the conscience-driven considerations were initially "introduced to support."[35]

Yet, given what Rawls actually says about how the public reason of a democratic society is constituted, it is difficult to understand how either the nineteenth-century case for abolition, or the twentieth-century case for racial equality, could have *initially* been made from "inside" public reason. Rawls writes, for example, that public reason is "characteristic of a democratic people," and that it is "the reason of its citizens, of those sharing the status of equal citizenship."[36] In a related passage, he explains that public reason is "the reason of equal citizens who, as a collective body, exercise final political and coercive power over one another in enacting laws and in amending their constitution."[37] To be fair, Rawls seems to have believed that struggles to end slavery and segregation certainly needed to achieve consensus on a reinterpretation of the "constitutional essentials" held to express the public conception of justice. He also seems to have hoped that the right kind of reinterpretation could come about within public reason. But in each of the struggles against injustice that interest Rawls most, the necessary revisions and "reinterpretation" involved fundamentally redefining the very notion of "citizen" and conceptually reconstituting the "collective body" of "equal citizens." What was required in each case was a fundamental *extension* of the bounds of public reason to make room for the legitimacy of new kinds and, perhaps especially, new *sources* of legitimate public claims.

Now, it is a fortunate truth about the ingenuity of human reason that the deliberative resources available within a particular public sphere—within a historically particular moment in any given political society—can never exhaust the stock of tools that makes rational persuasion possible. A great painting or a searching piece of music may require us to confront the horrors of war; a well-crafted novel or a moving personal memoir may deepen our understanding of the injustice of slavery; a moral exemplar's self-sacrifice may lead us to confront moral inconsistencies in our own belief and practice that have, for too long, lead us to unreflectively accept some mode of discrimination or oppression.[38] Iris Young was thus right to argue that, especially in a complex multicultural democracy, the public sphere must make room for ways of producing and deepening our understanding of others' experiences and legitimate claims that may not resemble "ordinary" discursive reason-giving and argument.[39] But it seems clear that when a movement must seek deliberative resources to produce a fundamental change in the way in which public reason is *constituted*, this will mean that the movement's initial essential case cannot be made within the bounds of existing public reason.

We learn in "The Letter from Birmingham Jail" that Martin Luther King had a sophisticated understanding of this truth. We also learn that he had a rich appreciation of the deliberative resources to which democratic dissenters might turn when the resources of public reason proved insufficient. Principled compromise—including the mutually respectful "negotiation" with Birmingham merchants that King was actually calling for in the "Letter"—is one such deliberative resource, and there is powerful evidence that King appreciated this fact. I contend, moreover, that King conceived of the non-violent civil disobedience that he defines and defends in the "Letter" as *itself* a public call for national engagement in a broader, and hence more complex, national project of principled compromise.

To fully display the appropriateness of the language of principled compromise here, it is important to note, first, that the
movement demanded great sacrifice from its participants. Like
Gandhi before him, King understood that non-violent civil disobedience was a complex expression of *agape*—disinterested love—
that demanded the capacity to genuinely "love thy enemy." King
also knew that non-violent direct action demanded remarkable
self-discipline and a readiness to accept the idea that unearned
suffering could ultimately be redemptive. Moreover, in my view,
it is not clear how one might fully deliver on the Rawlsian requirement to translate the belief in the redemptive value of suffering,
and the "ultimate community" that King thought it might make
possible—into a fully secular public reason. But second, it must
also be stressed that the first phase of the Civil Rights movement
was rooted in a clear vision of the social "improvement" that ought
to result from new policies on access to public accommodations,
and full access to the power of the ballot. Third, non-violent civil
disobedience clearly embodied respect for democratic institutions
and practices in the readiness to accept any reasonable legal penalties that might follow on disobedience. Finally, the movement's
principles explicitly called for mutual respect and negotiation in
return for the sincerity of the sacrifice it demanded, the clarity of
its vision about desired outcomes, and the respect that it expressed
for democratic cooperation and democratic institutions.

What this means is that the Civil Rights movement was not simply an embodiment of the spirit of democratic compromise. For,
taken together, these considerations show that King, along with
many other civil rights leaders, came to understand that in a large,
complex democracy, public deliberation is a multi-layered, multi-
stage, temporally extended process.[40] Of course, especially at the
start of the movement, King often despaired of the fact that the
sacrifices of those who risked arrest and violence to adhere to principles of non-violence were not broadly recognized or accepted
as, in fact, an invitation to principled compromise. The "Letter"
also reveals King's frustration at the fact that social reforms laid
out by the leaders of the Civil Rights movement were often met
with incredulity as too "radical," sometimes even by the clergy, to
be acknowledged as genuinely plausible improvements on the status quo. As King argues in the "Letter," the Civil Rights movement

needed to harness the power of the Socratic *elenchus* to produce a "tension in the mind" that might rationally compel Americans to examine their unreflective commitments, confront the inconsistencies inherent in segregation, and contemplate a fundamental reimaging of the social world.

It must be noted that, in contrast to the focus on principled compromise that determines King's tone in the "Letter," many of King's most influential public speeches expressed a hope that the movement would not simply inspire "improvement" on the status quo, but that it might ultimately yield an integrative consensus capable of unifying the deepest convictions and aspirations of all Americans as part of a shared national self-understanding.[41] This is the idea implicit in King's references to the possibility of "ultimate community," or–in a phrase drawn from the work of Josiah Royce—the "beloved community." The frustrated, and sometimes violent, protests that took shape in the aftermath of King's death suggest that his assassination was seen by many as an expression of the futility of that hope for that integrative consensus (in more than one sense of "integrative"). Many also interpreted his assassination as the dissolution of the principled compromise that he helped bring about by means of non-violent direct action, and as regrettable evidence of the fundamental fragility of that compromise. It may also have confirmed suspicions—like those expressed in Bayard Rustin's internal criticisms of the Civil Rights movement—that a principled compromise on access to public accommodations was a far cry from fundamental changes in "the American socio-economic order" that would be necessary to produce substantive and not merely formal equality.[42]

Yet the agreements that resulted from the initial invitations to negotiation that shaped the first phase of the Civil Rights movement helped to produce more than a decade of dramatic social and political change—from *Brown v. Board of Education* in 1954 to the Civil Rights Act of 1964 and the Voting Right Act of 1965—that would have been unlikely, if not impossible, without those initial protests. Moreover, in his 1960 essay, "Pilgrimage to Nonviolence," King made the compelling argument that reason, "devoid of the purifying power of faith, can never free itself from distortions and rationalizations," and that the Christian doctrine of agape operating through the Gandhian method of nonviolence was an indispensable element of the power of the protests.[43] Of course, the broader movement would have had little hope of success if the national press had not played a pivotal *deliberative* role, publicly exposing the unrestrained violence of Southern efforts to suppress the "unruly" idea that racial segregation is fundamentally unjust. But the struggle catalyzed by that conviction provides a powerful counterweight to the idea that we should try to purge the public forum of substantive individual convictions or the comprehensive conceptions which give them their content and much of their initial "corrective" power in the sphere of public reason.

IV. Principled Compromise and Conscientious Objection

I have claimed that relying on the resources of principled compromise can enrich democratic deliberation in ways that fully acknowledge the power of substantive conscientious convictions—at least sometimes—to bring about constructive change in democratic institutions. I turn now to those conflicts in which democratic dissent yields something closer to conscientious objection than civil disobedience as defended in the "Letter from Birmingham Jail."

We can find some successful, and relatively uncontroversial, examples of principled compromise in the agreements typically reached when a society officially recognizes conscientious objections to military service. The examples I have in mind are those cases in which the compromise involves allowing the objectors to perform alternative service that still advances an important collective goal. More controversial examples—in need of careful scrutiny to confirm that they meet the demands of *principled* compromise— are cases in which parents seek exemptions from various demands of public education on the grounds that those demands unduly interfere with their ability to pass their religious beliefs on to their children.[44] In such cases, appropriate scrutiny must focus not just on the value of parental religious liberty, but also on the question of the extent of the sacrifices, and even harms, that might be imposed on the affected children. But this just reminds us that the acceptability of a principled compromise cannot be measured solely by the nature and extent of the sacrifices or improvements for the deliberating parties alone.

Yet principled compromise is not always a requirement of robust respect for dissent. Even in a democracy guided by meaningful respect, and committed to meet the prima facie requirement to accord meaningful public respect to individual convictions, there are legitimate constraints on the sacrifices that democratic majorities must make to express that respect. In particular, a democratic people is sometimes entitled to deny that systematically excusing objectors from public obligations is a reasonable requirement of democratic respect, especially when to do so would endanger realization of legitimate and important democratic ends.

The argument against systematic excuses of this sort is especially strong in two kinds of cases. First, the case against systematic excuses can be compelling when those who object are in a position to do so principally because of previous choices of their own. This is an especially convincing consideration, in my view, when the relevant choices lead them to take on a publicly necessary role, or to pursue a profession, that is known to rely (at least in part) upon public support. In such contexts, I contend, any occupant of the role or any member of the profession is legitimately subject to regulation by reference to democratically agreed upon ends. This means, for example, that—whatever the policies that have, in fact, been adopted by some jurisdictions—it can be entirely justifiable not to enact a policy that systematically protects pharmacists who object to prescribing certain kinds of contraception. In fact, it is often the case that to enact the exclusion wrongly ignores the fact that we have the responsibility to weigh the costs of entering a profession, when those costs are a matter of public knowledge.[45]

But, second, the case against extending systematic excuses from public obligations can be strengthened when the social importance attached to the profession can be publicly known, and the kinds of personally challenging decisions that an individual professional might be asked to confront can be appreciated in advance. What counts as evidence of public commitment to the social importance of the profession is often largely a function of the level of public investment in the complex set of institutions and practices that are essential to training those intending to go into that profession. Equally important is the frequency of expressions of *social respect* for the expertise of those who undergo the training.

Anyone who decides to train as a pharmacist, for instance, cannot plausibly claim ignorance of the social importance of the role, of public commitment to supporting and promoting the expertise of those who occupy the role, or to the fact that taking on the role may commit one to promoting ends that may conflict with one's private convictions.

Denying systematic exceptions to those who choose to take up a profession made possible in large part by public investment, and underwritten by social valuation of the relevant professional expertise, is not a veiled expression of disrespect for the deliverances of conscience. Nor is it an attempt to treat the deliverances of conscience as a purely "private" matter. In fact, my argument in this chapter is an extended defense of the opposite view. I accept that the meaning-giving commitments that shape people's identities and define their loyalties are not appropriately deemed essentially "private." I also insist that, given the fallibility of democratic majorities, it would be dangerous to do. Further, I would argue that even in nation-states claiming officially "secular" identities, it is often difficult to understand how such conduct as wearing a religious symbol, or adopting certain modes of dress inspired by religious traditions, could *in itself* constitute an unacceptable "interference" with the pursuit of any *legitimate* public purposes.

Yet, however any society decides such cases, it must not ignore the full extent of the politically weighty considerations at stake in such disputes. Democratic deliberation may result in a policy that legalizes access to a contested medicine or medical procedure, or that legalizes a state-sanctioned marriage for those who were historically denied access to it. Individual convictions that involve objections to such legislation should almost always carry some weight in a society's deliberations. But when we examine some actual controversies, we discover that there is a politically weighty asymmetry between, on one hand, the pharmacist who objects to prescribing the "morning-after pill" or the county clerk who seeks to deny a marriage license to a same-sex couple and, on the other hand, a religious dissenter conscripted into military service. The authority that the pharmacist and the clerk demand as a way of grounding a right to refuse in these cases is rooted in the most fundamental way on their *choices* to participate in ways of life that are deeply dependent on processes of democratic decision-making and the pursuit of democratically agreed-upon ends. We must thus be cautious in assuming that the conscientious objections they might have should be accorded the same weight—as a matter of course—as the objections of the religious dissenter who has been *conscripted* into military service against his (or her) individual will.

Any adequate contribution to the normative theory of democracy must anticipate the deliberative challenges that will remain for any democratic society that might seek to deny a right of refusal to pharmacists opposed to the morning-after pill, or to a county clerk opposed to same-sex marriage, even on democratically legitimate grounds. No stable democracy can ignore the possibly divisive and destabilizing effects that even democratically legitimate denials of petitions for systematic excuses may produce. As I argue in section V, this is why complex democracies must more intentionally, and more substantively, integrate multiple forums for principled compromise into their deliberative processes. These are the only deliberative mechanisms that can be reliably expected to give dissenters an authentic voice in deliberations about collective ends, and to leave them feeling confident that their dissenting voices have in fact been heard.

V. Principled Compromise as a Tool for Authentically Democratic Deliberation

The best way for a democracy to minimize the risk of destabilization in response to any such decisions is to make an explicit national commitment to principled compromise as a deliberative resource. This commitment must be taken seriously at all levels: by educational institutions, civic groups and religious communities, responsible news media, and by private foundations, as well as by local and national governments. It must also inform debate in the multiple deliberative networks that, over time and on many different levels, shape deliberation in complex democracies.

An informal consensus on the importance of such networks seems to have emerged in some contemporary democracies. It is instructive that on some of the most important and divisive political conflicts, principled compromise often remains an unreachable goal. The problem is that, for far too long, many "debates" have been carried out in a manner that can only poison the wells:

damaging any prospect that those who disagree might retain respect for, or acknowledge the moral legitimacy of, the "other side." Fortunately, those involved in the informal deliberative networks have recognized that, in such contexts, the primary goal of democratic deliberation must be to repair the social and political damage resulting from a socially widespread failure to appreciate the deliberative importance of principled compromise.

One of the most remarkable examples of such an effort began shortly after an act of deadly violence at a Planned Parenthood clinic in Massachusetts in 1994, when an organization called the Public Conversation Project quietly convened several meetings of a group of civic leaders (all of them women) on both "sides" of the abortion debate. In a jointly authored account of what transpired, published under the provocative headline "Talking with the Enemy," the participants reported that they began by agreeing that "our talks would not aim for common ground or compromise":

> Instead, the goals of our conversations would be to communicate openly with our opponents away from the ... spotlight ...; to build relationships of mutual respect and understanding; to help de-escalate the rhetoric of the abortion controversy; and, of course, to reduce the risk of future shootings.[46]

The meetings continued for more than five and a half years, and involved 150 hours of conversations that were kept secret until a Boston newspaper published the participants' joint account in 2001. That account concludes with two observations that are worthy of note in this context. First, the participants observe (perhaps predictably) that, by the end, they came to believe that their positions "reflect two world views that are irreconcilable." But they also reported that they nonetheless planned to continue meeting, in the hope of contributing "to a more civil and compassionate society." I will briefly explore a few instructive elements of the exercise that led to these conclusions.

It deserves notice, first, that although the participants were all prominent leaders of influential organizations known for forceful public stands in the debate, they all approached the project as citizens with a fundamental stake in the cooperative project of democracy.[47] They wrote about how difficult this proved to be. But their resolve reminds us of how important it is, in such contexts, to understand that "citizen" is a political role defined (however informally) by normative standards. But, second, they squarely confronted familiar concerns that, in political conflicts rooted in deep moral disagreement, even being willing to talk to someone from the "other side" might be thought to reveal a lack of moral integrity. One participant who identified as pro-life worried that, if the fact of her participation became public, she would be interpreted as "treating abortion merely as a matter of opinion." Another feared being viewed as morally tainted for "sitting with people who were directly involved with taking life." Of course, the conversations continued for more than five years, and the participants expressed the intention to continue talking even after that. This is surely evidence that they came to understand that, far from being a violation of moral integrity, granting reasonableness and moral legitimacy to those with whom we disagree is in fact a confirmation of moral integrity.

Regrettably, none of the participants seemed willing to allow that granting moral legitimacy to the other is also an important way of expressing the fact of human fallibility.[48] Indeed, the published account suggests that, given the framing of the exercise, none of the participants believed that she *could* concede this point, and at least one pro-life participant believed that she *should not* concede the point. But let us suppose, for the sake of argument, that any participant in the abortion debate could be confident of possessing an unimpeachable grasp of a relevant truth. It is nonetheless *always* possible that she might be mistaken about how to apply that truth in the world. One of the many strengths of Mario Cuomo's 1984 speech on "Religious Belief and Public Morality" is the care with which he raises this possibility and courageously draws out its profoundly important political implications.[49]

Yet some things that the participants did not say are as instructive as what they did say. In particular, they never considered the possibility that, despite the initial framing, they were in fact engaged in a process of "principled compromise" (though not, of course, any sort of compromise on what constitutes a legitimate political decision on abortion). This "absence," in my view, predictably reflects the cultural ascendancy of the mistaken idea that compromise is always about "trimming one's conscience" to fit the consensus of the moment. Moreover, many features of a principled compromise are evident in their interactions. For instance, it was surely a sacrifice to spend 150 hours of time over five years, talking and listening in a way that required the bracketing of their identity-defining commitments, and (as they report) being in constant fear that merely to be in the conversation might be to endanger those commitments. Further, it surely constituted an improvement on the context of fear and mistrust in which the exercise began that each participant became able to "talk with the enemy" long enough to stop seeing her *as* an enemy, but instead as a fellow citizen who shares a common interest in creating a "more civil and compassionate society." Indeed, the participants reported that, even as they kept their conversations secret, their participation nonetheless began to soften their public rhetoric and led them to encourage their respective organizations to do so as well. This is certainly a profound improvement on the status quo that led to their deliberative exercise.[50] Indeed, in my view, it provides helpful support for my claim that contemporary liberal democracies cannot afford *not* to create more deliberative space for this kind of project.

VI. Compromise and Democratic Humility

Critics will rightly insist that accepting the moral legitimacy of one's opponents, and even securing broad agreement on the superiority of civil discourse over acrimony and violence, are not equivalent to successfully negotiating agreement on a "solution" to the question of what a democracy can legitimately do on the matter of abortion, for instance. They may also object that even if it were possible to achieve a principled compromise on some substantive political outcome concerning abortion, compromises are unstable and, in Follett's words, "if we only get compromise, the conflict will come up again and again in some other form."[51] Finally, it may be objected that history is full of examples in which the willingness to live with compromise—even when it might have seemed to some to actually be principled compromise—has turned out to make the participants potentially (and sometimes actually) complicit in injustice. Thus, as thinkers like Avishai Margalit and Sanford Levison remind us, it is very much a live question whether the "Great Compromise" that led to the US Constitution ought to be understood as a "rotten compromise" for its recognition of a political order that allowed the cruelties and indignities of chattel slavery.[52]

But I have already conceded the point about the difference between ending socially divisive hostility about abortion and reaching a principled compromise on a political solution to the debate about abortion. The continued inaccessibility of such a compromise on abortion confirms my earlier claim that it presents the kind of deliberative challenge that *for now* outstrips our capacity to provide a rationally constructive response. If a constructive principled compromise is to be possible, all parties to the abortion debate will need to rethink not only the way that all of us talk about the moral dimensions of the human capacity to reproduce, but also how we understand the interests, responsibilities, and rights of *everyone* in society who can be substantially affected by the exercise of that capacity. This process will require extraordinary efforts of self-scrutiny, good will toward the "opposition," and creative moral imagination.[53] For the time being, the best way to create deliberative space for such efforts is to help people learn to stop seeing those with whom they disagree as "the enemy."

Regrettably, it is not currently clear how or whether it might be possible to disentangle political conflict about abortion from the unruly and intractable moral debate that has fueled the conflict for a very long time. Yet, as I have argued elsewhere, the idea that we might definitively "solve" such a complex moral problem involves a fundamental misunderstanding of how moral argument and moral reasoning actually work.[54] Even if we proved able to resolve this kind of serious moral conflict *now*, this would not and could not guarantee that some aspect of the disputed issue would not reemerge at some point in the future, as a source of newly serious disagreement. When we adopt any policy on matters such as abortion, or physician-assisted suicide, or even a particular national configuration of healthcare, we effectively begin to alter the data of moral and political experience, and in time we will very likely need to revisit many of the central issues again. This is why Hilary Putnam is right to argue that words like "solution" and "problem" may be leading us astray in these contexts. Moral "problems," he urges, are not like "scientific problems"; they do not, and cannot, have "solutions" in the sense that scientific problems do. Putnam therefore contends that we adopt a different way of conceiving of moral argument—in particular, a conception relying on the idea of adjudication.[55] In my view, this is a conceptual shift best translated into political contexts by means of the idea of principled compromise, for what we need when we address deep moral disagreements in political life is precisely a mode of deliberation that can acknowledge the recurring character of the conflicts. To be sure, we choose in contexts of ever-present risk. Even when we seek *principled* compromise, we sometimes rely on flawed assumptions about what sacrifices it is reasonable or morally right to impose on others. Further, we often make unreliable predictions about the likelihood that allowing sacrifices to continue now may allow us to pursue a peace that is likely to bring such suffering to an acceptable end. Our fundamental, inescapable fallibility may mean, in the end, that *humility* may be the most important political virtue. This is the wisdom expressed by the Chorus in Sophocles' *Antigone* when they observe that "the mighty words of the proud are paid in full with the mighty blows of fate."

The kind of humility relevant to democratic life is not to be confused with any kind of personal trait that—in religious and secular contexts alike—might be associated with an attitude of servility, perhaps as some kind of "corrective" to the dangers of human pride. Rather, as Mark Button has argued, the humility relevant to democratic life embodies a set of dispositions, attitudes, and beliefs that "put us on guard against the ethical and political dangers of complacency, premature closures and dogmatism"— especially against those forms of dogmatism that "express a will to mastery or domination."[56] This kind of humility is not the "monkish virtue" that Hume rejected, but a political virtue that is critical for the survival of any complex, multicultural democracy, so I follow Button in calling it "democratic humility." What democratic humility requires most in the realm of democratic governance, whether at the level of political elites or in the everyday decisions and actions that citizens take in the realm of quotidian democracy, is that we acknowledge the depth of human fallibility by setting out the terms under which our most politically fundamental compromises can be revised. With American history as our guide, we can recognize that this kind of humility—as embodied in a

Constitution that could be revised—has the extraordinary power to transform even a "rotten" compromise into a rational blueprint for a genuinely democratic way of life.

NOTES

1. Edmund Burke, *Burke's Speeches and Letters on American Affairs*, ed. Ernest Rhys (New York: J.P. Dutton, 1950), pp. 76–144.

2. Mary Parker Follett, "Constructive Conflict," *Dynamic Administration: The Collected Papers of Mary Parker Follett* (1925; reprint) (Mansfield Centre, CT: Martino Publishing, 2013;) pp. 30–49.

3. Ibid., pp. 45–49.

4. Amy Gutmann and Dennis Thompson, *The Spirit of Compromise* (Princeton, NJ: Princeton University Press, 2012).

5. Ibid., pp. 3–4.

6. A "mindset" for Gutmann and Thompson is "a cluster of attitudes and arguments that incline an individual to organize thinking an action in a way that makes some considerations and choices more salient than others." See *The Spirit of Compromise*, pp. 64–65. Mindsets are compromising or uncompromising to the extent that they "aid or impede" the making of compromises. The most concise definition of the compromising mindset appears on pp. 16–17 of *The Spirit of Compromise*.

7. Ibid., pp. 189–199.

8. Ibid., pp. 199–202.

9. Russell J. Dalton and Hans-Dieter Klingemann, "Citizens and Political Behavior," in Dalton and Klingemann, editors, *The Oxford Handbook of Political Behavior* (Oxford, UK: Oxford University Press, 2007), p. 3.

10. Dalton and Klingemann, "Overview of Political Behavior," in Robert E. Goodin, editor, *The Oxford Handbook of Political Behavior Science* (Oxford, UK: Oxford University Press, 2009) pp. 321–344.

11. The term "quotidian democracy," as I will show, is a way of capturing a Deweyan notion that democracy is best understood not by reference to external institutions but, as he says in "Creative Democracy," a way of life. It is also an obvious nod to the value of the idea of "middle democracy" developed in Guttman and Thomson, *Democracy and Disagreement* (Cambridge, MA: Harvard University Press, 1996). See especially pp. 12–13, where they write that "The forums of deliberation in middle democracy embrace virtually any setting in which citizens come together on a regular basis to reach collective decisions about public issues—governmental as well as nongovernmental institutions. They include not only legislative sessions, court proceedings, and administrative hearings at all levels of government but also meetings of grass roots organizations, professional

associations, shareholders meetings, and citizens' committees in hospitals and other similar institutions."

12. The conflict remains whether one interprets it as conflict between religion and human law, or between the demands of family and the demands of the polis. A compelling analysis of Antigone's transition from righteousness to self-righteousness is offered by Patricia M. Lines in her essay "Antigone's Flaw," *Humanitas* XII, no. 1: 1999. See also George Steiner, *Antigones* (New Haven, CT: Yale University Press, 1984), p. 5.

13. One of the most influential of these critics was Fr. Richard Neuhaus, in *The Naked Public Square: Religion and Democracy in America* (Grand Rapids, MI: Eerdmans, 1988). The idea certainly informs both the "strict interpretation" interpretation of the First Amendment Establishment Clause, as well as the demand made by much contemporary political thought for government neutrality between competing conceptions of the good. But the idea itself is not essentially a critique of religion.

14. *Antigone,* line 912.

15. Hobbes, *Leviathan,* part II, ch. 29, "Of Those Things that Weaken or Tend to the Dissolution of the Commonwealth," C. B. Macpherson, editor, 1651; rpt. Penguin Classics 1968, p. 366.

16. See Michele Moody-Adams, *Fieldwork in Familiar Places: Morality, Culture and Philosophy* (Cambridge, MA: Harvard University Press, 1997), ch. 5.

17. Mary Parker Follett, "Constructive Conflict," *Dynamic Administration: The Collected Papers of Mary Parker Follett* (1925; reprint Martino Publishing, 2013), pp. 30–49.

18. Martin Golding argues that in any compromise process "some degree of moral legitimacy is accorded to the other side." See Martin Golding, "The Nature of Compromise: A Preliminary Inquiry," *Compromise in Ethics, Law and Politics: Nomos XXI,* J. Roland Pennock and John W. Chapman, editors (New York: New York University Press, 1979), p. 17. Theodore Benditt develops further implications of this view, in "Compromising Interest and Principles," also in *Nomos XXI,* pp. 26–37. I contend that according full moral legitimacy is something that comes only when we seek what I call principled compromise.

19. Barber discusses the notion of democracy as "self-correcting" in Benjamin Barber, "Foundationalism and Democracy," in Seyla Benhabib, editor, *Democracy and Difference: Contesting the Boundaries of the Political* (Princeton, NJ: Princeton University Press, 1998), pp. 348–359; especially p. 354.

20. These passages draw on an argument I make in an as-yet-unpublished paper of mine entitled "Cultural Diversity, Globalization and the Future of Democratic Citizenship."

21. Elizabeth Anderson, "Democracy: Instrumental vs. Non-Instrumental Value," in Thomas Christiano and John Christman, editors, *Contemporary Debates in Political Philosophy* (Oxford: Wiley-Blackwell, 2009), pp. 216–217.

22. John Dewey, "Creative Democracy: The Task before Us," in J. A. Boylston, editor, *The Later Works of John Dewey*, Vol 14 (Carbondale: Southern Illinois University Press, 1988).

23. This view is defended primarily in Dewey, *The Public and Its Problems* (New York: Holt and Company, 1927).

24. Michael Lipsky, *Street Level Bureaucracy: Dilemmas of the Individual in Public Services*, 30th annual edition (New York: Russell Sage Foundation, 2010), p. xi.

25. Mario Cuomo, "Religious Belief and Public Morality: A Catholic Governor's Perspective," 1984. www.archives.nd.edu.

26. Judith Skklar, *Ordinary Vices* (Cambridge, MA: Harvard University Press, 1984), pp. 4–5.

27. Eva LaFollette and Hugh LaFollette, "Private Conscience, Public Acts: Does Private Conscience Trump Professional Duty?," *Journal of Medical Ethics* 33:5 (2007): 249–254.

28. This is one of the most important lessons of Mill's defense of liberty of expression in John Stuart Mill, *On Liberty* [1859] (Indianapolis: Hackett, 1978), ch. 2; See also Eva LaFollette and Hugh LaFollette, "Private Conscience, Public Acts."

29. Cuomo, "Religious Belief and Public Morality."

30. Barber discusses the notion of democracy as "self-correcting" in Benjamin Barber, "Foundationalism and Democracy," in Seyla Benhabib, editor, *Democracy and Difference: Contesting the Boundaries of the Political* (Princeton, NJ: Princeton University Press, 1998), pp. 348–359; p. 354.

31. Anderson, "Democracy: Instrumental vs. Non-Instrumental Value," p. 217.

32. Martin Luther King, Jr., "Letter from Birmingham City Jail" [1963] in James M. Washington, editor, *A Testament of Hope: The Essential Writings and Speeches of Martin Luther King, Jr.* (New York: Harper Collins, 1986), pp. 290–292, esp. 292. 1.

33. The arguments of this section draw on and respond to the conception of public reason defended in John Rawls, *Political Liberalism: Expanded Edition* (Cambridge, MA: Harvard University Press, 1996), esp. lecture VI, "The Idea of Public Reason," pp. 212–254. The relevant arguments from Gutmann and Thompson are contained in their *Democracy and Disagreement*, esp. ch. 2, pp. 52–95.

34. This argument is developed by Stanley Fish, "Mutual Respect As a Device of Exclusion," in Stephen Macedo, editor, *Deliberative Politics: Essays*

on *Democracy and Disagreement* (Oxford: Oxford University Press, 1999), pp. 88–102.

35. Rawls, *Political Liberalism*, exp. edition, Introduction to the paperback edition, pp. xlix–l. Conversation and engagement with the work of Brandon Terry helped me appreciate the importance of Rawls's remarks on these matters.

36. *Political Liberalism*, exp. edition, lecture VI, p. 213.

37. *Political Liberalism*, exp. edition, lecture VI, p. 214.

38. I develop this view in Moody-Adams. "The Idea of Moral Progress." *Metaphilosophy*, 30, No. 3, (July 1999), esp. pp. 176–178.

39. Iris Young, "Communication and the Other: Beyond Deliberative Democracy," in Benhabib, editor, *Democracy and Difference* (Princeton, NJ: Princeton University Press, 1996), pp. 120–135; p. 120.

40. A related view of democratic deliberation as similarly complex is developed in the essays in Jane Mansbridge and John Parkinson, editors, *Deliberative Systems* (Cambridge: Cambridge University Press, 2010).

41. What I describe as "integrative consensus" may be what Henry Richardson means by "deep compromise" in chapter 11 of his *Democratic Autonomy* (Oxford: Oxford University Press, 2002). My differences with Richardson's rich account concern the issue of categorization. What he calls "deep compromise" seems to be, instead, a form of agreement that somehow unifies the meaning-giving commitments that underwrite serious political disagreement in such a way that the idea of "sacrifice"—so central to the idea of compromise—seems to lose its relevance. Thus, what he calls deep compromise I would call integrative consensus.

42. Bayard Rustin, "From Protest to Politics: The Future of the Civil Rights Movement," *Commentary*, February 1965.

43. Martin Luther King, "Pilgrimage to Nonviolence" (1960), in Washington, editor, *A Testament of Hope*, pp. 36 and 38.

44. I am thinking here of the issues raised by *Wisconsin V. Yoder* 406 U.S. 205 (1972) and *Mozert v. Hawkins* 827 F. 2d 1058 (1987).

45. Eva LaFollette and Hugh LaFolllete offer an especially rich analysis of the central issues, even as they take a stand in arguing (I think correctly) for the idea our moral responsibilities as professionals are "not identical" to our moral responsibilities as individuals. See "Private Conscience, Public Acts," esp. p. 253.

46. Anne Fowler, Nikki Nichols Gamble, Frances X. Hogan, Melissa Kogut, Madeline McComish and Barbara Thorp, "Talking with the Enemy," *Boston Sunday Globe*, January 28, 2001 pp. F1–F3.

47. Ibid., p. F2.

48. Theodore Benditt draws important links between the fact of human fallibility, the consequent need for humility, and the notion of moral

integrity. He argues that compromise is connected with recognition of the need for humility. See Benditt, "Compromising Interests and Principles," *NOMOS XXI*, esp. pp. 340–336.

49. Cuomo draws this distinction with clarity and care, and with insightful attention to the relevance of his position for other debate. See Mario Cuomo, "Religious Belief and Public Morality: A Catholic Governor's Perspective," reprinted in *More Than Words: The Speeches of Mario Cuomo* (New York: St. Martin's Press, 1993).

50. It does not constitute an objection to this claim to note—as some commentators have done—that the exchanges did not continue, and that the discussants' serious disagreement about abortion did not disappear. The argument of the final section of the chapter explicitly acknowledges that this kind of disagreement may demand repeated discussions extended indefinitely in time.

51. Follett, "Constructive Conflict," p. 35.

52. Avashai Margalit, *On Compromise and Rotten Compromises* (Princeton, NJ: Princeton University Press, 2010), pp. 54–61. Sanford Levinson, "Compromise and Constitutionalism," 38 *Pepperdine Law Review* 821: 2010–2011.

53. This passage draws on arguments in my *Fieldwork in Familiar Places* (Cambridge, MA: Harvard University Press, 1997), esp. pp. 143–154.

54. Ibid., ch. 3.

55. Hilary Putnam, *Realism with a Human Face* (Cambridge, MA: Harvard University Press, 1990), pp. 181–183.

56. Mark Button, "'A Monkish Kind of Virtue'? For and Against Humility," *Political Theory*, 33 no. 6 (December 2005): 861.

8

THE CHALLENGES OF CONSCIENCE IN A WORLD OF COMPROMISE

AMY J. SEPINWALL

The process of crafting and passing legislation might be thought to be the locus of compromise par excellence.[1] Yet, where the law that results impinges upon moral or religious belief or practice, the issue of compromise arises anew, in both senses of the word: Individuals who oppose the law on moral or religious grounds believe that their political obedience will compromise them in a fundamental way. Their plea for an exemption from the objectionable legal requirement is, then, a bid for further compromise.[2] Compromise in the first sense concerns an undercutting of the self, while compromise in the second sense involves a grant of concessions. Yet, unlike compromises that arise in the legislative process, or at least in some ideal version of it,[3] the compromise involved in an exemption from a neutral law of general application involves neither an exchange of benefits nor the prospect of mutual benefit—two hallmarks of compromise in, say, political (and other) negotiations.[4] There are several reasons to doubt the wisdom or fairness of the requested exemptions, then.

First, why should government confer a "private right to ignore [a] generally applicable law[]"?[5] Further, why defer to conscience at all? The claims of conscience compel from a first-person perspective; they have no hold over anyone but their bearer. And there is no necessary connection between these claims and moral truth—one might be just as gripped by a conscience dictating virtue as one demanding vice. Worse still, where the exemption would impose burdens on third parties, accommodating his claims of conscience threatens not just political obedience but oppression of others too. Finally, if compromise embodies the best of politics, as at least some theorists contend, then conscientious exemptions might well embody its worst—instances of favoritism that offend against commitments to neutrality and equality too.

These are all concerns that would support significant restrictions on the exercise of conscientious objection, or perhaps its elimination altogether, as some theorists have proposed.[6] In this chapter, I seek to defend robust rights of conscientious objection, first by arguing in favor of a highly, though not completely, deferential stance toward pleas for accommodations on conscientious grounds, and then by taking up in turn the challenges lodged against granting conscientious exemptions.

I frame the discussion through the challenges and requests for accommodations that have been raised in response to the Patient Protection and Affordable Care Act (PPACA), focusing in particular on the employer mandate—the legal requirement that employers with 50 or more employees provide health insurance that meets a minimum set of standards.[7] Among these standards are rules requiring coverage for women's healthcare, including all 20 FDA-approved methods of contraception.[8] The most prominent challenge to the contraceptive coverage requirement—the so-called contraceptive mandate—is the one the US Supreme Court decided on the last day of its 2013 term, in *Burwell v. Hobby Lobby*.[9] Hobby Lobby is a closely held corporation owned by a family of evangelical Christians who object, on religious grounds, to the use of certain forms of contraception. The PPACA's employer mandate required that Hobby Lobby's insurance package provide coverage for these forms of contraception, but the Supreme Court held that this requirement substantially and unnecessarily burdened the family's freedom of religion, and that of its corporation by extension. As a result of the decision, Hobby Lobby was permitted to exclude contraceptive coverage from its employee healthcare plan.[10]

Challenges to the employer mandate involve three features that render them especially difficult, and so fruitful, for an inquiry into the place of conscientious objection within a democratic polity. First, these cases turn upon an atypical conception of complicity. In the standard case of conscientious objection, the objector seeks to avoid

having to participate directly in conduct he deems wrong. Paradigmatically, pacifists seek to avoid fighting in a war. But the employer
mandate cases involve complicity in an asserted wrong that occurs at
a far greater remove: The employer claims that simply by subsidizing an insurance package through which his employees access medical interventions he deems wrong, he is complicit in their wrongs—
and indeed complicit enough, he thinks, for him to warrant an
exemption. Historically, courts have denied pleas for exemptions
where the objector's connection to the conduct he believes wrong
is attenuated in the way that the employer's is. Thus, those opposed
to war may not withhold the portion of their tax burden meant to
fund the military,[11] and those opposed to abortion may not withhold
that portion of their university fees that fund campus health services
where the health services provide abortions or abortion counseling.[12] *Hobby Lobby* marked a shift from these cases. Recognizing complicity through subsidization, as *Hobby Lobby* does, opens the door to
a whole host of opt-outs, with potentially vast implications for much
of our regulatory regime.

The second challenging, and so illuminating, feature of the
employer mandate cases is that the exemptions sought threaten to
impose costs upon third parties. If employers are released, on conscientious grounds, from their obligation to cover certain forms of
healthcare, their employees will have to secure subsidization for,
or provision of, the excluded drugs or treatment elsewhere, possibly at their own expense and inconvenience. Historically, however,
cases of religious accommodation have involved claimants who
have wanted to be left alone; they have not sought to impose their
convictions, or the implications of their convictions, on others.[13]
In this way, the employer mandate cases raise issues that courts
have not yet had significant occasion to think through.[14] As such,
these cases invite us to work out the appropriate balance between
the employers' interests in purity of conscience and the material
(and perhaps also expressive) costs of being denied what is otherwise a statutory entitlement.

Finally, the employer mandate challenges exemplify a kind of
conscientious objection that is especially threatening to democratic politics. The typical case for an accommodation involves a
claimant pressing a marginal religious or moral commitment, and
an exemption can be granted to him with little or no disruption to

anyone else, and so no worries about government partiality. Thus, when we permit Native Americans to use peyote (an otherwise illegal drug) in their religious ceremonies, we can congratulate ourselves on our benevolence and cultural sensitivity.[15] When we honor the pacifist employee's objection to manufacturing tanks even though he evidenced no objection to manufacturing the steel used to make these tanks, we can celebrate our deference and humility.[16] In both cases, accommodation implicates no one else's legitimate interests. But when the government faces a conflict between respecting religious freedom and women's reproductive rights, any outcome it pursues threatens an intolerable favoritism. This conflict is perhaps the most vexing (and belabored) one in the literature on democratic disagreement. The employer challenges to contraceptive provision crystallize the conflict and allow us, perhaps, to see a way out.

I aim in the first part of the chapter to defend a qualified, albeit quite deferential, stance on conscientious accommodation. But that does not mean that we should offer exemptions to all comers. The second half of the chapter explores limits to the presumptively deferential exemption regime that the first part defends.

In sum, the aspiration here is to find a balance—a suitable compromise—between claims of conscience and the foundational commitments of a liberal democracy. The outcomes at which I arrive may not find widespread favor among political liberals, but I believe that they maintain faith with the spirit of political liberalism nonetheless.

I. Conscience and Accommodation

A. *Defining and Defending Conscience*

Thomas Hill defines "conscience" as "a capacity, commonly attributed to most human beings, to sense or immediately discern that what he or she has done, or is about to do (or not do) is wrong, bad, and worthy of disapproval."[17] This definition seems overly cognitive, however. For one thing, conscience is more than mere judgment, or the formation of a belief that something is "wrong, bad, and worthy of disapproval."[18] If I have not internalized a particular moral prohibition—if I have no conviction in regard to it—I may

well know that an act I have done, or am about to do, is wrong and
worthy of disapproval and yet feel no compunction about it. That
is, it forms no part of my conscience. Further, if I *have* internalized
the prohibition, then my conscience is likely to elicit more than
just the belief that what I am about to do is wrong; it will also provide motivation to refrain from committing the wrong, and antici-
patory guilt or fear at the prospect of doing wrong. In other words,
"conscience," as I shall understand the term, is a complex of cognitive, conative, and emotional dispositions.[19]

In addition to the dispositions that conscience requires, we
should also attend to its content. The commitments constitutive
of one's conscience are those that are central to one's identity.[20]
These can be non-moral (e.g., "never let the fire in one's soul
die,"[21] or "may what I do flow from me like a river, no forcing and
no holding back, the way it is with children"[22]), moral ("I will recognize the inherent dignity of all people and treat them all with
equal respect") or "I will not unjustifiably harm another"), or religious (e.g., "I will treat all human life from the moment of conception as sacred"). Moreover, each of these can be specified in a
multitude of ways. For example, "I will not cheat" is a specification
of "I will play fair" (a moral commitment).

I doubt that non-moral commitments could justify a conscientious exemption, for we do not take it to be the state's role to
facilitate our efforts at self-actualization. By contrast, moral and
religious commitments are typically other-regarding and, for good
or ill, we privilege commitments motivated by concern for others
over commitments motivated by concern for self.[23] As such, we
have more reason to exempt someone from a law binding on the
rest of us where that law conflicts with a moral or religious commitment than where it conflicts with a commitment aimed at self-
actualization that does not have religion or morality as its source.[24]
At any rate, since most claims for an accommodation turn on
moral or religious commitments, I do not consider non-moral
commitments further.[25] On the other hand, I follow those theorists who argue, despite much law to the contrary, that we should
be willing, where appropriate, to accommodate not just religious
claims of conscience but moral ones too.[26] I seek to elucidate, in
what follows, when and why we should conclude that these claims
should ground an accommodation.

To begin, one might wonder why any conscientious commitments ought to command our respect. Andrew Koppelman argues that conscience poorly tracks the cases where we feel exemptions should or should not be granted.[27] Thus, some claims that we are inclined to think worthy of accommodation are not claims of conscience per se. For example, those who seek an exemption from the ban on peyote, because peyote is used in religious ceremonies, do not claim that their consciences mandate peyote use so much as their religion does. On the other hand, conscience can be strongly felt in favor of claims that we would not want to grant. Thus, Koppelman offers the rationale provided by a man who murdered his sister-in-law and her infant daughter because, as the murderer recounted, he received a divine command that he felt he could not disobey.[28]

The first half of Koppelman's puzzle seems readily resolved once we note that the dictates of conscience may be specified in a multitude of ways and the reasons we have for accommodating these dictates provide at least prima facie reason for accommodating their specifications. Thus, we allow Native Americans to use peyote because peyote use is a central part of their religious observance and we believe religious observance worthy of accommodation in the face of the federal drug laws.

The second half of Koppelman's puzzle, however, which turns on the questionably moral nature of the contents of a conscience, is more troubling. And Koppelman is not alone in noting that claims of conscience need not track objective, or even commonly held, moral truths. Other theorists invoke Huck Finn as the paradigmatic instance of someone whose conscience would have led him astray had he heeded it, because he had internalized the law of his day, and so felt deep inner turmoil about not turning Jim in.[29] And Hannah Arendt's great and devastating insight in *Eichmann in Jerusalem* is precisely along these lines. She writes, "it was not his fanaticism but his very conscience that prompted Eichmann to adopt his uncompromising attitude [i.e., his unwavering devotion to the "final solution"] during the last year of the war."[30]

Moreover, for Koppelman, it is not just that there is no reason to expect that the dictates of anyone's conscience will be worthy of deference but also that conscience itself—the capacity, rather than its contents—is hardly worthy of respect. Koppelman defines conscience as "an imprecise word for an internal compulsion to act that is specified only by the possessor's internal psychology."[31] Conscience, that is, is the capacity that turns one's convictions—whatever their source—into authoritative commands. But so defined, Koppelman argues, conscience can play no compelling role in justifying accommodations: "Neither conscience . . . nor volitional necessity necessarily points toward anything that other people have any obligation to respect. . . . Perhaps it is very hard for someone to resist the force of volitional necessity, and perhaps that counts as a (rebuttable!) reason not to ask them to do it. But in that case, the appropriate response is not respect. It is pity."[32] In sum, the problem with conscience for Koppelman is that it "is entirely unmoored from any objective value"[33] and it is heeded automatically, and not because its possessor reflectively endorses its commands.

Contrary to Koppelman, I believe that the process of heeding one's conscience is not as reflexive as Koppelman contends, and more valuable than he allows. The notion that we follow our conscience merely as a matter of compulsion fails to track both the phenomenology of, and our discourse around, conscience. Our most prominent experiences of conscience arise when we face a conflict between two incompatible norms—for example, secular law and religious conviction. There is no proceeding automatically in the face of this conflict. If we see both as normative—if we have adopted an "internal point of view" with respect to each[34]—the conflict will call us to attention. We will be forced to decide which norm to follow, and the process of so doing will require that we engage in conscious deliberation.

With that said, some people do take their claims of conscience to be automatic trumps. Even here, however, we should not treat reliance on conscience as a matter of brute compulsion. For the automatic adherence to conscience would quite likely have been preceded by a moment when the individual in question did deliberately decide that conscience would prevail. This is just the way it is with commitments—we deliberately adopt them precisely so that, from the moment of their adoption, they will operate for us as non-starters:[35] To adopt a commitment is to decide once and for all that it will function as a trump. Should a commitment be implicated at some time thereafter, we will not need to go through the deliberative exercise of deciding what weight to give it, less still whether to heed it at all. That work was done the moment we adopted the commitment. It is efficient to proceed in this way, but it is also appropriate to do so: What it is for something to be a conviction is for it to preempt our considering whether it should dictate our conduct. Having been made a conviction, it just does dictate. Other commitments work the same way. For example, the marriage vow, along with its commitment to fidelity, is intended to take off the table each spouse's recurring evaluation of whether to stay in the relationship. While the marriage is well functioning at least, the question should not even arise; the vow short-circuits it. And convictions are just commitments of a particular kind—as I have already said, commitments are central to one's identity. In sum, Koppelman is right that there is something automatic about the exercise of conscience. But there is nothing unusual or embarrassing about the deliberative elision that conscience involves.

Turning now to the other complaint, that conscience fails to track objective value. One can agree with those who express the worry and yet still believe that conscience itself is intrinsically valuable. The project of living one's life in accordance with a set of values one chooses (or at least affirms) is a distinctive trait of persons. Living according to one's conscience gives meaning to our lives, making them about more than the peripeteia of everyday existence. The fact that we are meaning-creating creatures, that we can and do play a role in shaping our life stories, is valuable in its own right. Insofar as conscience, which again consists of our identity-defining commitments, is central to the direction our lives take,[36] it too is valuable in its own right. We can grant all of this even while acknowledging that countervailing considerations might, at the end of the day, mandate that we deny the conscientious objector an accommodation. The connection of conscience to self, that is, confers a presumption in favor of claims of conscience. I shall go on to specify the circumstances where the presumption may be defeated. First, though, I seek to argue that conscience should always get a thumb on the scale.

B. *Deferring to Conscience*

When it comes to blaming one another for participation in, or facilitation of, a wrong, both legal and moral practice set the necessary threshold for complicity in light of the gravity of the sanctions that a finding of complicity entails.[37] Thus, under much domestic criminal law, for example, the predicates for complicity are quite demanding, given the gravity of a criminal conviction. In particular, one will be found complicit only if one shared the perpetrator's purpose in seeing the crime completed and one at least attempted to assist or encourage its commission.[38] More generally, the harsher the sanction, the more strongly connected one must be to the wrong—causally and psychologically—in order for one to be held morally or legally responsible for it.[39] In this way, third-personal judgments of complicity—those judgments we form about others—are both standardized and appropriately sensitive to commonsense ideas about individual culpability.

But our first-personal complicity judgments—each of our assessments of our *own* culpability in another's wrong—are nowhere near this regular, and this is so in light of three possible points of divergence. First, in a pluralistic society like ours, there is often widespread disagreement over what counts as a wrong. Contraceptive use is a paradigmatic case.

Second, we might disagree about the empirical facts. For example, the medical establishment rejects the Hobby Lobby owners' belief that the four contested forms of contraception are abortifacients. This is not a dispute about whether destroying embryos is morally permissible; it is a dispute about whether these four contraceptive devices work by destroying embryos. So it is a factual, and not a moral, dispute.

Finally, there is a third kind of disagreement, and it is the one of greatest relevance here—disagreement about the kind of connection one must bear to another's wrong in order for one to be complicit in that wrong. As described above, standard moral and legal accounts proceed with relatively demanding conceptions of complicity. But conscientious objectors to insurance subsidization under the PPACA, or conscientious tax resisters, operate with a conception of complicity that is far more encompassing than the standard account. These individuals believe that mere facilitation in a wrong (or in conduct they believe wrong) is sufficient to render them morally responsible for that wrong, and this is so even if their contribution is made at several layers of remove from the wrong. Thus, in the contraceptive mandate challenges, the employer believes that merely by subsidizing an insurance plan through which its employees or their dependents have access to contraception, the employers become complicit in contraceptive use. Even if we are prepared to allow individuals to decide for themselves on matters of value (e.g., whether contraceptive use is wrong), we might question why we should defer to those with non-standard accounts when it comes to articulating the relevant standard of complicity.

I have argued elsewhere that we should not judge the strength of claims of conscientious objection on the basis of the strength of the complicity claims underpinning them, for the pain the objector would experience in contributing to a wrong may be insensitive to the extent of her anticipated contribution.[40] Being made to act against conscience produces a certain kind of pain—the pain of a loss of integrity, or a dislocation from the self.[41] It is easy for many of us to imagine how compelled participation in a wrong might produce this sense of self-transgression, and yet difficult for us to fathom how a compelled remote and minor contribution might do so. But, from the perspective of one who holds a more expansive view of complicity, and so more readily sees herself as implicated in a wrong, the pain of facilitation in a wrong may be no less than that for the person who is made, against his will, to participate in the wrong. For example, the Quaker pacifist might view paying taxes to fund a war as no less violative of his commitments than is fighting in that war. And what should matter for purposes of conscientious accommodation is the objector's felt sense of complicity, not the sense of complicity we would have were we in her shoes.

Put differently, conscience is tied up with the self, so it is ineluctably subjective. Individuals may differ with respect to how readily their consciences are activated even where they agree on matters of substantive morality or religion—e.g., where all the individuals in question believe that contraceptive use is wrong. One will think that she bears responsibility only for her own contraceptive use; another will think she bears responsibility for any contraceptive use that she has facilitated, through its provision or subsidization. But the subjective experience of both may well be the same—each may think that she has done wrong in light of her connection to contraceptive use, and the breach of conscience may feel equally severe for each of them.

There are circumstances where we think the law should, all else equal, protect individuals from having to contribute to conduct they deem wrong and the feelings of guilt to which that contribution would give rise. This is the rationale for which we permit conscientious objection to a military draft. But if the foregoing is correct, we have no reason to think that an objection to fighting in a war is more *intrinsically* compelling than is an objection to funding that war. To be sure, there may be extrinsic considerations that would justify our more readily exempting someone from military service than from paying taxes to support a war. For example, it may be easier to find a replacement for the conscientious objector to a draft than it would be to find alternative funds to cover all of the tax dollars that would be withheld if we were to allow individuals to resist paying taxes for every government initiative they oppose. I shall have more to say about when countervailing considerations should restrict our accommodating conscientious objections. The point for now, however, is that, looking at the objections on their own merits, the very reasons we accommodate objectors to the draft obtain for objectors to more remote contributions to war, like taxes. In both cases, the objector believes that he would be complicit in war, which the objector believes wrong. In both cases, the objector anticipates that his complicity will violate some of his most fundamental commitments, and so he conceives of his prospective complicity as a source of deep pain. If the experience of contributing would be the same for draftee and taxpayer alike, we have no reason—again, on the intrinsic merits of their claims—to yield to the first and not the second. All else equal, each has an equally compelling claim for accommodation.

The foregoing treats both military participation and military funding as differing only in degree of contribution. But one might contend that they are different in kind: The draftee *performs* the controversial act; the taxpayer merely funds it. The same might be said of the doctor who objects to abortion or physician-assisted suicide (PAS) and some other individual who contributes to it more remotely—e.g., the taxpayer who funds Medicaid abortions or the store clerk who rings up the PAS prescription. When it comes to complicity, the former are like principals to a crime and the latter are only accomplices. Surely this difference should make the objection of the person who would be made to perform the objectionable act more compelling than the claim of the person who would contribute to it more remotely, the thought would go.

I maintain, however, that it is no less tendentious to refer to the draftee or the physician as someone who would be made to "perform" the objectionable act than it is to characterize both draftee (or physician) and taxpayer as "contributors" or "participants." For medical care—in particular, the decision whether to have an abortion and especially whether to avail oneself of PAS—is typically a joint endeavor, involving physician and patient. Both are participants in the treatment decisions. The taxpayer or pharmacy clerk contributes far less directly, to be sure. But the difference in question is just one of degree, not of kind. The point is even clearer in the face of the two objectors to military conduct—the draftee and the taxpayer. The draftee does no more than participate in the war. Indeed, it is conceptually impossible for any one person to wage war; instead, war is, by definition, a collective endeavor. Again, the draftee's participation is more direct than is the taxpayer's. But again, that fact alone does not make an objection to the draft more compelling than an objection to funding the military. And, indeed, if the law did not recognize that different kinds of participation in a war might nonetheless lead to reasonable feelings of complicity, it would require all pacifist draftees to fulfill their service in noncombatant positions, rather than exempting those who object to facilitating war from military service altogether. That is, the fact that drafted pacifists may elect to perform community, rather than military, service shows that what matters is participation—including mere facilitation—and not perpetration.

Legal and moral thinking go wrong, I have argued, in distinguishing between different instances of facilitation on the basis of the strength of the causal connection between the objector and the asserted wrong. But they do not restrict conscientious exemptions to those who would be made to perpetrate the asserted wrong. Nor should they. Participation may be a matter of degree, but the sense of guilt may not—and indeed need not—track the extent of one's causal involvement.

In sum, if we think that the law, at least all else equal, should protect people from having to participate in conduct they deem wrong, then we have reason to defer to the objector's subjective sense of implication even if it is one we do not share. We have, that is, presumptive reason to exempt the person who objects to funding contraceptive use just so long as she would view funding as a significant source of complicity in conduct she deems wrong. With that said, the deference I urge is merely presumptive. I turn now to the considerations that can and should defeat it, and the policies and values that should accompany, inform, and constrain a regime of moral or religious accommodation.

II. Conscientious Exemptions and Liberalism

One might grant that there is a case to be made in favor of conscientious objection and still contend that a robust exemption regime offends against fundamental liberal values. In particular, one might argue that such a regime conflicts with three key liberal commitments: First, one might worry that granting exemptions is unfair because oftentimes the exemptions will impose significant costs on individuals who do not share the objectors' religious convictions. Second, insofar as the exemptions sought impose burdens disproportionately on historically oppressed groups—women, in the contraceptive mandate cases, or homosexuals in the cases where business owners seek to deny employment or goods and services to gays and lesbians—one might worry that exemptions involve discrimination, and governmental complicity therein. And, finally, one might see in an exemption regime a more widespread failure of governmental neutrality: Had the law evolved in more neutral ways, the thought would go, there would be no need for customized departures from it in the first place. I address each of these worries in turn.

A. *Externalizing the Costs of One's Moral or Religious Convictions*

I have sought to argue that we should, all else equal, grant an exemption from a legal requirement if adhering to it would contravene an individual's deeply held moral or religious convictions. But often all else is not equal. In the employer mandate context in particular, granting the employer an exemption might well leave his employees without adequate healthcare coverage.[42] Thus, in the cases where employers object to having to fund contraception, we would have reason to deny their bids for an exemption if the women covered by these employer plans could then obtain contraception only at significant cost or inconvenience to themselves. Happily, this was not the likely outcome in the *Hobby Lobby* case as the Obama administration had already developed a workaround, whereby the insurance companies would offer contraception for free, and so courts could grant exemptions without imposing any costs on the plan beneficiaries. Matters would surely be otherwise if the employer objected to life-saving treatment (e.g., blood transfusions, which Jehovah's Witnesses oppose), and there was no alternative arrangement.

More generally, claims of conscience ground at most a presumption in their favor. That presumption will be defeated when the cost of an exemption for third parties exceeds some threshold. Just where this threshold lies is a matter for us to decide through democratic deliberation. We need to determine together the extent to which we value freedom of conscience, and the burdens we are therefore willing to incur, or impose upon others, in order to respect it. Once we have done so, we will have identified a level of burden below which exemptions should be granted in the face of sincere conscientious objection and beyond which exemptions may be denied. In short, one constraint on our exemption regimes arises in light of the material consequences an exemption might entail for third parties.

B. Political Oppression and Animus

Even if we need not worry about third-party costs, though, one might still find exemptions objectionable, for they look to provide a way for individuals who lost in the democratic sphere to evade the outcome they opposed.[43] A plea for an exemption is, in other words, the enemy of compromise: The pleading party is unyielding, and granting him the exemption can undermine the prospect of compromise in future efforts at legislation. After all, why

should a party dissatisfied with some proposed legal requirement
settle for a second-best version of his preferred outcome when he
can instead, as a conscientious objector, seek to evade the resulting law altogether? The worry about evasion is especially compelling where one suspects that the objectors aim not just to preserve
the purity of their souls by ensuring that they do not have a hand
in, say, facilitating contraceptive use; they aim to right this (supposed) wrong through their objections and (what they hope will
be) the ensuing denials of access. The concern, in short, is that
these moral or religious objectors intend sabotage.[44]

And there is a more cynical worry still lurking in some of the
reaction to exemptions to the contraceptive mandate. On this
thought, what motivates opposition to contraceptive use is not
genuine concern for nascent human life but instead animus
against women. It is plausible to see certain efforts to restrict
access to abortion as evidence of misogyny.[45] And some commentators understand efforts to evade the contraceptive mandate in
a similar way: As Ilyse Hogue, director of NARAL, says about the
challenges, "The truth is that this is not about religious freedom,
it's about sexism, and a fear of women's sexuality."[46]

The worry here is not, as it was above, about discrete third parties who bear direct consequences if the government grants an
exemption. Instead, the concerns suggest that all citizens may have
reason to feel aggrieved by the intransigence of the objectors. In
this way, these concerns should prompt us to question the viability
of a liberal democratic regime in the face of deep and widespread
division. To address these concerns, I consider in turn two possible
policy responses: (1) no exemptions; and (2) public provision.

1. No Exemptions
Given the threat of sabotage, and the difficulty in discerning the
objectors' true motivations, we might decide to grant no exemptions at all. Andrew Koppelman proposes as much when he argues
that we should not permit any exemptions if the legal requirement
from which the exemption is sought can function only with complete, or at least near-complete, compliance.[47] And this is just the
way courts have traditionally proceeded, denying religious accommodations where the requested exemptions would undermine the
system or program the legal requirement aims to support. Thus,

courts do not permit tax evasion on religious grounds because the tax system could not survive a multitude of exemptions.[48] So too they have denied exemptions from Sunday closing laws on the ground that allowing employers to close on any day they choose would undermine the effort to grant citizens a *common* day of rest.[49] In this way, Koppelman's concern about subverting the law through a grant of too many exemptions makes sense.

At the same time, the notion that the prospect of being granted an accommodation should turn on how many others share one's objection has the counterintuitive consequence that widespread opposition garners less deference than does opposition that is idiosyncratic or unusual. Because intersubjective convergence upon a proposition is at least some evidence of the proposition's truth, one might instead have thought that widespread opposition ought to be more compelling than opposition voiced by a few. And, at any rate, oppression of a significant minority is surely worse than oppression of an insignificant one.

The problem, writ large, is that compelled employer subsidization of healthcare that includes elements about which there is deep disagreement cannot be squared with the commitment to neutrality underpinning liberal democratic politics, and the tensions to which the employer mandate gives rise will be felt on both sides of the ideological spectrum.

From the perspective of the employer with conscientious objections to some of the forms of healthcare he is mandated to cover, the difficulty is just the obverse of the problem of dirty hands: In the classic case of dirty hands, politicians compromise themselves in order to carry out our political will. As a result, they bear the moral stain and suffer the transgression of self on our behalf.[50] Those who believe that contraceptive use (or other medical care that employers are mandated to cover) is wrong might think of the employer mandate as just the other side of the coin. Under the mandate, the government recruits employers to subsidize contraception and thereby outsources the moral stain to them.

The government might seek to protect these employers from having to incur this stain by allowing them to exclude contraception from their insurance plans, as the Court did in *Hobby Lobby*. But excusing employers from contraceptive coverage because they would otherwise feel implicated in a wrong involves symbolically denigrating women's rights. In other words, having a woman's access to contraception turn not on her own convictions but instead on those of her employer puts them both in a contest, and has the government choose the victor. This is the kind of choice that a government committed to neutrality and equality should at all costs seek to avoid.

The exemption/no-exemption options, then, arise after we have already made a choice—that provision of basic healthcare will fall to private employers, rather than the government. It is time to revisit that choice.

2. Public Provision
Given the controversy over contraception, one might well wonder why providing coverage for it should have fallen within the employer mandate in the first place. Had the government, from the outset, undertaken the obligation to provide contraception to all women who needed it, the conflict between employers' conscience and employees' reproductive freedoms would have been avoided. More generally, the government should not recruit its citizens to provide goods or services that a significant portion of the populace opposes on conscientious grounds. Instead, providing these goods and services should be a core government responsibility, and it should have been recognized as such during the debates over the PPACA.

It would be naïve to overlook the role that special interests played in defeating a public option, under which government would have competed with private insurance companies for healthcare subscribers.[51] We can anticipate that these interests would work even more strenuously to impede a regime under which government was the only game in town, even if government played the role of sole provider for only some, but not all, of the healthcare coverage individuals might seek. For good or ill, however, I am concerned here only with the principled merits of government contraceptive provision, not with its political feasibility. After all, if government provision is indefensible on the merits, then we need not worry about whether it could be implemented in practice. In any event, the issue of government healthcare provision—for contraception or other medical care—is largely illustrative. The discussion that follows should illuminate more generally the appropriate role of government in issues around which there is deep disagreement. One might worry that having government, rather than private employers, provide coverage for contraception does not so much resolve complicity concerns as displace them. For employers who oppose contraception might have just as much reason to object to having to fund it through taxation as through insurance subsidization. In fact, however, I believe that concerns about complicity through taxation are more easily met.

For one thing, the government might be able to provide contraception without relying on tax dollars at all. For example, in an effort to develop a work-around for religious non-profit institutions that object to contraception, the Obama administration convinced insurance companies to offer contraception at no cost either to the religious non-profits or their plan beneficiaries. Insurers were amenable to footing the bill because the costs to them of complications arising from unintended pregnancies are far more significant than the cost of contraception itself.[52]

Moreover, even if the government must draw on the public fisc to provide contraception, there are still principled reasons for thinking complicity claims less compelling here than in the insurance subsidization context. The relevant line of argument draws upon liberal egalitarian responses to libertarian arguments against taxation.[53] Briefly put: It is reasonable to see a commitment to distributive justice as immanent in our tax scheme; in particular, our tax scheme aims to mitigate or eradicate the effect of brute luck, and it does so by claiming, as a matter of right, a portion of the earnings of those who are favored, through pure good luck, by features of our social and economic arrangements. As such, one's tax burden consists, at least in part, of money one has earned in fulfillment of one's obligations of justice to compensate those who are disadvantaged in our scheme. Since the money used to cover this part of one's tax burden is not, and never was, one's own, one cannot say that handing it over to the government connects one to conduct one deems wrong. Covering the costs of female contraception can be seen as part of a redistributive scheme. By some lights, structural injustices make it the case that women are all too disempowered with respect to deciding whether they will have sex at all.[54] At any rate, women currently bear disproportionate healthcare costs resulting from unwanted pregnancies, and disproportionate childcare burdens. On this way of understanding the objectives of a tax scheme, then, the person who objects to contraceptive use has no legitimate complicity claim against taxation used to cover others' contraceptive costs. In particular, he cannot argue that using tax dollars to cover contraception forces him to spend *his* money on a wrong since the money was never his in the first place.[55]

Further, even if one rejects the liberal egalitarian rationale for taxation, there is still a practical distinction between taxation and subsidization: Taxation, we have seen, is not subject to an exemption on conscientious grounds because the system would collapse were such exemptions to be granted. So, even if one concludes that the conscientious objector's complaint is strong, it is not one to which a court can yield. And the notion that the objector loses not on the merits but instead on practical grounds should serve to undercut concerns about government partiality.[56]

In short, the contraceptive mandate challenges expose the limits of both compromise and conscientious objection. The concerns of those who object to funding contraception do not admit of compromise; reducing the amount these employers contribute will not mitigate their concerns. And exempting them altogether might implicate the government in an expressive harm, at least where it is animus that motivates the objectors. As such, government provision might well be the most defensible response. Making contraceptive provision a government responsibility in the first instance would both allow those who object to contraception to maintain clean, or at least cleaner, hands, and would ensure universal access to it under an exemption-free regime. While expanding the government's role in women's reproductive choices might not be the obvious liberal solution, it is, I believe, the one that most maintains fidelity with the foundational core of our political morality.

NOTES

1. Alin Fumurescu, *Compromise: A Political and Philosophical History* (Cambridge: Cambridge University Press, 2013), 28; T.V. Smith, *The Ethics of Compromise and the Art of Restraint* (Chicago: University of Chicago

Press, 1957) 50. See also Amy Gutmann and Dennis F. Thompson, *The Spirit of Compromise* (Princeton, NJ: Princeton University Press, 2012), 42 ("Far from being a necessary evil, contentious politics is an essential part of the democratic process, and an inevitable context for compromise").

2. Martin Benjamin refers to these two senses of compromise as internal (i.e., occurring within one person) and external (i.e., occurring between individuals or parties). Martin Benjamin, *Splitting the Difference: Compromise and Integrity in Ethics and Politics* (Lawrence: University Press of Kansas, 1990), 20. See also Chiara Lepora and Robert E. Goodin, *On Complicity & Compromise* (Oxford: Oxford University Press, 2013), p. 27 (referring to "interpersonal 'compromises with'" and "intra-personal feelings of 'being compromised'").

3. For the view that there are principled reasons to affirm compromise in politics, see, for example, Joseph Carens, "Compromise in Politics," in *Nomos XXI: Compromise in Ethics, Law, and Politics*, ed. J. Ronald Pennock and John Chapman (New York: New York University Press, 1979), 135; Richard Bellamy and Martin Hollis, "Consensus, Neutrality and Compromise," in *Pluralism and Liberal Neutrality*, ed. Richard Bellamy and Martin Hollis (London: Frank Cass & Co., 1999), 76; and Stephen Macedo, *Liberal Virtues: Citizenship, Virtue, and Community in Liberal Constitutionalism* (Oxford: Clarendon Press, 1990), 71.

4. See, for example, Richard Bellamy, *Liberalism and Pluralism: Towards a Politics of Compromise* (London, UK: Routledge, 1999), pp. 93–114.

5. Emp't Div. v. Smith, 494 U.S. 872, 885–86 (1990). Or, in the more florid words of Brian Leiter, allowing for exemption on conscientious grounds "would appear to amount to a legalization of anarchy!"— especially if, as Leiter believes, secular claims of conscience warrant no less respect than religious ones. Brian Leiter, *Why Tolerate Religion?* (Princeton, NJ: Princeton University Press, 2012), 91.

6. See, for example, Brian Barry, *Culture and Equality: An Egalitarian Critique of Multiculturalism* (Cambridge, MA: Harvard University Press, 2001).

7. The full text of the PPACA can be found here: 42 U.S.C. §§ 300gg–13(a)(4); 45 C.F.R. § 147.130(a)(1)(iv) (2012). For a description of the employer mandate, see "Health insurance for businesses with more than 50 employees," Health Care, www.healthcare.gov.

8. Group Health Plans and Health Insurance Issuers Relating to Coverage of Preventive Services Under the Patient Protection and Affordable Care Act, 76 Fed. Reg. 46621–01 (Aug. 3, 2011) (to be codified at 45 C.F.R. pt. 147).

9. 134 S.Ct. 2751 (2014).

10. In using *Hobby Lobby* for illustration, I set aside two unique features of the case. First, the owners of Hobby Lobby objected not to all forms of contraception but only to the four that posed a risk of acting after fertilization, by destroying the embryo that had formed. Other employers have sought exemptions from the employer mandate because they object to all contraceptive use. For purposes of the discussion here, I assume that the employer under consideration opposes all contraception.

Second, while much of the critical reaction to *Hobby Lobby* focuses on its extension of religious freedom rights to a for-profit corporation, I do not attend to those questions here. Employers organized as sole proprietorships or partnerships might also object to having to fund contraceptive use, and so the question of whether to accommodate an employer's objections to aspects of a mandated employee health plan turn in significant part on considerations that have nothing to do with *corporate* religious exercise. For critical engagement with the notion of corporations and freedom of religion, see Amy J. Sepinwall, "Corporate Piety and Impropriety: Hobby Lobby's Extension of RFRA Rights to For-Profit Corporations," in 5 *Harvard Business Law Review 173* (2015).

11. Marjorie E. Kornhauser, *For God and Country: Taxing Conscience,* 1999 *Wisconsin Law Review* 939, 972 (1999) (surveying cases and concluding that "[e]ach has held that . . . RFRA . . . does not require the income tax laws to accommodate religious beliefs, specifically those of conscientious objectors to war"); Michelle O'Connor, "The Religious Freedom Restoration Act: Exactly What Rights Does It 'Restore' in the Federal Tax Context?," 36 *Arizona State Law Journal* 321, 329 (2004) ("the Supreme Court never has held that the Free Exercise Clause requires the government to grant a person an exemption from a generally applicable, neutral tax law").

12. Goehring v. Brophy, 94 F.3d 1294, 1300 (9th Cir., 1996) (use of university registration fee to fund student health insurance plan that included abortion coverage did not substantially burden free exercise rights of students who objected to abortion on religious grounds because, in part, "plaintiffs are not required to accept, participate in, or advocate in any manner for the provision of abortion services"), *overruled* on other grounds by City of Boerne v. Flores, 521 U.S. 507; Erzinger v. Regents of Univ. of Cal., 137 Cal.App.3d 389, 187 Cal.Rptr. 164, *cert. denied,* 462 U.S. 1133 (1983).

13. For example, in one of the seminal cases grounding the test for religious accommodation, Amish parents successfully challenged a Wisconsin law requiring education through age 16, arguing that they needed their children to be free to fulfill the farming obligations incurred in later adolescence, and that they feared the corrupting influence of a secular

education. See Wisconsin v. Yoder, 406 U.S. 205 (1972). Their request involved only an effort to insulate their religious community, not an impingement upon anyone else's rights or entitlements.

14. I discuss the relevant case law at length, with an eye to establishing that the current doctrine neglects third-party costs, in "Conscience and Complicity: Assessing Pleas for Religious Exemptions in Hobby Lobby's Wake," 82 *University of Chicago Law Review* 1897 (2015).

15. Emp't Div. v. Smith, 494 U.S. 872, 881 (1990).

16. Thomas v. Review Bd. of Indiana Employment Security Div., 450 U.S. 707, 715 (1981).

17. Thomas E. Hill, Jr., "Four Conceptions of Conscience," in *Nomos XL: Integrity and Conscience* 14, ed. Ian Shapiro and Robert Adams (New York: New York University Press, 1998). For other theorists who view conscience exclusively in cognitive terms, see Thomas Aquinas, *Summa Theologiae, Ia IIae*, q. 19, a. 5, v. 18, 63 (Cambridge: McGraw-Hill/Blackfriars, 1966) (defining conscience as an exercise of reason); James F. Childress, "Appeals to Conscience," *Ethics* 89(4), 1979, pp. 315–335.

18. Hill, "Four Conceptions of Conscience."

19. See, e.g., C. D. Broad, "Conscience and Conscientious Action," in *Philosophy, XV, No. 58* (New York: Humanities Press, 1952), 118. I argue elsewhere that corporations lack conative and emotional dispositions and it is for this reason that we may deny that they have rights of free exercise in their own right. Sepinwall, "Corporate Piety and Impropriety."

20. See, e.g., Joseph Raz, *The Authority of Law: Essays on Law and Morality* (Oxford: Oxford University Press, 1979) ("The areas of a person's life and plans which have to be respected by others are those which are central to his own image of the kind of person he is and which form the foundation of his self-respect"); Kwame Anthony Appiah, *The Ethics of Identity* (Princeton, NJ: Princeton University Press, 2005) (arguing that claims of conscience are "likely to represent deeply constitutive aspects of people's identity"); Kent Greenawalt, "Refusals of Conscience: What Are They and When Should They Be Accommodated?," *Ave Maria Law Review* 9(1) (2010): 47–66, 49 (Conscience, in its "modern usage connotes something stronger, that she would disregard a deep aspect of her identity if she went along"); Peter Fuss, "Conscience," *Ethics* 74(2), 1964, pp. 111–120; Benjamin, *Splitting the Difference*, pp. 53–60.

21. *The Letters of Vincent van Gogh*, ed. Ronald de Leeuw, trans. Arnold Pomerans (London: Penguin Books, 1997), 54.

22. Rainer Maria Rilke, *Rilke's Book of Hours 65*, trans. Anita Barrows & Joanna Macey (New York: Riverhead Trade, 2005).

23. For the view that the hierarchy between moral and non-moral commitments should trouble us, see Bernard Williams, *Moral Luck* 23 (Cam-

bridge: Cambridge University Press, 1981) ("While we are sometimes guided by the notion that it would be the best of worlds in which morality were universally respected and all men were of a disposition to affirm it, we have, in fact, deep and persistent reasons to be grateful that that is not the world we have").

24. Jeremy Waldron offers a possible rationale for having the state treat moral or religious commitments more seriously than non-moral ones. He has argued that a conscientious bid for an exemption is not a bid to escape law; it is a request that secular officials recognize that the objector owes obedience not just to the law of the state but also to the laws of one or another religious (or, I would add, moral) authority. Jeremy Waldron, "One Law for All: The Logic of Cultural Accommodation," 59 *Washington and Lee Law Review* 3 (2002). According to this way of thinking, religion and morality have an authority of their own, sometimes even one that is as weighty as, or even weightier than, the state's. There is reason to doubt that one's self-chosen commitments—one's crafted mission statement, as it were—can claim this much authority.

25. I note, at least in a preliminary way, that, for some deeply held personal commitments, it will not be easy to discern whether they are moral in nature or not. For example, one can stake her identity on her strict adherence to one or more moral rules—e.g., "I am the kind of person who would never cheat." Further, one can treat one's personal commitments as if they were moral imperatives, such that in violating such a commitment—e.g., "I will be true to myself"—one not only endures a personal failure but also commits a wrong. This way of viewing personal commitments suggests that they are something like promises to self. (See Connie Rosati, "The Importance of Self-Promises," in *Understanding Promises and Agreements: Philosophical Essays*, ed. Hanoch Sheinman (Oxford: Oxford University Press, 2011), pp. 124–155, for an account elucidating the structure and grounds of self-promises). Perhaps the distinctive mark of type 4 rules, then, is that their content is not, or not merely, self-regarding. In the secular moral context, these rules typically concern how we should treat others. In the religious context, the "others" whom the rules concern might include a deity and its creations.

26. For support for the idea that the law should not distinguish between moral and religious convictions when it comes to exemptions, see, for example, Michael J. Sandel, *Democracy's Discontent: America in Search of a Public Philosophy* (Cambridge, MA: Belknap Press, 1996), pp. 65–71; Kathleen Sullivan, "Religion and Liberal Democracy," 59 *University of Chicago Law Review* 195 (1992); Leiter, *Why Tolerate Religion?*, 54–67; Christopher L. Eisgruber and Lawrence G. Sager, *Religious Freedom and the Constitution* (Cambridge, MA: Harvard University Press, 2007), pp. 51–77. For argu-

ments on the other side, see Chad Flanders, "The Possibility of a Secular First Amendment," 26 *Quinnipiac Law Review* 257 (2008); Michael W. Mc-Connell, "The Problem of Singling Out Religion," 50 *DePaul Law Review* 1, 1–3 (2000). For an especially searching inquiry into whether religion is special, see Micah Schwartzman, "What If Religion Is Not Special?" 79 *University of Chicago Law Review* 1351 (2012). See also Andrew Koppelman, "Conscience, Volitional Necessity, and Religious Exemptions," 15 *Legal Theory* 215, 215 & n. 1 (2009) (noting that "[m]any distinguished legal theorists and philosophers have been drawn to the idea that it is conscience rather than religion that is entitled to special protection, and the U.S. Supreme Court has sometimes embraced the same position," and collecting sources and cases).

27. Koppelman, "Conscience, Volitional Necessity, and Religious Exemptions." See also Christopher L. Eisgruber and Lawrence G. Sager, "The Vulnerability of Conscience: The Constitutional Basis for Protecting Religious Conduct," 61 *University of Chicago Law Review* 1245, 1269 (1994).

28. Koppelman, "Conscience, Volitional Necessity, and Religious Exemptions," at 221–222.

29. Jonathan Bennett, "The Conscience of Huckleberry Finn," *Philosophy* 49 (1974): 123–34; Hill, "Four Conceptions of Conscience," p. 45 note 22.

30. Hannah Arendt, *Eichmann in Jerusalem* (New York: Viking Press, 1963), p. 131.

31. Koppelman, "Conscience, Volitional Necessity, and Religious Exemptions," p. 234.

32. *Id.*, p. 237.

33. *Id.*, p. 239.

34. H.L.A. Hart, *The Concept of Law*, at p. 89.

35. The description of commitments in this paragraph borrows from David Owens's account of obligations in David Owens, *Shaping the Normative Landscape* (Oxford: Oxford University Press, 2012), pp. 79–89.

36. Or, more precisely perhaps, conscience may be central to determining the features that our life stories will *not* include. Thus, the conscientious objector to war does not want a life story in which he has engaged in military action; the conscientious objector to physician-assisted suicide does not want a life story in which she has used her medical training to help someone else end his life; and so on.

37. The account advanced in this section is developed at greater length in Sepinwall, "Conscience and Complicity."

38. Model Penal Code 2.06.

39. See, e.g., Lepora and Goodin, *On Complicity & Compromise*, pp. 59–70 (providing a detailed account for grading complicity that turns in sig-

nificant part on the strength of the putative accomplice's causal connection to another's wrong).
40. Sepinwall, "Conscience and Complicity."
41. See, e.g., John Stuart Mill, *Utilitarianism* (New York: Liberal Arts Press, 1957), p. 36 (describing as the "essence" of conscience the feeling of "a pain, more or less intense, attendant on violation of duty, which in properly cultivated moral natures rises, in the more serious cases, into shrinking from [the violation] as an impossibility"); Childress, "Appeals to Conscience," p. 321 (describing the reaction that would attend a breach of conscience as an "ache of guilt").
42. Sepinwall, "Conscience and Complicity."
43. As Douglas NeJaime and Reva Siegel argue, this was just the strategy underpinning the Hobby Lobby case: "After failing to achieve a complicity based exemption through legislation, lawyers turned to individual complicity-based claims to exemption through litigation under RFRA." Douglas NeJaime and Reva B. Siegel, "Conscience Wars: Complicity-Based Conscience Claims in Religion and Politics," 124 *Yale Law Journal* 2516, 2552 (2015).
44. NeJaime and Siegel compellingly identify sabotage as the ultimate objective in bids for exemption from having to participate in contraceptive provision, abortion, or gay weddings. They quote the strategy as articulated by Bishop James Conley, who described *Hobby Lobby* as an exercise of religious liberty intended not to protect conscience so much as an effort to evangelize: "If we want to protect our religious liberty, the very best thing we can do is to use it—to transform culture by transforming hearts for Jesus Christ." *Id.* at 2552 (quoting Bishop James Conley, "Hobby Lobby Decision Is Also a Mandate," *Southern Nebraska Register: Bishop's Column*, July 11, 2014. NeJaime and Siegel describe this strategy as an instance of "preservation through transformation": "when an existing legal regime is successfully challenged so that its rules and reasons no longer seem persuasive or legitimate, defenders may act to preserve elements of the challenged regime through new rules and reasons." *Id.* at 2553.
45. See, e.g., Catharine A. MacKinnon, *Feminism Unmodified: Discourses on Life and Law* (Cambridge, MA: Harvard University Press, 1987); Reva Siegel, "Reasoning from the Body: A Historical Perspective on Abortion Regulation and Questions of Equal Protection," 44 *Stanford Law Review* 261, 377 (1992) ("when the state enacts restrictions on abortion, it coerces women to perform the work of motherhood without altering the conditions that continue to make such work a principal cause of their secondary social status").
46. Jessica Valenti, "Birth Control Coverage: It's the Misogyny, Stupid," *Nation*, November 26, 2013. Available online at www.thenation.com (quot-

ing Hogue). See also Marci A. Hamilton, "The Republican War Against Women," *Justia,* October 3, 2013. ("This is not simply a move to ensure that contraception isn't paid for; it is an all-out war on women. This is the pushback to the feminist revolution, and it is being fostered by the religious organizations that believe that women should be subservient to men"); Ruth Rosen, "The War Against Contraception: 'Women Must Be Liberated from Their Libidios,'" *Huffington Post,* February 19, 2014.

47. Andrew Koppelman, "Gay Rights, Religious Accommodations, and the Purposes of Antidiscrimination Law," 88 *Southern California Law Review* 619 (2015).

48. See, e.g., Emp't Div. v. Smith, 494 U.S. 872, 881 (1990) (stating that the "tax system could not function if denominations were allowed to challenge the tax system because tax payments were spent in a manner that violates their religious belief" and invoking United States v. Lee, 455 U.S. 252 (1982) and Hernandez v. Commissioner, 490 U.S. 680 (1989) as support).

49. See, e.g., Braunfeld v. Brown, 366 U.S. 599, 607 (1961).

50. Michael Walzer, "Political Action: The Problem of Dirty Hands," *Philosophy and Public Affairs,* 2 (1973): 160–180.

51. For an overview of the reasons for the demise of the public option, see Helen A. Halpin and Peter Harbage, "The Origins and Demise of the Public Option," *Health Affairs* 29 (6): June 2010, pp. 1117–1124.

52. "Good for Business: Covering Contraceptive Care Without Cost-Sharing Is Cost-Neutral or Even Saves Money," *Guttmacher,* July 16, 2014.

53. The libertarian objection is given voice in, for example, Robert Nozick, *Anarchy, State and Utopia* (New York: Basic Books, 1974), p. 169. The liberal egalitarian response can be found, for example, in Liam Murphy and Thomas Nagel, "Taxes, Redistribution, and Public Provision," *Philosophy and Public Affairs* 30(1): 53–71, 53–54 (2001) ("Taxes do not take away from taxpayers what is antecedently theirs; pretax income has no status as a moral baseline for the purpose of evaluating the justice of the tax system"); Ronald Dworkin, *Sovereign Virtue: The Theory and Practice of Equality* (Cambridge, MA: Harvard University Press, 2000), p. 349 ("It is a ruling principle of equality that it is unjust when some people lead their lives with less wealth available to them, or in otherwise less favorable circumstances, than others, not through some choice or gamble of their own but through brute bad luck"); G. A. Cohen, "On the Currency of Egalitarian Justice," *Ethics* 99 (1989): 906–944.

54. See Catharine A. MacKinnon, "Privacy v. Equality: Beyond Roe v. Wade," in *Feminism Unmodified: Discourses on Life and Law* 93, 185–194 (Cambridge, MA: Harvard University Press, 1987).

55. There is another way to understand the objectives of the tax system: On this understanding (which need not operate to the exclusion of a re-

distributive understanding), we pay taxes at least in part to fund public goods, costs for which are shared among all taxpayers, even if not every taxpayer benefits from every public good. The idea here is that it is efficient for taxpayers to pool their money and to use the resulting funds to pay for all public goods, instead of having the government operate on a pay-as-you-use system. See generally Arye L. Hillman, *Public Finance and Public Policy: Responsibilities and Limitations of Government*, 2d edition (Cambridge: Cambridge University Press, 2009).

Even though (at least currently) healthcare plans contemplate only female (and not male) contraceptives, it is not undue to consider coverage of these devices a public good. For one thing, contraception is needed only for heterosexual sex, so these devices protect both the men and women who want to have non-procreative sex. And there is no more problematic favoritism in having the government subsidize sexual activity than in having the government mandate that private insurance packages include coverage for contraception, as the PPACA does. Under either arrangement some citizens are made to defray the costs of other citizens' contraceptive use, and their doing so is no different—from the standpoint of concerns about government subsidization of certain "lifestyle" choices—from their defraying healthcare costs stemming from obesity, accidents incurred through extreme sports, and so on.

56. One might worry that the argument proves too much. If government provision avoids concerns about complicity, why not socialize any and every program generating opposition from some citizens? Why stop at contraception? Elective abortions, physician-assisted suicide, and so on all might be paid for from the public fisc, independent of the beneficiary's ability to pay for the service in question herself.

In response, it bears noting that the foregoing arguments might well entail government provision not only of contraception but also other elements of the mandated healthcare packages to which a significant number of employers object. If it turned out that enough employers objected to blood transfusions that exempting them all would undermine the employer mandate altogether, then it might make sense to have the government provide coverage for blood transfusions. (If, on the other hand, the number of objecting employers were trivial then, as I have argued, it would make sense to offer these employers an exemption—assuming that doing so does not impose undue third-party costs—rather than having government take over provision completely.)

But government subsidization of elements of the PPACA's mandated coverage is a far cry from having the government pay for non-Medicaid elective abortions, PAS, etc. With the contraceptive mandate, the government had already decided that women should have cost-free access to contraception. And I have argued that there are good reasons, compatible with political liberalism, for providing contraception at no cost to the women using it (again, reasons that sound in distributive justice or theories of public financing for public goods). The distinctive and problematic element arose because the government had also mandated that private employers help defray contraceptive costs. The predicate for government provision then is that the government has decided—correctly—that citizens should be given no-cost access to a particular good or service and the question is whether the government should provide it directly. No such decision has been made about elective abortions for women who are not Medicaid beneficiaries, or about PAS. So the arguments here do not in fact lead to the objectionable implications that the worry raises.

9

NECESSARY COMPROMISE AND PUBLIC HARM

ANDREW SABL

An actor who engages in political compromise concedes some-thing—an interest, a principle, a favored interpretation of a principle—for the sake of something he or she regards as more important.[1] Much has been written regarding the first half of this trade-off: regarding the kinds of interests, principles, or identity-defining commitments that may, or may not, be considered subject to compromise. Less has been said about the second half: about that for the sake of which compromise typically occurs.

In other words: the debate over why compromise raises acute and powerful moral questions has crowded out the debate over why there is often such an urgent need to answer (or brush aside) such questions—to reach the determinate, though provisional, decisions that only compromise makes possible. In fact, both of the main schools regarding compromise have reason to avoid talk of the ends that compromise serves. Those who view politics in chastened or skeptical terms, such that its typical currency is something like interest—though not necessarily *self*interest in a narrow sense—deny that compromise is a serious moral or politi-cal problem, and often suggest that those who worry about com-promise are merely utopian, selfish, or weak. There is no particu-lar need to examine the ends or purposes served by compromise, since the means raise no special concern. From the other side, there are those who view compromise as a potentially profound threat to identity, integrity, or principle.[2] From that standpoint, it seems like a temptation or corruption, when such things are in

248

danger of being sacrificed, even to think about any ends that compromise might further.[3] On this latter view, one may consider the ends of compromise without risking corruption only if those ends themselves involve promoting, or affirming, some aspect of one's identity or principles—ideally, some version, perhaps transformed or reconceptualized, of the *same* principle, or the same piece of one's identity, that the compromise sacrifices.[4] Thus, those who see politics as the play of interests see little need to ask about the urgent situations that make compromise necessary; those who see it as the expression of identities and the vindication of moral principles are reluctant to acknowledge how common those situations may be and how pervasively they affect the everyday practice of compromise.

This chapter will discuss the case in which compromise is *necessary*, demanded by circumstances. While readily granting that there are circumstances that render compromises moral or desirable even when they are not necessary, it will argue that we should stop worrying about many of those (real or alleged) preconditions of moral or desirable compromise when compromise is necessary.

In the first section, I discuss well-known treatments of the circumstances of politics (also known as circumstances of compromise) and introduce the idea of compromise as a response to necessary decision. In the second section, I briefly canvass why existing accounts of compromise fail to give proper accounts of this necessity: they define this necessity in terms that are either too moralized or too subjective. In the third section, I put forth my own account of necessity as rooted in the prevention of public harm. In the fourth section, I explore how this account helps explain the desirability of compromise when other accounts fall short. In the fifth section, I explain how this account helps make sense of the claim that the only alternative to compromise is violence; that claim, I argue, is well founded when it comes to necessary compromises and those alone. The concluding section essentially amounts to an error theory; it explores some possible reasons why an account along the current lines has not seemed convincing up to now, and why we should nevertheless be convinced.

Necessary compromises, speaking loosely for now, are those motivated by the knowledge that failure to meet a deadline to act would result in public harm. One satirical take on how politicians think (or panic) has been called the Politician's Syllogism: "We must do something. This is something. Therefore we must do this."[5] Provided that we sufficiently define "must"; define "something" as "a solution to the problem that authoritative parties can agree on"; and face a deadline by which one solution among many must be reached if a public harm is to be prevented, this syllogism is, I argue, not as silly as it seems—in fact, valid.

I. THE CIRCUMSTANCES OF POLITICS AND THE CIRCUMSTANCES OF COMPROMISE

Philip Pettit has described the "compromise predicament" as one in which "everyone prefers that all choose the same alternative . . . but among the different alternatives, they divide on which should be the option selected."[6] Game theorists will recognize this as a bargaining game. (Think of negotiations between labor and management, in which both sides would prefer to avoid a work stoppage but disagree strongly on which package of wages and benefits they prefer; the parties' interests are partly common, partly conflicting.) But in bargaining games, negotiations not infrequently *break down*: each of the parties ultimately judges that accepting the other side's final offer is so unfair, or economically untenable, that letting negotiations fail, resulting in a strike or lockout, is the least bad option. If the compromise predicament is to be, as Pettit hopes, the kind of thing that can define political "common interests," the consequences of such a breakdown must, with regard to certain interests, be regarded by relevant actors as so awful that *any* plausible solution would be better than failure. And indeed, Pettit suggests as much.[7] But we seem to need an account of how to distinguish the particular interests that are common, in this sense, from the many interests—the kind of interests subject to normal bargaining—that are *not* common. When it comes to the latter kind of interests, the kind at stake in many normal economic and private negotiations, reasonable people might allow negotiations to break down if the threat to let them break down is useful in bargaining, i.e., if that threat has the potential to further their partial aims.

Jeremy Waldron, writing in almost the same year as Pettit but independently, defined the "circumstances of politics" in almost exactly the same way as Pettit defines those of compromise: "The authority of law rests on the fact that there is a recognizable need for us to act in concert on various issues or to co-ordinate our behaviour in various areas with reference to a common framework, and that this need is not obviated by the fact that we disagree among ourselves as to what our common course of action or our common framework ought to be."[8] Waldron's work draws striking and compelling conclusions about the nature and status of legislative debate and decision from the—fully justified— assumption that this need for coordinated action is, and ought to be, recognized. It does not, however, fully spell out the contours of this need, and of what makes it "recognizable," in the detail one would need to apply this account to the political ethics of compromise. At issue is *who* recognizes the need, regarding *which* issues, at *what* potential cost (surely not any cost) to the programs and principles of the parties who disagree. Above all, the question is, what is to be done when some assert a "need" for common action while others deny it. As I argue in the next section, Waldron tends to answer this question in terms of an irreducibly subjective political judgment. I shall argue that this is normatively (as well as phenomenologically) inadequate, and shall suggest an alternative.

II. The Circumstances of Compromise: Three Alternatives to Necessity

I have said the compromise literature has been relatively silent regarding the circumstances that render compromise necessary. That said, it does contain, at least by implication, two very plausible treatments. Despite their plausibility, however, each fails in my view to give a full account.

A. Political Urgency as Subjective Felt Need

Waldron in several places implies a subjective standard of when compromise is necessary. The circumstances of politics operate when there is a "*felt need* for common action . . . in circumstances of diversity and disagreement"; when members of an ethnically diverse society "share some *sense* of common purpose" (or at least a "foreboding" that going separate ways would court "frightful dangers and difficulties"); when "large numbers . . . *believe* we should act, or organize things, together"; when we have, in spite of confidence in our own particular views, "a *firm determination*—at times . . . a *ferocious determination*—to go on sharing a social world with those who differ from us."[9]

When all parties indeed feel the need to act in common, come what may, this no doubt is enough to motivate compromise (and in some cases it may be dangerous to demand a reason to ground the sentiment, as opposed to leaving well enough alone). But a problem occurs when the need is itself controversial. We want guidelines to distinguish cases in which the circumstances of politics do not obtain, even though some think they do, from those in which they do obtain, even though some think they do not. In the first case, some who assert a duty to compromise would probably do better to stick to their principles (or bargain harder); in the second case, those who persist in sticking to their principles are flouting their actual duty: to compromise. Absent such guidelines, circumstances-of-politics arguments risk tautology or triviality: compromise will be a good thing when, but only when, everyone already agrees that overriding political considerations render it a good thing.[10]

One way of rescuing something like the subjective standard would be to raise it to a higher level of political abstraction. Gutmann and Thompson cite evidence that ordinary voters of all political persuasions are much more willing to endorse compromise in general than to accept particular compromises, which they tend to regard as involving sellouts by politicians.[11] Though public opinion surveys rarely compare the two questions, one suspects that just about *every* compromise will be less popular than compromises in general. For one thing, people tend to be "egomorphic," overestimating the extent to which their own views are widely shared[12] (thus making compromise seem less pressing than it is; the opposing view surely "must be" a fringe view or "special interest" that will soon have to yield). For another, because precise knowledge of the best terms available is specialized, it is likely to be confined to negotiators. But rational citizens who realize these tendencies of human nature, their own and others', might consciously or unconsciously choose to grant those who reach political compromises on their behalf—particularly legislators—the benefit of the doubt. Or, in a less rationalist and more evolutionary account, societies may be more stable and better off over time if they develop a norm of such deference (perhaps coming to understand its rational basis after the fact). In any case, our subjective desire to live in a society in which compromise works *in general* could be said to provide normative justification for swallowing our objections to particular compromises. The former sentiment could be seen, in roughly Humean terms, as more calm or impartial than the latter.

However, two reasons count against this solution. The first, perhaps intellectually trivial but politically formidable, is stressed by Gutmann and Thompson and concerns voter rage: ordinary citizens, especially voters in partisan primaries, are likely to punish politicians for what they see as particular betrayals rather than rewarding them for their more long-term role as professionals whose task includes skill at compromise generally. The pressures of campaigning undermine governing.[13]

The second reason to avoid basing compromise on a subjective "felt need" for common action seems more fundamental, as well as likely to count against many other arguments in praise of compromise for its own sake: what this sentiment requires is radically indeterminate. The problem is that the conviction that a decision must be reached does not give proper direction to the (partly adversarial) actors trying to reach it. On the one hand, one can say that such a conviction should rule out extreme threats or hostage-taking, since such make a failure of common decision more likely. But one can also run the argument in precisely the opposite direction, so that it *licenses*, in fact encourages, threats and hostage-taking. If I know, or think I know, that all parties are determined to reach a decision no matter what, I can insist on quite extreme terms—terms that may include concessions on matters unrelated to the main business ("side payments")—because I calculate that my opponents must accept those terms or else risk a no-common-action alternative that we all acknowledge to be worse. Thus, if a felt need for common action is both strong and common knowledge, it can enable endless games of chicken.

Consider the US "debt ceiling": a statutory limit, requiring annual adjustment by law, on borrowing the funds needed to pay back government obligations already incurred. As is well known, Republican legislators from 2011 through at least the end of the

Obama administration have sought substantial cuts in spending, or concessions on unrelated issues, as the price of raising the ceiling and avoiding a default. While some such legislators have denied, or else seemed confused about, the need to raise the debt ceiling at all—and Democratic partisans have made much of their denial and confusion—a much more common mode of making the argument has been to agree that the debt ceiling "must be" raised, while claiming that responsible Democrats who agree that it must be raised *must accept Republican proposals for spending cuts*—since a "clean" bill raising the debt ceiling "could not" win Republican votes. As this argument goes, the party that stands in the way of compromise is not the Republicans, for trying to tie the debt ceiling to demands in other areas, but the Democrats, for refusing to accept such a linkage.[14] The problem is analogous to a common objection against legal positivism: that it may instruct ordinary citizens to regard as law whatever is duly passed by a proper authority, but does not instruct lawmakers on what *they* should decide to adopt as law. Similarly, even a strong subjective belief in the need for a common decision in a certain case does not give proper direction to the (democratic, diverse) legislative deciders, nor guidance to citizens trying to judge who is to blame for a given breakdown of compromise—or for a compromise reached at an extreme cost. As we shall see, a necessity standard can ground a normative argument against playing chicken in the first place.

B. The Moral Progress Standard

In their recent book *The Spirit of Compromise*, Amy Gutmann and Dennis Thompson recommend a moral progress standard for legitimate compromise. Their position is complex, at once less moralistic than some other theorists have demanded and more moralistic than it appears.

On the anti-moralistic side, (1) Gutmann and Thompson argue that any serious compromise will take place among people with fundamentally different principles. Therefore, no serious compromise can be fully justified against the background of any coherent system of moral principles. In fact, if it were fully coherent, a compromise would not really do what it needs to do, namely, "respec[t] competing principles and values." Accordingly,

Gutmann and Thompson reject many aspirational standards for compromise that are commonly (but unrealistically) put forth: that compromise involve "common ground or overlapping consensus," such that no real sacrifice of one's deepest principles is required, or that it be what has been called "integrative"—so creative that all parties are able to recognize the outcome as what they really wanted.[15] (2) Gutmann and Thompson admit that compromise cannot avoid some sacrifice of principle. To the extent that compromises "respect" principles, they will do so only to the extent that the actors involved "adapt" or "trim" their principles, sacrificing the particular form that the agent imagined those principles would take, though with luck retaining some of those principles' moral core.[16] (3) Gutmann and Thompson tacitly marginalize deontological principles, which rule out participation in certain solutions altogether, in favor of principles understood as something like regulative ideals. The principles that can be largely preserved in the face of political compromise are those that operate as "directional signals," not "roadblocks."[17] The effect is to ameliorate the tension between an ethic of principle and the practice of compromise. Once strictly deontological principles are sidelined, treated as not very relevant to or useful for political life, life is made safe for the kind of principles that orient political programs, as opposed to those that rule out altogether certain political means. (4) Gutmann and Thompson repeatedly stress the costs of standing on principle to a degree that makes compromise impossible. From a progressive perspective, "[p]rivileging the status quo does not mean that nothing changes. It just means that politicians let other forces control the change." Nor is this desirable, on their view, from a conservative standpoint: "it would take massive positive action to reduce the size of government, cut the deficit, and curtail government regulation."[18] This double argument is meant to undermine the psychological comfort that might otherwise attach to a bias toward the status quo. One might say that if our political order is less like a forest, which evolved without our help and does best without our interference, than like the Golden Gate Bridge, a collectively constructed artifact that is both beautiful and useful but subject to rust unless constantly painted, the "normal," rational default position is not inaction but common action—facilitated by compromise. A failure to act will preserve not the status quo but costly decay or decline, a failure to perform regular and required maintenance *on* the status quo. So far, so pragmatic. In fact, Gutmann and Thompson's repeated insistence that the point of compromise is to "improve on the status quo"[19] from the perspective of all sides might seem to involve a wholesale substitution of some sort of pragmatic standard for a moral one. But Gutmann and Thompson restore with one hand the moralism they remove with the other. By "improve on the status quo," Gutmann and Thompson mean "to *morally* improve on the status quo."[20] A failure to compromise is culpable because defaulting to the status quo is undesirable. But its undesirability it to be understood in moral terms: "to fail to compromise in politics is to privilege the status quo . . . a compromising mindset opens up opportunities to promote *greater justice*."[21]

Gutmann and Thompson's moral progress framework, adapted to the pluralistic and messy world that compromise entails, potentially does much to justify the "mindset" of compromise in the face of a bias, common among both rank-and-file political activists and moral theorists, that is suspicious of compromise and calls on political actors to "stand firm on principle" despite the predictable costs of that stance. Yet it does not go far enough in a direction of acknowledging the claims of political necessity, which may or may not track moral progress.

First, the argument that the status quo involves costs reflects a Deweyan bias: it assumes that conscious collective action is morally and pragmatically superior to the unintended, aggregated results of action by market actors and voluntary associations.[22] But one of the United States' great ideological parties does not share this assumption. Its partisans suspect that many, perhaps most, collective decisions involve not the solving of common problems by the public-spirited but the grabbing of rents by the well-organized.[23] And they believe that society is best served by the unintended outcome of dispersed decisions by private actors, who in turn will find their long-term planning easier if the role of government is not so much small, in absolute terms, as *stable and predictable*.[24] On this account, even if policy could in theory be better, the constant desire to make it better undercuts the very great benefits of keeping it predictable. While Gutmann and Thompson rightly portray conservatives as having an interest in common action to the extent that they oppose existing government policy, they ignore the differential importance conservatives and progressives place on getting policy exactly right. A certain type of mildly libertarian and relatively non-ideological conservative—unlike progressives—believes that the market and society can, given time and the predictability that comes with lack of change, work around bad policy. They simply do not care as much as progressives do about how rational government policy is and what purposes government action expresses, for they never regarded those purposes as fully public to begin with, and see self-government in individual and social rather than political terms.

Second, and more simply, a compromise that respects every major party's principles, even suitably adapted and redefined, simply may not be possible, as those principles may be not only different but opposed. On issues ranging from the estate tax to assistance for the poor to amnesty for undocumented immigrants who have long lived in the country, not only the two sides' policy stances but also the principles that underlie them are not just different but opposed. While we can literally split the difference, as in zero-sum bargains, we cannot hope that both sides will advance their principles, because one side has a principled commitment to X and the other to not-X. The demand that all parties regard a compromise as involving progress from the perspective of their own moral principles—call this the criterion of "multi-partisan" moral progress—actually involves, in my view, a softer form of the vain hope that no fundamental principle need be sacrificed. In situations of urgency, under ideologically adversarial conditions, compromise may be possible if and only if the parties give up on the demand that any compromise embody moral progress. Quite often, parties will only be able to reach a compromise on particular cases if they agree for the day to put aside their deepest principles altogether in favor of preventing the severe harms that a failure to reach a compromise would inflict.

The hope that all compromises will represent moral improvements seems to arise out of the common need for political myth, for a story that would explain every particular action according to its place in a larger story: "in every instance good shall triumph over evil." Belief in such myths may stand in the way of actually existing compromise, since the myths promote the belief that a less disagreeable compromise than the one on offer "must be" available even if none is apparent. (On the other hand, one must admit, the belief may also sometimes help facilitate compromise, depending on the time frame it covers. That is, if each of two apparently irreconcilable parties to a dispute also believes in a myth of *long-term* moral progress, the parties may be able to reach a compromise that seems principled to both because each can tell an unlikely but hopeful story about how the compromise paves the way toward progress in the future.)

III. PUBLIC BUSINESS AS REQUIRED COMMON ACTION: URGENCY, NECESSITY, AND THE PREVENTION OF PUBLIC HARM

> The path of compromise is indicated to avoid dictatorship and death.[25]

Discussions of compromise often stress the link between compromise and time pressure. Because political decisions must sometimes be reached within a given time, a non-ideal method of decision is often acceptable (if perhaps not exactly moral). In situations of diffuse party control—"divided government" in a presidential system that separates executive from legislative power; unruly or unstable multi-party coalitions in a multi-party parliamentary system—one test of government competence, and one focus of civic anger in cases of incompetence, is the ability (or failure) to pass a timely budget to keep government functioning. (In common parliamentary practice, a full or partial coalition agreement necessarily involves a prior commitment to do this, to vote for what Commonwealth usage pithily calls "supply.") The necessary compromise standard explains why this is so important. In contrast, democratic theory's common neglect of budget crises displays a certain indifference to the competent performance—as opposed to the perfection—of public business.

But a mention of time limits does not settle the question of urgency or necessity, because it does not tell us what exactly will occur if the deadline is missed. Say that the business of government is to provide public goods, and that a bias against government action interferes with optimal decisions regarding those goods.[26] This granted, inaction will still typically result in *some* level of public good provision. Roads may deteriorate, but will still exist in some state; the army may be too big or too small, poorly trained or equipped, or focused on the wrong threats, but will still be on duty in the event of attacks from abroad. Even when government inaction does result in a temporary halt in public goods provision, a temporary halt is sometimes tolerable and parties will sometimes risk it to accomplish their purposes. Education is widely agreed to be a public good, but policy makers are not therefore insane to risk a teacher's strike that temporarily cuts off that good, any more than steelworkers are always wrong to risk a strike that temporarily cuts off their private livelihood.

Beyond this, claims regarding the need or necessity to reach a political decision often do not even arise to the level of a public good. Those who think existing policy in some area is very bad claim that reform is "necessary" (and that the status quo is a crisis), while those who think it is less bad deny the necessity and mock the alleged crisis.[27] So the mere existence of a deadline does not entail urgency or necessity in a morally or politically relevant sense. To assert that it is *necessary* to reach a compromise is to say something about the consequences of failing to reach a decision by the deadline. And if the assertion is to have a chance of persuading across ideological divides, the dire nature of those consequences must rest on grounds that do not track those divides.

When it comes to certain crises, the parties in question are attached to different causes that happen to affirmatively overlap, so that a compromise may be reached that all relevant parties independently affirm. (Such was the need to protect civil rights for African Americans in 1964, which united the majority of a Democratic party by then predominantly devoted to racial equality with a majority of Republicans devoted to formal equal liberty and assuring the preconditions for economic striving.[28]) But in the normal case, what potentially unites partisans around a shared sense of urgency is not affirmative, cross-partisan commitment to a solution but grudging recognition of the possible consequences of *not setting aside* most partisan commitments. Compromise is necessary when missing a deadline for public action would cause public harm.

Broadly in line with Joel Feinberg, we may define harm as wrongful setback to interests.[29] This may seem to beg the question of what is wrong and what counts as an interest. One could try to define interests in terms of objective human needs—or, even more stringently, Rawlsian primary goods—at the cost of arriving at a theory of compromise that adherents to conservative parties would uniformly reject. Or one could define them so minimally that only violent death counts as an interest, thus arriving at a libertarian solution in which the only necessary compromise is the one needed to preserve funding for the police, the courts, the prisons, and basic homeland defense—an outcome that progressive and centrist parties would uniformly reject. (Such parties probably would, and historically often do, refuse assent to such a compromise, and would hold this minimal outcome hostage to the provision of greater public goods and welfare benefits.) Given the practical, political occasion, I would propose a standard in between: substantial enough to provide critical purpose, and to go beyond the subjective standard canvassed above, but not so demanding as to leave large swaths of the political spectrum behind.

The idea is a kind of two-level political intuitionism. The goal is an account of compromise that could command wide assent given political actors who already endorse, explicitly or implicitly, a common account of public harm—even if they might in practice culpably risk public harm. The critical purchase of the argument in fact rests precisely in this gap between principle and practice.

To get to it: *Compromise is necessary when inaction by a certain deadline would cause either diffuse but substantial and pervasive harm to the citizenry as a whole, or acute and dangerous harm to a subset of it.*

Harm that is diffuse but substantial and pervasive involves substantial and irreversible damage to the provision of an uncontroversial public good. Such harm involves the loss of police, courts, and prisons but also the loss of (though not the failure to promote) many public goods beyond that. Harm of this kind would include not the delay of bridge maintenance but collapse of the bridge; not cuts to military procurement but failure to fund troops actively engaged in a conflict or prepared to be so engaged, or else needed for homeland defense; not a teacher strike lasting a few days but one lasting a more substantial portion of a school year, risking permanent educational deficits. Foreign invasion is obviously a harm, but so is an avoidable economic recession, since the costs of such are often permanent, involving costs to people's lives that no recovery will fully recoup. Harm that is acute and danger-ous to a subset of the population includes some but not all welfare benefits: subsistence-level aid to the elderly, disabled, and desti-tute; such housing assistance as is necessary to avoid homelessness (not, say, mortgage interest subsidies); and emergency medical care. I would also include as acute and dangerous harm to a subset of the population deprivation of a group's basic civil rights, to the extent that these require government action in excess of standard police protection against injury. (When the rights of members of a particular group face disproportionate threats, depriving them of protection against those threats constitutes harm.) While those who have an expansive notion of universal human rights are free to claim (from their ideological or partisan standpoint) that any failure to achieve those rights constitutes harm, the public harm standard can only successfully motivate compromise, and shame its absence, if a less ambitious conception of harm is proposed.[30] There is no claim here that what constitutes harm is "given" or factual. Whenever serious policies are at stake, claims of harm will involve a potentially controversial political and moral stance (and will provoke political and moral argument). It seems possible, however, that a rough consensus on whether certain types of inac-tion will result in harming some, or all, citizens is more likely to be attainable than a similar consensus on what, affirmatively, should be done to promote the public good.

Two things must be clarified. First, I am far from claiming that preventing the above categories of harm is all that government is for (nor does any mainstream political actor make such a claim). I argue only that preventing such harms defines a narrower thing: what is necessary, a small subset of what is beneficial, just, or good. Necessary compromises are therefore also a small subset of *benefi-cial* compromises. When compromise might be beneficial but is not necessary, Gutmann and Thompson's standard of multi-partisan moral improvement may be appropriate. Of course, in those cir-cumstances no solution that advances the principles of all major parties, or even a sufficiently large coalition, may be available. For what strikes one party as beneficial may strike another as the reverse.

Second, prevention of public harm so defined includes many things that are currently funded during one of the United States' recurring "government shutdowns." But the reverse is not the case, since the legislation providing emergency funding during shutdowns also funds many things that are politically sacrosanct but arguably involve neither irreversible damage to public goods nor acute or dangerous harm to anyone (for instance the uninterrupted payment of full Social Security, i.e., old age, benefits to recipients, regardless of wealth). Again, my claim involves not first-order intuitionism, such that we should consider matters of necessity or emergency whatever currently goes by that label, but intuitionism at one remove. When certain harms are socially recognized as such, and perhaps in some few cases before they are fully recognized, we should regard compromise as necessary when failure to compromise would result in such harms—whether or not those acknowledging the harms in fact strive, as they should, for the necessary compromise.

IV. CASES

I believe that the above standard illuminates political compromise in ways that other accounts do not. On the empirical level, it shows how counsel that we cultivate the virtues or attitudes conducive to compromise may fail to bring about compromise, since the dispositions of those contemplating compromise matter less than the circumstances in which they find themselves. Normatively, the standard of necessity helps distinguish defensible refusals to compromise from unforgivable ones.

A. Circumstances of Compromise vs. the Virtue of Compromisers

Britain during the Second World War represents a rare case in which compromise for necessity and compromise for the sake of multi-partisan moral progress briefly coincided. Because Britain very plausibly feared German invasion (launched from occupied France), partisan disagreement bore potentially dire costs. Even normal electoral competition was widely seen as risking direct and palpable collective harm: the danger of invasion both explains and justifies why Britain did (and its Commonwealth and other allies mostly did not) cancel the election that was normally due to take place, governing throughout the war through an all-party War Cabinet. The case also represents one in which all major parties saw victory as genuine progress (from an appalling starting point) toward the values they held dear: for the Conservatives, the war was a battle of civilization against barbarism and represented the only chance of holding the Empire; for Labour, the cause was democracy and equality against fascism.

After the war, the parties and politicians were much the same as they were during the war. If the amount of compromise practiced in politics had been a matter of cultivating certain political virtues, or derived from the shared experience of interparty cooperation, the country's voters and political leaders presumably possessed *more* such virtue, and more such experience, after the war than they did before. Yet interparty cooperation and a propensity to compromise did not in fact survive the war: the voters immediately kicked out Churchill and elected Labour, which proceeded to adopt thoroughgoing reform proposals that the Conservatives bitterly opposed. Compromise was driven by a situation involving necessity, not by politicians' or voters' mindsets or virtues.[31]

B. *Necessity vs. Choice: The Bush Tax Cuts and the Debt Ceiling*

At the end of 2010, Americans will recall, income tax rates were scheduled to rise for every taxpayer. (The tax cuts passed by a Republican House and Senate after George W. Bush's victory in 2000, though intended by Republicans to be permanent, had been given an expiration date to obscure their long-term cost.) Gutmann and Thompson applaud the compromise that was struck to avoid this. Tax cuts for the wealthiest were allowed to expire; the cuts were made permanent for everyone else; an exemption from estate tax for all estates except the largest was extended. As the price paid for extension of most of the income tax cuts, Republicans agreed to fund a Democratic "wish list" involving various spending items, but in particular extended unemployment benefits as well as a temporary cut in the payroll tax, which falls heavily on non-wealthy citizens.[32]

Gutmann and Thompson praise the compromising mindset that gave rise to this outcome, and give a plausible account of the political virtues and practices that made it possible. But why, exactly, was reaching a compromise in this case a good thing? This was not an example where failure to compromise risked some sort of catastrophe; the consequences of inaction would have been not a government shutdown but a reversion of tax rates to their 2000 level. Nor is Gutmann and Thompson's claim that reaching a compromise built momentum for a later grand bargain on deficit reduction very persuasive. Stipulating for argument that they are right to regard as desirable "comprehensive tax reform and deficit reduction, which would require major changes in tax policy and entitlement programs (Social Security, Medicare, and Medicaid),"[33] it seems odd for the authors to claim that the 2010 tax deal made such a grand fiscal bargain more feasible. It was hard to see how a deal that greatly increased the deficit and enshrined the Republican priority of lower taxes—as well as lowering the payroll taxes that fund Social Security—would make such a grand bargain more likely. In fact, it shifted baseline assumptions in the opposite direction, and was widely attacked by deficit hawks. Nor, in hindsight, does it seem that the habit of compromise is something that builds on itself as easily as Gutmann and Thompson believe. Exploiting the fact that the 2010 tax deal did not include a raising of the debt limit, Republicans less than a year later, in 2011, proved themselves willing to hold the debt limit hostage to cuts in government programs, including many that helped the poor, and showed almost no inclination to meet the Democrats halfway on either distributional issues or the latter's preferred programs.

The case for the 2010 tax compromise can in fact be made, but only by appeal to the public harm standard. Though ideological debate at the time focused on partisan principles involving taxes and distribution, we now know that the Obama administration was focused above all on *macroeconomics.* Tax increases would have threatened a renewed recession. Spending increases, on the contrary, would maintain a policy of Keynesian stimulus; accordingly, as part of the deal, parts of President Obama's Recovery Act (a.k.a. "stimulus") that had been slated to expire were extended. Though it opposed the distributional consequences of preserving cuts in the estate tax and in upper-middle-income taxes, and knew that downwardly redistributive reductions in the payroll tax would only be temporary, the Obama administration cared less about such matters of ideological and moral principle than about avoiding the diffuse but pervasive harm of a double-dip recession.[34] In addition, the deal prevented acute danger to a specific subgroup, namely the unemployed, given that the United States lacks a permanent dole for the able-bodied. It was the need to avoid both diffuse and acute harm that justified a compromise that without such considerations would seem baffling.

Regarding the debt ceiling fight of 2011, it is again tempting but misleading to see a propensity or refusal to compromise as an illustration of the "uncompromising mindset," as Gutmann and Thompson do. In fact, *once one accepts the legitimacy of threatening* a debt default, one must acknowledge that Republicans in Congress *did* display a fair willingness to compromise. After initially standing firm on a staunchly ideological policy of "cut, cap, and balance," they settled for something less.[35] While Gutmann and Thompson are right to note that the 2011 deal "kicked the can down the road" in the sense of avoiding permanent deficit reduction, and that the parties' attempt (through a "supercommittee") to find terms for a grand budget bargain in the future was a complete failure (stipulating, again, that fiscal conservatism was desirable),[36] the 2010 tax deal that the authors praise was actually worse in this respect: it greatly increased the deficit.

Whether or not the way that the 2011 negotiations *proceeded* exhibits a compromising mindset, what is more important is that the way they *started* reveals a culpable insouciance toward public harm. House Republicans in 2011 constituted the first legislative majority in American history to threaten default by holding the debt limit hostage; they did so twice more, in 2013 and 2014. Essentially, the party controlling one branch of government threatened deliberately to throw the country into a deep recession, through a massive government default not seen since the Tyler administration, if its demands were not met. And it stuck by this demand fervently enough that many of its demands were in fact met. It is the *first step* in this process that merits condemnation. What was unconscionable was not the substance of negotiations, nor whatever unhelpful mindsets might have been displayed during them, but House Republicans' *substantive*, deliberate, and gratuitous threat to risk grave public harm. Here the public harm standard provides more bite than the "felt need" standard rebutted above. The former, but not the latter, tells us which kinds of threats must be avoided altogether by responsible politicians. We are not permitted to play chicken with public harm, even if we have a good chance of winning that game (perhaps precisely because the other side takes public harm more seriously). In the case of the debt limit, an absurd institution that essentially requires an affirmative vote every year *not* to default, any politician purporting to care about avoiding public harm must simply call for its abolition. Those who do not are failing to observe the spirit of necessary compromise, regardless of how they conduct themselves under the threat of a catastrophe that they themselves have courted.

C. Abortion: Harm and the Pathos of Compromise

The abortion issue is sometimes said to be intractable because it involves a clash of asserted fundamental rights: it pits unborn children's right to life against women's rights, essentially liberty rights, to choose whether or not to sustain the burden of childbearing.[37] But it is not the case that questions involving rights admit of no middle ground. Consider same-sex marriage. Though considered a matter of equality rights by its proponents (and, one supposes, a matter of divine law, or as a fallback religious liberty, by its opponents), it progressed, until the *Obergefell* decision, according to a fairly normal legislative process. Different states adopted different policies. Many adopted the intellectually disreputable but politically attractive half-measure of allowing same-sex couples to form "civil unions" that provided legal and economic privileges but withheld the formal status of marriage. The tendency to regard rights as trumps, or quasi-absolute, is probably a lawyer's fetish to begin with; ordinary citizens probably view rights as more like signposts than like guardrails, and as precisely the kind of things we can and do compromise about.[38]

It seems more precise to say that abortion is intractable because it involves such strong alleged *harms*. US opponents of legal abortion regard themselves not primarily as supporting life as an abstract value but as protecting children against murder. Supporters of legal abortion regard themselves not as maintaining general values of equality but as protecting the liberty of female fellow citizens, their rights to free movement and self-determination in the face of prohibitions that seem akin to kidnapping.[39]

Failure to reach compromise here is not a sign of ill-will or lack of virtue. To the extent that compromise is necessary to prevent public harm, what is "necessary" in this case *cannot be achieved.* There is no action, no possible compromise, that both sides will judge as preventing such harm. In this case, thinking and acting in ways conducive to compromise, e.g., by respecting those who disagree and fairly portraying their positions and their sincerity, provides little help. Such habits of mind and action might reduce social incivility, enable potential side-bargains on peripheral issues (e.g., aid to single mothers), and promote political stability. But they will not enable anyone to *resolve the dispute* through compromise, because the nature of the question, involving conflicting public harms, does not admit of compromise. Preventing what one side sees as grievous harm to children would require laws that the other side sees as grievously harmful to women. That may be one reason why abortion remains an irreducible partisan issue even as same-sex marriage seems well on its way to becoming an object of peaceful consensus: nobody can quite articulate a specific group of people who are harmed when same-sex marriage is allowed.[40]

In accord with this account: when the issue is *not* articulated in the language of competing harms, compromise *can* be reached. As Mary Ann Glendon has pointed out, the lower status of rights talk (she might more accurately have said harm talk, with its notions of common-law injury) in Continental Europe, compared to Anglo-American countries, allowed European countries during the 1970s and 1980s to reach halfway solutions that seemed impossible in the United States. In most European countries, abortion was permitted during early stages of pregnancy only; in most but not all, it was funded through a national health system, so that poor women bore no disproportionate burden. In (West) Germany, abortion was not legal but was de facto decriminalized, with much state-level variation in how easy it was to get. In France, notably, life was treated as something like a signpost, a serious but abstract value. The French abortion law, drafted by a lawyer renowned for his serious and rhetorically powerful style, started by proclaiming the public's attachment to the right to life. It went on to say that in recognition of the value of life, women seeking to terminate their pregnancy must obtain counseling, and be told about social programs for mothers, before they could go ahead and have abortions.[41]

This is not to say that compromise is superior to lack of compromise on these questions. (I in fact find the continental solutions'

ANDREW SABL

lack of sympathy for claims of harm on both sides quite baffling.) The point is that a standard of acute and dangerous harm properly illuminates the boundary of compromise. *If* one thinks such harm is involved on both sides of an either-or question, compromise will be elusive. If not, not. The presence of harm does, as talk of principles, identities, feelings of political community, or compromising mindsets does not, easily distinguish the American from the continental cases.

While abortion may be unusual in its tendency to evoke moral extremes, it is not unusual in being zero-sum. Thus *Bush v. Gore*, a case that determined which of two candidates would be named president, concerned a matter of urgency that did not admit of compromise.[42] In such zero-sum cases, we are lucky if we have an authority whose decisions are regarded as binding even by those who regard its reasons as absurd. This brings up the final topic.

V. COMPROMISE AND AUTHORITY

Given that I have defined "harm" in ways that some find controversial (so as to include, for instance, not just security from violent death but civil rights and educational goods), the current argument might seem to elide the difference between compromises that are literally necessary and those that would merely be a good idea. Similarly, the idea that the alternative to compromise is violence might seem both empirically falsifiable and, in fact, false: a society can, for instance, fail to enforce certain rights, and fail to provide everyone a decent education, without the result being anarchy or civil war. But the claim that failure to reach certain compromises courts violence can in fact be sustained if the threat of violence is understood in subtler and more indirect terms.

It cannot be true that the failure to reach a merely *beneficial* compromise must result in violence. If we fail to pass a bill increasing (or limiting) work visas for certain types of skilled labor, or enacting corporate tax reform, there will not be a civil war. But when we fail to reach *necessary* compromises, at the cost of public harm, matters may be different. When subsets of society face palpable injury, they are likely to take matters of self-defense, or the defense of others with whom they sympathize, into their own hands. When people face destitution, or deprivations of basic civil rights, they may revolt, demanding those rights, or engage in levels of nonviolent disobedience that approach violence in their ability to disrupt public business. (Such disruption is the point.) These are cases of acute or controverted harm, primarily affecting specific social subgroups. When diffuse and pervasive harm is at issue, the legitimacy of the government as a whole may be threatened: cases include mass unemployment (even when a dole prevents starvation); war, when one is on the losing side or casualties mount without apparent end; or a collapse in basic public services, which often enables partisan, sectarian, or even criminal organizations to usurp much of government's authority through their ability to provide those services.

To avoid these threats of extra-legal violence should compromise fail, we commonly license state violence: the exercise of authority in the absence of some or all of the legislative procedures that normally render it legal or legitimate. When we cannot decide matters through compromise and agreement, we defer to an authority that decides without agreement. The most famous case is late Weimar, where inability to compromise on the funding of unemployment taxes (reflecting of course a wider lack of commitment to democratic processes) led to years of emergency rule by the Reich President, followed ultimately by the Nazi takeover. But in less flamboyant cases the same principle operates, sometimes with an eerie lack of fanfare. For example: most pro-life activists accept the *authority* of the Supreme Court to decide the abortion question, even while regarding the substance of its decisions as evil. This can be seen as a standing authoritarian solution in which pro-life citizens accept mass murder as the price of political order. (A pro-life Supreme Court would find many, though far from all, pro-choice citizens acquiescing in what they regard as a kind of slavery, as the price of political order.)

This conclusion may seem dire. It is meant to be. In the case of abortion, I have argued, there is no alternative to a solution by authority because compromise is impossible: the fervent claims to harm on both sides of a zero-sum question are too strong. When it comes to other questions, however, the ugliness of such authoritarian solutions, little more than forms of acquiescence in sovereign force, should motivate us to seek the compromises that really are available: we can, and should, avoid harm through legislative agreement rather than mere authority.

When it comes to budget politics in the United States, the so-called extraordinary measures that Treasury Secretaries use to keep government running for a time in the absence of regular appropriations reflect a deliberate abdication by Congress of its power over the purse. To summarize bluntly a complex and largely hidden constitutional situation: Congress has rather quietly enacted laws empowering Secretaries of the Treasury to shift money around among certain federal asset accounts, even in default of specific appropriations by Congress, in order to enable the federal government to pay its bills should Congress fail to appropriate the money to pay them.[43] This prevents the breakdown of government functions at the cost of increasing executive power and abandoning a constitutional principle that has been enshrined, and regarded as crucial to liberty, since the English parliament's defeat of Charles I.

It is also an extraordinarily cumbersome, secretive, and dangerous expedient, a very poor substitute for what should be a political norm of retreating from budget crises before they become acute. It is as if the leaders of two youth gangs known to be fond of settling disputes through games of chicken lacked the courage to forswear the game (or to render it impossible by installing guardrails at the cliff edge), but instead advised the police to install hidden nets, of unknown strength, to catch drivers who might turn away too late. As with extraordinary budget measures, the presence of such dubious safety nets might encourage games of chicken rather than preventing them, while granting capricious, life-and-death power to authorities whom the leaders have little reason to trust or empower.

In sum: the claim that the only alternative to compromises of necessity is violence *in some sense* is stronger than it seems. The violence involved is merely pushed back a step: we resort to a less democratic, more nearly Hobbesian, authority to provide public goods, and to command a monopoly on legitimate force, when we lack the kind of agreement through regular legislative procedures that only compromise makes possible.

CONCLUSION

In the last analysis, the majority principle remains a principle of decision making. The majority is capable of deciding and resolving conflicts that do not have a solution within the simple process of confrontation and negotiation among different social forces. We cannot content ourselves with the idea that pluralism and the irreconcilable conflict of social forces are a necessity. If pushed to its extreme, such conflict and pluralism would mean the dissolution of society. On this point, Hobbes's argument has lost none of its force. There must be come locus of decision endowed with a will that can carry the day in a case of last resort. It does not follow that this institution must be all-powerful, or that it should settle everything. The pluralism of forces, and the conflict among them, form the very conditions for social liberty, while the unity of the ultimate decision guarantees political and social cohesiveness, and thereby liberty. Germany during the Weimar Republic was doubtless free, but it did not remain so for long.

—Bernard Manin[44]

With respect to the US system, in which separation of powers prevents "the majority principle" in its simple form from serving as a decision principle, the above insight remains but its implications shift. Under a presidential system—replicated fully in several countries, especially in Latin America, and partially in every country that has a bicameral legislature or an executive veto, or both— what serves as the guarantee of cohesiveness, and prevents conflict and pluralism from requiring Hobbesian solutions, is not the *majority* principle but a norm under which political actors reach *compromise* under conditions of necessity.

Rather than summarizing my arguments regarding necessary compromise, I would like to speculate on why those arguments might not seem compelling, in fact have not normally prevailed in the compromise literature.

First, under something like a hierarchy of political needs, progress and stability with respect in our political and social institutions may come to obscure the elemental problems that those institutions evolved in order to solve. Hobbes worried about the problem of anarchy—or, more precisely, warlordism; he posited the need to solve it through universal public acceptance of the priority of authority and order, and of Hobbes's preferred method (sovereign authority) for achieving such. Locke, whose natural law theory allowed him to assume that judgment of "civil interests" could be widely dispersed and potentially pre-political (rather than concentrated and a matter of political artifice as in Hobbes), took order to be a background problem and worried about guarantees for liberty and religious toleration. Adam Smith, taking for granted (while appreciating and praising) not only order but also the stable enjoyment of something like Lockean liberty, worried about what would come to be called economic growth. Later writers, taking for granted order, liberty, and levels of wealth far above subsistence, have concerned themselves—rightly—with an ever-expanding range of political goods: participation and democratization; equality for women and for racial, ethnic, linguistic, and sexual minorities; environmental protection and the welfare of nonhuman animals. But we lose sight of the fact that each of these achievements relies on respect for the institutions and practices that have solved previous ones. To rest compromise on urgency is to remind us, unpleasantly, of how much authority and order still count for economic stability; how crucial economic stability is for the achievement and extension of social rights; and so on. This is depressing. Reminding people of why certain compromises are truly necessary is like posting a sign outside a fine restaurant that says, "This establishment employs a reliable sewer system."

Second, since much work on the ethics of compromise has its origins in moral philosophy, it tends to be driven by moral philosophy's predominant, though not universal, conviction that the test of a good moral theory is that it guides action, tells us what to do. More precisely, it tends to be driven by a loose inverse of that conviction: that moral philosophy's unique task is to serve as the *only* thing that can tell us what to do. The urgency or public harm standard of course relies on some moral propositions: that war, depression, or the failure to guarantee certain basic rights and subsistence benefits are very bad; that government inaction resulting in such outcomes can be culpable. But the urgency standard admittedly calls for agents to put aside *many* of the positive moral reasons that lead most people who reason about political ethics to be interested in politics in the first place, in favor of a necessitarian ethics that is much more minimal. This "bare-bones" ethics, to use a phrase Judith Shklar employed in a different context, places priority on avoiding the worst[45] and does not particularly flatter our capacity to engage in nuanced, exhaustive moral reflection. (Put differently: in matters of necessary compromise, "injure no one" trumps the higher imperatives to render true justice and vindicate high principle.) To the extent that political leaders are expected to combine an ethic of responsibility with an ethic of conviction, the politician may also display, and feel, a version of the moral philosopher's characteristic unease: the social, ideological, or partisan causes that motivate politicians and their followers alike are to be put aside in favor of emergency repair work. For the moment, the ruling political virtue is not integrity or conscientious representation, but the ability to do a job and do it quickly.[46]

Third, the idea that compromise is a matter of preventing harms under conditions of urgency runs up against the attractive idea—my idea as well, in other work—that democratic politics is, normally, about democratic relationships.[47] Much of politics involves political professionals explaining their actions to ordinary citizens (while those citizens in turn challenge their explanations); the growth of political parties and movements, involving the cultivation of sympathies and the negotiation of conflicts; and practices of dissent and disagreement, in which citizens dissociate themselves from official actions or actors while proclaiming their willingness to display future allegiance to measures they support. That democratic politics involves these things more centrally than other kinds of politics, and under conditions of civic liberty and equality, is among its great attractions.[48] Situations of urgency involve slighting those relationships for a restricted time and for specific reasons. Such situations place a premium on simply getting things done, avoiding public harms, in a context where ordinary citizens are likely to be shut out. That the usual process of explanation, judgment, and disagreement can and will resume after the situation of urgency is over, and will shape the parameters of the next compromise, seems, under such circumstances, cold comfort.

Perhaps the single most cited American article on compromise, by T. V. Smith—a political theorist as well as a state legislator—portrays compromise essentially as a dirty job that someone has to do: namely, politicians. Ordinary citizens are advised, "Let these moral middlemen do this dirty work for you. They are paid to do it, and trained to do it."[49] This sentiment is often mentioned, but rarely endorsed. We would like to deny that the heady heights of political achievement presuppose the satisfactory accomplishment of dirty jobs. And we would like to deny that time, complexity, numbers, and the difficulties of collective action require that those jobs be done by professionals who are responsible to us but occupationally separate from us (and not even, at the moment they are doing their most urgent jobs, listening all that hard to us). But political theory, like political compromise, means admitting that we cannot always get what we would like. Smith wrote, "Compromise is necessary because we literally cannot live without it."[50] Almost all contemporary scholars of compromise do their best to edit out the word "literally." We should leave it in.

NOTES

1. Previous versions of this chapter were delivered at a workshop on "Political Compromise: History, Theory, and Practice," Yale University Center for the Study of Representative Institutions, New Haven, January 31, 2014; and at the American Society for Political and Legal Philosophy's Annual Meeting, Chicago, February 27–28, 2014. I would like to thank for excellent comments the participants at both, especially Kevin Elliott, Alin Fumurescu, Russ Muirhead, Danilo Petranovich and, in particular, Turku Isiksel.

That politicians may permissibly bargain over interests but not principles seems a common folk principle that lacks obvious scholarly defenders. Benditt argues that compromises over principle involve difficult but not insuperable ethical problems. Theodore M. Benditt, 1979. "Compromising Interests and Principles." In *Compromise in Ethics, Law and Politics: Nomos XXI:* 26–37. Ed. J. Roland Pennock and John W. Chapman. (He notes briefly that one way of transcending those problems is to appeal to overriding "pragmatic" considerations akin to those discussed in this chapter.) Smith as well as Gutmann and Thompson (73–78) argue more systematically that, and why, authors who have sought to defend compromise on matters of interest but not those of principle have found this distinction impossible to maintain. One basic problem is that every non-trivial political question seems a matter of deep principle to some. T. V. Smith, 1942. "Compromise: Its Context and Limits." *Ethics* 53, no. 1 (October): 1–13. Amy Gutmann and Dennis Thompson, 2012. *The Spirit of Compromise.* Princeton, NJ: Princeton University Press.

2. Alin Fumurescu offers a fascinating deep history of the alternatives just described. For obvious reasons, something like the latter viewpoint is likely to be overrepresented among those who write on compromise, since the more likely one believes this, the more likely one is to find compromise troubling and interesting. Alin Fumurescu, 2013. *Compromise: A Political and Philosophical History.* Cambridge, UK: Cambridge University Press.

3. As Fumurescu points out, this concern with corruption often leads theorists in the continental tradition to designate the state, fairly narrowly understood, as the sole locus of compromise (and sometimes, of politics itself): state actors may corrupt their souls, but everyone else remains pure. As shown below, an apparently pragmatic "Anglo-American" tradition can often end up in a similar place. Fumurescu, *Compromise*.

4. I take Martin Benjamin to make something like this argument in the name of integrity; Martin Benjamin, 1990. *Splitting the Difference: Compromise and Integrity in Ethics and Politics*. Lawrence: University Press of Kansas; Dennis Thompson, 2007. "Mill in Parliament: When Should a Philosopher Compromise?" In *J.S. Mill's Political Thought*, 166–199. Ed. Nadia Urbinati and Alex Zakaras. Cambridge, UK: Cambridge University Press; as well as Gutmann and Thompson, *Spirit of Compromise* (esp. ch. 3) make something like the same argument in the name of principle. Fumurescu's discussion of European politics shows how a similar argument can be made in the name of national identity: he argues that a growing identification with a European identity let Romania and Hungary in the early 1990s settle their differences, which implicated national identity, over Transylvania. Fumurescu, *Compromise*, 284.

5. See Wikipedia's entry on Politician's syllogism, accessed January 26, 2014. I defend the use of this source when it comes to jokes.

6. Philip Pettit, 2000. "Democracy, Electoral and Contestatory." In *NOMOS 42: Designing Democratic Institutions*, 105–144. Ed. Ian Shapiro and Stephen Macedo. New York: NYU Press, 110, citing further sources.

7. "[I]n many situations there will always be a further cooperatively avowable consideration available: viz, that everyone is worse off not agreeing at all than agreeing on one or another of the rival schemes and that some measure ought to be adopted, therefore, to break the tie. The situations where people will take this view are those situations of compromise where no one feels that his or her position is wholly undermined by the failure to get his or her preferred solution. The measure adopted for resolving a stalemate in such a situation of compromise may be *to toss a coin, for example*; or to go to adjudication of some kind; or of course to put the issue to a majority vote in the electorate or parliament." Pettit, "Democracy, Electoral and Contestatory," 109; emphasis added. Clearly, if we imagine the parties are willing to settle a matter by a coin toss, however much they might prefer legislative or judicial settlement, their interest in some common solution must be very strong indeed compared to their interest in, or commitment to, a particular or partisan outcome.

8. Jeremy Waldron, 1999. *Law and Disagreement*. Oxford: Oxford University Press, 7.

9. Waldron, *Law and Disagreement*, "Felt need" at 76 (compare 102, 189); "common purpose" at 73; "believe we should act" at 101; "ferocious determination" at 228 (emphases added).

10. Waldron in other work admits that claims of urgency are often dubious, used to rush through favored proposals and avoid critical scrutiny. Jeremy Waldron, 2008. "Parliamentary Recklessness: Why We Need to Legislate More Carefully." John Graham Lecture. Auckland: Maxim Institute. www.maxim.org.nz. Compare R[eginald] Bassett, 1935. *The Essentials of Parliamentary Democracy*. London: Macmillan, 142: "For the most part . . . the demand for action means little more than that action should be taken on the lines favoured by those who present the demand. To them, 'inaction' simply means that the actions *they* want taken have not been taken; it does not mean that no actions have been taken. The 'speed' they clamour for is speed only in the directions in which *they* want to proceed, although others may not think it wise to tread those particular paths at all" (emphases in original).

11. Ordinary citizens often distrust compromise out of fear that politicians are selling out ordinary voters for the sake of their own, elite interests. Carens stresses this; later treatments more typically neglect it (with some exceptions, e.g., Shapiro [2003: ch. 3] and, more unexpectedly, Gutmann and Thompson, *Spirit of Compromise*). Joseph H. Carens, 1979. "Compromise in Politics." In *NOMOS XXI: Compromise in Ethics, Law, and Politics*, 123–141. Ed. J. Roland Pennock and John W. Chapman. New York: New York University Press.

12. William H. Riker, 1986. *The Art of Political Manipulation*. New Haven, CT: Yale University Press, 60 (writing of "egomorphism"); John R. Hibbing and Elizabeth Theiss-Morse, 2002. *Stealth Democracy*. Cambridge: Cambridge University Press.

13. Gutmann and Thompson, *Spirit of Compromise*, passim. While those authors suggest many reforms that might ameliorate this dynamic, they do not seem very confident that those reforms would be politically possible and effective, and I share this lack of confidence. In an earlier era, the career of Pete Domenici (R-NM) showed how an expert budget negotiator, dripping with compromise, could overcome the distrust of purists through a reputation for general competence and public service. This quest was greatly helped by mainstream media outlets. Newspaper editorial boards, in particular, put forth something like the long-term or generalized argument for compromise just mentioned, and counseled respect for Domenici as an expert at reaching budget compromises. Richard F. Fenno, Jr., 1991. *The Emergence of a Senate Leader: Pete Domenici and the Reagan Budget*. Washington, DC: Congressional Quarterly Press. Trying to imagine how *any* steps of this process could be restored—budgets ne-

gotiated on time, through regular committee order; newspapers placing a sense of competence over the partisan affiliations of their readers; a senator enjoying relative immunity to intra-party challenge due to prospective extremist opponents' inability to raise money—only reveals how quixotic reform proposals seem.

14. "Michael Steel, a spokesman for [House Speaker John] Boehner, reiterated that the speaker does not want to get 'even close' to a default on the United States debt. But, he added, a 'clean' increase in the debt limit without some concessions to Republicans 'simply won't pass in the House.'" Jonathan Weisman, 2014. "Treasury Secretary Sends Warning on Debt Limit." *New York Times,* January 22, p. A17. Compare Robert Draper, 2012. *Do Not Ask What Good We Do.* New York: Free Press, ch. 22.

15. Gutmann and Thompson, *Spirit of Compromise,* 14f., 103, 207–8. Quotation on 103.

16. Gutmann and Thompson, *Spirit of Compromise,* 3,10, 76, 104, and ch. 3 passim. (Thompson, "Mill in Parliament," contains more on this theme.) Depending on how we cash it out, even the aspiration that all parties be able to see themselves as furthering trimmed or adapted principles, as opposed to having sacrificed some principles altogether, may be utopian.

17. Gutmann and Thompson, *Spirit of Compromise,* 84.

18. Gutmann and Thompson, *Spirit of Compromise,* 2, s211.

19. Gutmann and Thompson, *Spirit of Compromise,* 10; see similarly 17, 31, 47, 53, and elsewhere.

20. Gutmann and Thompson, *Spirit of Compromise,* 83 (emphasis added).

21. Gutmann and Thompson, *Spirit of Compromise,* 101 (emphasis added).

22. Compare Hacker and Mansbridge on the hazard of "drift" through failure to take collective action. Jacob S. Hacker, 2004. "Privatizing Risk without Privatizing the Welfare State: The Hidden Politics of Social Policy Retrenchment in the United States." *American Political Science Review* 98, no. 2 (May): 243–260. Jane Mansbridge, 2012. "On the Importance of Getting Things Done." *PS: Political Science and Politics* 45, no. 1: 1–8.

23. See Mancur Olson, 1982. *The Rise and Decline of Nations.* New Haven, CT: Yale University Press.

24. F. A. Hayek, 2011 (1960). *The Constitution of Liberty.* "Definitive edition." Ed. Ronald Hamowy. Chicago: University of Chicago Press.

25. Smith, "Compromise," 6.

26. Mansbridge, "On the Importance of Getting Things Done."

27. Bill Clinton in 1993 declared a healthcare crisis but a famous fax distributed by William Kristol rallied the Republican party around the proposition that no crisis existed. Though Gutmann and Thompson (*Spirit of Compromise,* 9) claim "nearly everyone agreed that . . . health care

[was] in dire need of change" in 2009, that was very far from the case. In fact, not just Republicans but moderate Democrats said we should either go slowly or avoid the issue altogether, the economy being the real crisis.

28. See Andrew Sabl, 2002. *Ruling Passions: Political Offices and Democratic Ethics.* Princeton, NJ: Princeton University Press, ch. 4, who describes the result as truly bipartisan.

29. Joel Feinberg, 1984. *The Moral Limits of the Criminal Law, vol. 1: Harm to Others.* Oxford: Oxford University Press.

30. In fact, those who press expansive and controversial interpretations of human rights rarely describe failure to protect the most expansive and controversial rights as "harms" or "injuries"—perhaps reflecting an implicit acknowledgment that some rights are less well grounded than others.

31. To be sure, a sophisticated treatment of the "compromising mindset" might see it either probabilistically—someone possessing the mindset to a greater degree is *more likely* to compromise—or as a matter of seeking out the *right sort* of compromise given circumstances that allow for it. (I thank Russ Muirhead for this point.) However, I am skeptical that political mindsets and dispositions are that stable, collectively and on average, under drastic changes in political circumstances. Nor am I persuaded that they ought to be. Where public harm is not at issue, being a tough negotiator—even at the risk of inaction—may be politically and ethically admirable, as may enacting a party program that commands majority support while being bitterly opposed by the other side.

32. Gutmann and Thompson, *Spirit of Compromise,* 133–140.

33. Gutmann and Thompson, *Spirit of Compromise,* 139; the present author regards "entitlements" as a dangerous, conservative term, embodying bias against welfare state provision, and believes that Medicaid, at any rate, should be expanded.

34. See Michael Grunwald, 2012. *The New New Deal: The Hidden Story of Change in the Obama Era.* New York: Simon & Schuster, 402–407.

35. Draper, *Do Not Ask What Good We Do,* ch. 22.

36. Gutmann and Thompson, *Spirit of Compromise,* 140.

37. Laurence H. Tribe, 1990. *Abortion: The Clash of Absolutes.* New York: Norton.

38. Bellamy is strong on this, though I differ with his overall account of compromise. Richard Bellamy, 1999. *Liberalism and Pluralism: Towards a Politics of Compromise.* London: Routledge.

39. Judith Jarvis Thomson, 1971. "A Defense of Abortion." *Philosophy and Public Affairs* 1, no. 1: 47–66.

40. This question of harm was actually important in litigating same-sex marriage cases. It was not clear that anyone had standing to appeal court

decisions striking down same-sex marriage bans, because no party could claim to be unambiguously injured by those decisions.

41. Mary Ann Glendon, 1987. *Abortion and Divorce in Western Law.* Cambridge, MA: Harvard University Press.

42. I thank Turku Isiksel for this point.

43. Anita S. Krishnakumar, 1998. "Reconciliation and the Fiscal Constitution: The Anatomy of the 1995–96 Budget 'Train Wreck.'" *Harvard Journal on Legislation* 35: 589–622. US General Accounting Office, 1996. "Debt Ceiling: Analysis of Actions During the 1995–96 Crisis." "GAO-AIMD-96-130 Debt Ceiling." August. Washington, DC; Thomas J. Nicola and Morton Rosenberg, 1995. "Authority to Tap Trust Funds and Establish Payment Priorities If the Debt Limit Is Not Increased." CRS Report for Congress. November 9. Washington, DC: Congressional Research Service.

44. Bernard Manin, 1987. "On Legitimacy and Political Deliberation." Trans. Elly Stein and Jane Mansbridge. *Political Theory* 15, no. 3: 338–68.

45. See Jonathan Allen, 2001. "The Place of Negative Morality in Political Theory." *Political Theory* 29, no. 3: 337–363.

46. One may speculate that a wider "post-materialist" shift in values, at least among elites, from the aspiration to do a job conscientiously and competently to the aspiration to find work that reflects a personal passion or source of meaning makes it that much harder to appreciate the value in necessity-driven compromises. When reaching such compromises, politicians are merely doing a job but are not performing that part of their vocation that makes them love it, nor furthering the causes that drive that love.

47. In addition to Sabl, *Ruling Passions*, see Nadia Urbinati, 2006. *Representative Democracy: Principles and Genealogy.* Chicago: University of Chicago Press; Eric Beerbohm, 2012. *In Our Name: The Ethics of Democracy.* Princeton, NJ: Princeton University Press.

48. Fumurescu may perhaps be faulted for neglecting how *democratic* politics allows for such relationships, which may allow ordinary citizens to preserve much of their integrity and sense of group belonging, in ways that an earlier, more elite Anglo-American culture of compromise did not. Fumurescu, *Compromise.*

49. Smith, "Compromise." Though Smith's article is often cited as if it contained only that single insight, it is in fact packed with matter (in an admittedly old-fashioned style) and is worth closer reading.

50. Smith, "Compromise," 1.

10

COMPROMISE AND REPRESENTATIVE GOVERNMENT

A SKEPTICAL PERSPECTIVE

ALEXANDER S. KIRSHNER

Compromise is the duct tape holding representative governments together. Without compromise, the ramshackle institutions of modern democracies would ground to a halt or, worse, collapse. A willingness to compromise plausibly resolves two related problems. First, compromises make public or reflect rival partisans' status as partners in the work of self-government. Second, compromises allow those who disagree vigorously with one another to get good things done. By contrast, bargaining and bare democratic competition, the chief rivals to compromise, are distressingly inadequate to these tasks. As long as our representatives take care to avoid reprehensible or morally rotten compromises, we should actively encourage them to come to terms.[1] At least this is what public intellectuals and political theorists often tell us.

Champions of compromise treat the fact that a decision was forged via a compromise as an additional reason to value that decision, an additional reason to trust in its wisdom. To warrant that special status, political compromises must be more effective at reflecting respect or advancing individuals' interests than other ways of making political decisions, like bargaining and voting. If that were not the case, or if we did not have good reason to believe it were the case, there would be little reason to consider whether a decision was a compromise.

One reason to think that political compromises are special is because interpersonal compromises may be. Certain valuable personal relationships, like a loving partnership or a true friendship, require compromise; compromise between individuals is fundamental, even constitutive of these relationships. Hard-won understandings and compromises distinguish a couple that has built a loving relationship from a couple that is merely in love. If a married couple never compromises with each other, we could infer reasonably that they were not properly participating in that relationship, that they lacked the requisite attitudes and commitments. It would raise a red flag if my colleague and his husband always made difficult choices by bargaining with each other. Moreover, in these relationships, compromises play a special role advancing and securing the welfare of the participants. We can be reasonably confident of this because, in theory, each party is deeply committed to the well-being of all those affected by their agreements. I assume, *arguendo*, the validity of these characterizations of interpersonal compromise.

Scholars are sometimes tempted to treat the political and interpersonal varieties of compromises as if they were interchangeable. Avishai Margalit's well-regarded work on rotten compromises illustrates the force of this temptation. Compromises, for Margalit, always convey recognition no matter who makes them.[2] He discusses the principal-agent problem and decries agreements that harm those not party to a compromise, but he still treats compromises reached by leaders of a state as if they had been reached by that states' citizens. In this chapter, I show the cost of this philosophical sleight of hand.

If we take the institutional setting of representative government seriously, we cannot overlook the fact that major political decisions are not made by the people themselves, but by their representatives, the people's agents.[3] Political compromises are not interpersonal compromises. And once we remove the step stool provided by the analogy with interpersonal compromises, political compromises must stand on their own. Though I will not consider every argument in their favor, as I will show, we have good reason to be skeptical of the claim that political compromises are especially valuable.

Consider the first political challenge ostensibly resolved by compromise, the need for decisions to reflect or communicate mutual respect. When citizens recognize each other's equality and their representatives forge a compromise that citizens embrace, those citizens can understand themselves to be involved in a relation of mutual respect or partnership. But in the political context, that relation might also be reflected in fair bargains, fair competition, or in any number of practices besides compromise. More importantly, common cause is not reflected when legislators and representatives get ahead of those who elected them or when citizens do not respect one another. F. W. de Klerk, an elected leader, forged a compromise that ended Apartheid. But many South Africans did not respect their fellow citizens and de Klerk's compromise did not evince white citizens' respect for their black and colored counterparts. Because citizens rarely forge agreements themselves, we cannot assume that compromises regularly reflect mutual respect or its cognate sentiments, like recognition. And when we are sure that a compromise instantiates respect, there is little reason to think that it is the only or even the best way to make that respect public.

Instrumental arguments for compromise, arguments that focus on what compromise achieves, do not fare much better; they are also complicated by the institutional setting of representative government. In the political domain, representatives make decisions in place of their constituents and constituents possess only imperfect ways of holding their representatives to account. By implication, we cannot treat as given that compromises systematically advance citizens' interests. Politicians often forge compromises at the expense of others and those compromises may attenuate the mechanisms used to keep them in check.

From this more realistic perspective, we can also consider the claim that the stability of representative government hinges on key political players' willingness to compromise. Even if one conceded that compromises might not be consistently more attractive than other kinds of decisions, if they are necessary for democratic stability, they might warrant their lofty reputation. But this is a dead end too. Any polity that was actually steadied by the spirit of compromise, any polity that depended on compromise to that degree, would likely possess fairly dismal prospects for longevity. And because many regimes are stable, we should conclude that they are planted in substantially firmer soil than individuals' willingness to compromise. Scholarly and journalistic paeans to compromise are conspicuously silent about the institutional setting in which consequential political compromises are forged. The potential risks associated with compromise, some of them quite substantial, are not given their due and the problems resolved by compromise are mischaracterized. As a result, the conclusions of these works are skewed in predictable ways—compromise is warmly embraced, when a more nuanced and cautious approach is warranted. Political compromises may be of value, but they may also be objectionable. And any credible theory of compromise should acknowledge both sides of the coin.

I. Defining Compromise

The process of compromising is a form of collective decision-making, like voting, deliberating, drawing straws, or bargaining. A compromise is the outcome of that process and, like the outcome of any decision-making process, a compromise can be evaluated in light of how it was achieved (was the process fair?) and with respect to its content and effects (is the new state of affairs more just?).

To assess the special character of compromises, I use a definition that allows us to distinguish compromises from other decisions. A compromise is the product of a negotiation in which at least one of the parties willfully accepts an outcome inferior to the outcome they would most prefer.[4] They accept this inferior outcome because they desire, for whatever reason, to reach an agreement. In the case of bargaining, where both sides seek as much as possible, there is a serious risk that their efforts will not produce an agreement. By contrast, with a compromise, each party prefers that the other side accept her position, but together they come to a mutually acceptable agreement that does not fully satisfy at least one of the parties' preferences.

If during a negotiation a party changes her mind, coming to think that the outcome of the negotiation is superior to her initial preference, it does not make sense to refer to the final agreement as a compromise.[5] Consider the following example. Imagine I am negotiating with my partner about what to eat for dinner. Initially, I prefer pasta. My partner prefers salad. Suppose that I am also worried, for whatever reasons, about eating too many carbs. During our discussion, I realize I probably should avoid the pasta and we agree on salad. In this case, I haven't compromised. I now prefer salad to pasta.

Compromise necessarily carries an element of disdain or dissatisfaction.[6] This distinctive element contributes to its evanescent quality, one it shares with the practice of toleration. As Bernard Williams observed: "If there is to be a question of toleration; there has to be some belief or practice or way of life that one group thinks (however fanatically or unreasonably) wrong, mistaken, or undesirable . . . [The tolerant] will indeed have to lose something, their desire to suppress or drive out their rival belief; but they will also keep something, their commitment to their own beliefs, which is what gave them that desire in the first place."[7] In the case of toleration, if one no longer feels the pull of disapproval, if one becomes indifferent or even positively disposed to the belief or practice in question, then one is no longer engaged in the practice. So too with compromise. And as with toleration, the equivocal set of judgments at the core of compromise gives rise to a series of theoretical knots that philosophers and political theorists have habitually untied and tied again (e.g., If it is morally right to compromise, then how can it be objectionable to do so? If a compromise is morally objectionable, then how can it be right to agree to it?).[8]

This chapter is not concerned with the conceptual possibility of principled or moral compromise. I will assume that compromises are possible and not incoherent. I grant that some compromises are morally reprehensible, but that this fact should not lead us to reject all compromises. Turning from these issues, I focus on the key problem representation poses for self-governance: a society's moral stakeholders are not identical with its decision makers. Rather than make policy directly, in modern representative regimes citizens elect officials who make decisions in their name. These facts are plain enough, but they raise serious complications for our consideration of compromise. The practice may be an especially valuable tool when used by small groups, but its character is less obviously beneficial in a democracy.

II. THE INTRINSIC VALUE OF COMPROMISES

One strategy for establishing the special qualities of compromise is to focus on what it is, not what it achieves. Intrinsic arguments for compromise generally contend that it instantiates a form of respect. Daniel Weinstock has argued, for example, that coming to agreements at the cost of our own preferences reflects our regard for the epistemic quality of our fellow citizens and our desire that they see themselves as authors of policy and law.[9] On this account, compromises are costly signals. By giving up something we value, we credibly communicate esteem for our partners.

This view of compromise might seem especially plausible if one adopts the perspective of certain ideal conceptions of democracy, conceptions that treat self-government as a joint activity in which everyone does their part. Scholars in this tradition contend that for democratic decisions to be obligatory, citizens must share a certain kind of attitude about their compatriots and a certain relationship with the institutions of the state. Ronald Dworkin developed a conception of democracy along these lines, one he called: partnership democracy.[10] In a partnership democracy, citizens will think of themselves as members and collaborators in a political community. When disagreements arise in a partnership democracy, Dworkin observes, we do not treat another citizen as an enemy or an obstacle. Instead, we seek to "understand the force of his contrary views or to develop our own opinions in a way that makes them responsive to his."[11]

Surely, in a democracy of this sort, one laden with mutual respect, compromises really would reflect the valuable character of one's political relations. A compromise really would possess intrinsic value. But it is not clear why compromise would be any more valuable, any better at instantiating mutual respect, than other reasonably fair modes of decision-making. Presumably a democratic process manned by citizens who respect one another instantiates mutual respect when majorities make decisions or when conflicting parties bargain over the best course of action. If I get a fair shot at winning an election or gaining an outcome I desire via bargaining, then I am being treated as an equal even if I do not compromise with anyone.[12] For example, my partners might respect me enough to tell me when I am wrong. They might compete to establish policies they believe will better serve the commonweal. Indeed, in an environment defined by mutual respect, I might feel condescended to if someone felt the need to compromise with me. When my weekend soccer game is running long, my friends sometimes let me score so that the game will end. But in that case they aren't really treating me as an equal. I cannot go home and boast to my family about my exploits.

Treating compromise as a singular way to acknowledge one's democratic partners requires one to accept an idiosyncratic conception of democratic practice. Weinstock, for example, suggests that compromises reflect the import of having one's own preferences reflected in law and policy.[13] To illustrate his point, he asks us to consider a winner-take-all society, a society in which political losers are completely shut out of influencing policy. In such a place, it is true, compromise might offer a special way of acknowledging our fellow citizens. But this conclusion is not generalizable. It only holds if we assume background institutions that are strictly majoritarian and characterized by a single election. Of course, many political systems do not completely exclude the losers of a single poll—e.g., any multi-level democracy (federal and local) or any polity with non-majoritarian features. And all plausibly democratic regimes hold repeated elections. Electoral losers can seek to influence policy by gaining more voters or building new coalitions. In these regimes, if I am an election winner, I can express my respect for the intelligence of my partners in self-government by competing against them. If my fellow citizens get more votes at the next election, I can leave office and respect their claim to rule, which is itself a costly signal of recognition.[14] As long as we all respect one another, our sense of partnership will take many forms. Of course, specific compromises might be valuable in the idealistic conditions outlined by Dworkin, but those compromises have no more intrinsic valuable than the comparable output of any fair decision-making procedure.

Wisely considering alternative paths to reach his argumentative goals, Weinstock treats the possibility that compromise might actually have greater intrinsic weight under non-ideal or imperfect circumstances, conditions in which the political process and political institutions are not already imbued with equal respect.[15] Citizens, on this view, can forge compromises as a way of acknowledging the moral equality of fellow citizens who have been the subject of historical injustices or who have been unjustifiably locked out of the democratic process. But this is not self-evidently the best strategy for defending the intrinsic value on compromise. Weinstock's gambit implies that we might only reap the intrinsic value of compromise when we compromise with certain sections of the populace, individuals who are not adequately acknowledged by a society's political institutions. If, on the other hand, we compromise with those who have benefitted from historical injustices and political inequalities—perhaps the main political players in a society—the compromise has no intrinsic value at all. Indeed, compromising with the privileged likely reflects not equal respect, but deference or collusion (depending on whether you are a member of the elite). This strategy cannot be the basis of an account of the special value of the compromise. Moreover, in cases where one of the parties in a negotiation has been systematically disadvantaged by the political system, it seems odd to hold that a compromise is an attractive way of respecting their political equality. Why not just meet their demands? To return to the South African case, the appropriate way to signal the political equality of those who had been harmed by Apartheid was not to compromise with them, but to attempt, in whatever ways feasible, to make them whole.

Once we shift our point of reference from partnership democracies to the flawed representative regimes observed in the real world, arguments concerning the intrinsic value of compromise become tangled in the intricacies of the principal-agent problem. In representative regimes, politicians, professional activists, and bureaucrats typically make compromises. In many cases, these compromises will not track the preferences of constituents (otherwise there would often be no need to compromise—one could just reach a mutually acceptable agreement). Perhaps one's constituents would not reach the compromise in question because they dislike their fellow citizens or because they are indifferent to the issue. Of course, this does not mean a representative should reject the compromise. The deal might still be in the interest of her constituents. It might advance the cause of justice. But if compromises do not reliably track constituents' preferences, we should be skeptical of the claim that they generally possess intrinsic worth. For a compromise to be valuable as such, the parties to the agreement must understand that they have come to a compromise and have intended to do it. This seems uncontroversial to me. If I do not mean to compromise or somehow fail to realize that I am doing so, then it would be a mistake to interpret my agreement as reflecting either respect or concern. Part of what distinguishes compromise from other forms of decision-making is the way participants self-consciously embrace inferior outcomes. And if we accept that constituents would not reach a particular compromise on their own, then that compromise is devoid of intrinsic value.

It may be that some political compromises are intrinsically valuable. My claim, however, is that we lack grounds to conclude that compromising is a superior or morally special form of decision-making. Under ideal conditions, compromise is no more praiseworthy than any other way of reaching agreements. And under less than ideal conditions, a significant proportion of the compromises that are achieved—compromises reached with those who have benefited from unjust conditions and compromises that would not be reached by the constituents in question—lack intrinsic value. One might think that I have been insufficiently charitable to the advocates of compromise. Perhaps their claim is not that actual compromises consistently reflect citizens' moral equality, but that citizens have a duty to forge compromises that do so. This argument is not especially problematic. Individuals possess a duty to establish conditions consistent with their fellow citizens' moral status. They can fulfill this duty via compromise but also by any number of other avenues, including negotiation or principled obstruction. In other words, the character of compromise is irrelevant to the duty in question.

The distance between constituents and their representatives complicates our ability to assign intrinsic value to political compromises. But that distance does not make decisions reached by representatives unauthoritative. The intrinsic value of compromise depends on the active assent of parties to that compromise. But the ability of political institutions to generate decisions that individuals have an obligation to obey regardless of their content does not depend on whether citizens agree with a particular decision; it depends on whether the system of representative government as a whole is generally better than individuals at determining the best course of action or on whether the system objectively instantiates some morally valuable quality—like our common political equality.

III. The Instrumental Value of Compromises

Real-world conditions make life difficult for defenders of the intrinsic value of compromise. But they also complicate the task of those who focus on the instrumental benefits of compromise. Two related instrumental arguments for compromise are generally advanced. The first depends on the value of getting things done and the second on the way compromise contributes to the stability of democratic government. The next two sections of this chapter discuss each of these arguments in turn.

In their recent book, *The Spirit of Compromise: Why Governing Demands It and Campaigning Undermines It,* Amy Gutmann and Dennis Thompson focus on shortcomings of the status quo. Inspired by the legislative trench warfare that marks American politics, the authors are particularly troubled by politicians' aversion to compromise. They contend that the "chief reason to be concerned [about this problem] is that the greater resistance to compromise, the greater the bias in favor of the status quo." This bias, they argue, is deeply problematic because the world keeps moving. Even if law and policy remain unchanged, the conditions those laws and policies were meant to address shift inevitably, reducing the effectiveness of government action. Regardless of one's position on the ideological spectrum, or one's beliefs about the effectiveness of government policy, they contend, "few would argue for legislative inertia as a general policy."[16] Their claim is not that all shifts from the status quo are commendable, but that, all else equal, we should favor those shifts to stasis. It is not difficult to see why compromise could be a solution to this problem. Compromise implies that parties are willing to give something up to reach an agreement. They still regard the outcome as distasteful—otherwise the agreement would not be a compromise—but they have become receptive to the benefits of agreement for agreement's sake. That willingness plausibly greases the wheels of the democratic process. The logic of the argument can be summarized in the following way: the more politicians are willing to compromise, the more agreements they will reach, the more frequently a society will move from the status quo, the better off citizens will be.

Gutmann and Thompson's approach, I believe, depends on the assumption that political compromise is akin to interpersonal compromise. It is relatively unproblematic to assume interpersonal compromises will generally advance the interests of those who are party to them. As long as we believe individuals have a decent, if imperfect, sense of what will advance their common interests and are committed to doing so, we would be justified in thinking that the agreement improves their well-being, that reaching some agreement is generally better than reaching no agreement at all. Gutmann and Thompson have to presume that the same logic applies to large-scale, collective compromises. In other words, they have to believe that political compromises consistently advance citizens' interests more effectively than the alternatives.

Of course, citizens rarely forge political compromises. Representatives do that work. What keeps politicians from reaching agreements that are not in the interest of their constituents is the shadow of future elections.[17] Because politicians are accountable to those who they represent, their actions are likely to track the preferences and therefore the interests of their constituents, we hope. Gutmann and Thompson's argument depends on this assumption. Without it, it would be not reasonable to expect political compromises to make a special contribution to the well-being of the populace.

Gutmann and Thompson's argument, and others like it, suffer from the following problem: elite compromises may not advance those interests better than other forms of decision-making. The authors point to the 1986 Tax Reform in the United States as an example of beneficial compromise. No group was perfectly satisfied by the outcome, but most reasonable people now believe, the authors claim, that the agreement was better than no deal at all. I accept this description of the 1986 Tax Reform Act. Still, to ensure that we get a full sense of the topic, it makes sense to consider other instances of legislative compromise. Between 2003 and 2013, for example, members of the US Senate weighed the possibility of the "nuclear option." The nuclear option entailed a Senate majority voiding, via parliamentary maneuver, the requirement that 60 votes be cast to cut off unlimited consideration of Senate actions—such as the approval of legislation or the appointment of executive branch officials. In the future, a simple majority would be required to take such action, making it easier for the Senate to act. For individual senators, however, the nuclear option would diminish their capacity to block legislation. They would lose opportunities to extract special deals for their constituents and supporters. For more than a decade, despite all of the recent handwringing over partisan enmity, a bipartisan group of senators managed to temper their distaste for compromise and block the nuclear option.

The insider deals that saved the filibuster reveal two flaws that hobble status-quo-based arguments for compromise. First, in the context of representative government, compromises may preserve or even further entrench the status quo. The conditions required for such an outcome are unexceptional. As long as both sides of the negotiation would prefer: (a) an alternative to the status quo; (b) the status quo to the alternative favored by their rivals—then the two sides can compromise by agreeing to the status quo. My party might want to cut funding for school lunches and your party might want to increase it and, flushed by the spirit of compromise, we might agree to keep things just as they are. To be sure, compromises that maintain the status quo are less likely to draw attention than those that cause dramatic shifts in policy or law. But there is no abstract or definitional reason to assume that a willingness to compromise should lead to shifts away from the way things are currently done. Additionally, members of a single party might forge compromises with each other, compromises that ensure their joint opposition to policy changes. Whether compromises actually lead to change is therefore an empirical question. It is not one that proponents of compromise have answered. And given the difficulty of identifying compromises that maintain things as they are, it may prove impossible to answer.

Second, the ignominious history of the filibuster shows that cross-party compromises may exacerbate the principal-agent problems bedeviling representative government. In the political context, the principals, the people, have different interests than their agents—elected officials—and they face serious challenges monitoring those agents. The compromises reached by representatives may benefit representatives at the expense of their constituents. Presumably, what keeps representatives from making decisions that are too far afield from voters is the prospect of a lost election. And polities can establish institutional measures to mitigate the costs of monitoring representatives (e.g., Prime Minister's questions, publishing credible official statistics, supporting independent news sources, and so forth). But compromise may make this monitoring more challenging and more costly. By coming together across party lines to defend the filibuster, senators made it harder for their constituents to assign responsibility for government inaction. This phenomenon is not peculiar to the argument under discussion. Compromises between parties, certainly between two dominant parties, likely attenuate mechanisms of accountability. In other words, we might expect compromises to be worse, or at least no better at advancing citizens' interests than normal bargaining or voting.

The deep-seated tension between the spirit of compromise and political accountability can be illustrated in another way. For the sake of argument, we might accept that compromise is an effective method for bringing about political change. But there are other plausible strategies for increasing the frequency of such changes. For example, we might alter the institutional structures that define decision-making. Electoral rules can be manipulated, increasing the chance that elected representatives' policy preferences will overlap. Reducing the number of veto players—the number of actors whose agreement is needed to take action—might also increase the likelihood of policy shifts. Though modern scholars such as Keith Krehbiel, Kenneth Shepsle, George Tseblis, and Barry Weingast have traced how the multiplication of veto players can thwart change, the idea can be plausibly attributed to proponents of checks on political power, like the founders of the American republic.[18] The logic of the claim is straightforward. The more parties to an agreement there are, the more difficult it will be to satisfy all the parties. In this context, reducing the number of veto players is especially interesting, because it would simultaneously diminish adherence to the status quo and the import of compromise.

Imagine nine friends. Every night they have to decide where to go for dinner. Each friend has the power to reject a decision. Normally, they bargain among themselves, but sometimes this bargaining fails and they end up staying in. Everybody would prefer to eat out, but sometimes they cannot identify an option each one prefers to staying at home on the couch. To increase the frequency of their dinners, members of the group could commit to compromise more often—e.g., normally, I will only eat Spanish, and now I am willing to accept Italian, in the name of going out somewhere together. Alternatively, we might think a rule change is in order. The entire group should go out if five friends agree to do so. This approach reduces the number of veto players from nine to five. We expect the compromise-based approach to produce moderate outcomes—e.g., Italian every night. By contrast, with the veto-player approach, we broaden the range of possible results, increasing the likelihood of more extreme shifts as the pivotal voter changes—e.g., German one night, Japanese the next. If this is correct, it seems that calls for inter-party compromise are not merely that; they also carry, if covertly, an additional feature—a strong substantive preference for political moderation.

Like white gym socks worn with expensive leather shoes, a bias toward political moderation does not flatter democratic arguments for political compromise. To see why, consider the problem compromise is meant to resolve. Gutmann and Thompson contend politicians are overly wedded to the legislative status quo. Presumably, representatives are wary of compromising with members of other parties or even members of their own parties because they fear their constituents will punish them at the polls. On this telling, the constituents, or at least an electorally significant number of them, are not moderates—at a minimum they are more likely to support a candidate who makes extremist rather than moderate appeals. If constituents were moderate by nature, their representatives would, presumably, be willing to compromise. A spirit of compromise, in other words, is meant to embolden representatives to break from their constituents. In the context of representative government, establishing substantive goals for officials to pursue in the face of public opposition inevitably conflicts with the idea that representatives should be accountable to the citizens—the actual moral stakeholders in question. But once we argue that politicians should forge compromises that conflict with their constituents' preferences, we are left with the question of whether those compromises will advance citizens' interests better than the alternatives.

It seems to me that there are two ways defenders of compromise could salvage their position. First, one might claim that electorates would, in general, favor compromise but are often trapped in institutional contexts that encourage their representatives to respond solely to extremists or individuals and groups wielding outsized political power. If so, if politicians' incentives are skewed in this way, then it might appear that a spirit of compromise could ameliorate the impassive character of the political process. But what would be the character of those compromises? Wouldn't they be systematically warped and weakened by the very same incentives and character flaws that have skewed representatives' actions in the first place? Presumably those agreements would not advance the commonweal—but like the American Congress's foolhardy Sequester—they would achieve outcomes that favor extremists, powerful constituents, and, in all likelihood, representatives themselves.[19] Second, one might argue that compromises should be reached because democratic accountability is less valuable than political moderation. But for this strategy to work, one needs to offer an independent theory for why we ought to value political moderation even when moderation conflicts with the views of the people. In other words, that theory, for better or worse, would not be democratic and it would not stand or fall on the character of compromise.

IV. COMPROMISE AND DEMOCRATIC STABILITY

Collective self-government, it is said, is not sustainable without compromise. It is easy to see why an argument of this sort is attractive. And this claim is at the heart of a different strategy for defending compromise. If compromise is necessary to maintain a morally valuable form of government, then compromise is especially praiseworthy. I certainly accept that self-government is morally valuable. But since necessity is a redoubt of otherwise unpersuasive moral arguments, it is worth critically analyzing the claim that democratic stability depends on compromise.

One version of the argument—which I will refer to as the strong thesis—is that a paucity of compromises (or a lack of willingness to find compromises) will cause a democratic regime to fail. In other words, compromise is necessary, if not sufficient, for democratic stability. There are formidable difficulties involved with determining whether the strong claim is true. In practice, it will be difficult to distinguish between a failure to compromise and a lack of sufficiently shared interests to allow a compromise. Suppose that my colleagues and I are considering topics for next year's courses. Perhaps not surprisingly, I want all the classes to focus on my research. My colleagues believe, unreasonably to my mind, in introducing our students to the works of Plato, Aristotle, Hobbes, Hume, and Rousseau. Even if I assign a non-trivial value on reaching an agreement, our beliefs about the relative merit of undertaking a particular course of action might be so divergent that no compromise is feasible. How can proponents of the strong claim discriminate between uncompromising attitudes and divergent interests? It is hard to say. Along the same lines, the structural factors that political scientists generally associate with the failure of democratic regimes, extreme inequality and poverty, may reduce individuals' desire and ability to forge compromises. When we observe the collapse of democracy, we might also observe political leaders who are unwilling or unable to forge a compromise. But both outcomes might simply be the effects of a more fundamental cause—i.e., inequality and poverty.

Ignoring these empirical difficulties may lead political theorists to credit misleading arguments. Adam Przeworski, for example, has long argued that democratic stability is underwritten by wealth. The wealthier a democracy is, the less likely it is to fail, Przeworski contends. Many recent paeans to compromise have been inspired by the contentious character of politics in the United States (per capita income over $40,000) (Penn World Tables 8.0). Since 1950, no democracy with a GDP per capita above $8,100 has failed.[20] At a certain point, undermining democracy just isn't worth the trouble. For wealthy countries, the likelihood that a failure to compromise would threaten the regime is not great.

More generally, basic differences separate the theories of political stability that dominate contemporary political science from the theories motivating normative discussions of compromise. Democracies are stable, political scientists now contend, when individuals with the capacity to undermine the regime believe that it is in their interest, and in the interest of other similarly placed individuals, to sustain the regime.[21] In other words, a democracy is stable when it is self-enforcing. By implication, even if officials are unwilling to compromise, if individuals have an interest in maintaining the regime, it will persist. This approach to democratic stability can account for the remarkable longevity of wealthy democracies since 1950.

By contrast, advocates of the strong thesis believe that democracies will be stable only if individuals highly value agreement. The strong thesis implies that democracies might fail if individuals are unwilling to compromise, even if those individuals value living in a democracy. This view does not seem especially plausible. Consider the United States. It has become commonplace for journalists and political theorists to bemoan the inability of American politicians to work together. For argument's sake, let's accept the validity of the concern. If we do, the relative stability of the American republic in the aftermath of 9/11 and the "Great Recession" should lead us to doubt the claim that compromise is a bearing wall of democracy. It is normal for political regimes to confront political, economic, and military crises. Any regime that is substantially bound together by individuals' willingness to compromise is probably not stable. And that regime will likely be felled as soon a change in the political environment separates stakeholders' interests in ways that cannot be papered over by feelings of solidarity.

There is a less ambitious version of the claim about compromise and democratic stability. Compromises are not necessary for democratic stability, but they can help achieve it or sustain it. Perhaps this argument is true, although I am not sure how one could support it with evidence. Still, even the weaker thesis ignores the dark side of compromise. A willingness to compromise may help democracies to *fail.* Autocrats must act collectively too. Compromises may determine who will be the new dictator, how the new junta will make decisions, and which party will get to rule first. Democracy may not be observed in situations where individuals are unwilling to compromise. But one could say the same for autocracies. They will not last if autocrats do not compromise with their partners (in crime).

CONCLUSION

Without compromises, long marriages and strong friendships would be inconceivable. Compromises are constitutive of these committed personal relationships. Based on the arguments I have surveyed in this chapter, I suspect compromises play a less important role in self-government. They can be beneficial and they can reflect valuable forms of respect. But bargains and majority decisions can achieve much the same ends. Of course, bargains and out-and-out competition can be detrimental to citizens' interests and reflect disrespect. But I hope this chapter makes clear that much the same can be said about compromises. In the democratic context, it appears that there is no general reason to value compromise over other modes of decision-making.

NOTES

1. Avishai Margalit, *On Compromise and Rotten Compromises* (Princeton, NJ: Princeton University Press, 2009).

2. Margalit specifies that this only applies to what he refers to as "sanguine" compromises. Other compromises, compromises that do not convey respect, are the outcome of normal bargaining. In this chapter, I do not treat the latter kind of agreements as compromises. Ibid., 41–44.

3. Simon Căbulea May raises a related objection to the analogy between interpersonal and political compromises. He argues that the relationship between friends is not akin to the relationship between citizens. Simon Căbulea May, "Moral Compromise, Civic Friendship, and Political Reconciliation," *Critical Review of International Social and Political Philosophy* 14, no. 5 (December 1, 2011): 581–602, doi:10.1080/13698230.2011.617120.

4. Some authors hold that both sides must accept an inferior outcome for an agreement to be a compromise. All of the characteristic benefits of compromise can be achieved if only one party yields. After giving the issue much thought, I think it is preferable to employ the simpler definition.

5. My conception of compromise as a form of decision-making may or may not apply to decisions reached by those with compromising attitudes. Individuals infected by the spirit of compromise might be more likely than others to reach agreements of all sorts because, relative to their peers or to their non-infected former selves, they have become relatively indifferent to their principles. But in those cases, the agreements they reach will no longer be distasteful; they will not be compromises in the sense I am concerned with. For better or worse, the relative merit of being unprincipled is not something I will address at length in this chapter. I am grateful to Sam Bagg for his very insightful comments on this issue.

6. Margalit, *On Compromise and Rotten Compromises*, 6.

7. Bernard Williams, "Toleration: An Impossible Virtue?," *Toleration: An Elusive Virtue* 18 (1996): 19.

8. James Roland Pennock and John W. Chapman, eds., *NOMOS XXI: Compromise in Ethics, Law and Politics* (New York: New York University Press, 1979); Simon Căbulea May, "Principled Compromise and the Abortion Controversy," *Philosophy & Public Affairs* 33, no. 4 (September 1, 2005): 317–48, doi:10.1111/j.1088–4963.2005.00035.x.

9. Daniel Weinstock, "On the Possibility of Principled Moral Compromise," *Critical Review of International Social and Political Philosophy* 16, no. 4 (September 1, 2013): 537–56, doi:10.1080/13698230.2013.810392.

10. See also Eric Beerbohm, *In Our Name: The Ethics of Democracy* (Princeton, NJ: Princeton University Press, 2012).

11. Ronald Dworkin, *Is Democracy Possible Here?: Principles for a New Political Debate* (Princeton, NJ: Princeton University Press, 2006), 133.

12. May, "Principled Compromise and the Abortion Controversy," 347.

13. Weinstock, "On the Possibility of Principled Moral Compromise," 549.

14. May, "Principled Compromise and the Abortion Controversy," 347.

15. Weinstock, "On the Possibility of Principled Moral Compromise," 548.

16. Amy Gutmann and Dennis Thompson, *The Spirit of Compromise: Why Governing Demands It and Campaigning Undermines It* (Princeton, NJ: Princeton University Press, 2012), 30.
The validity of Gutmann and Thompson's claim is not incontestable. Geoff Brennan and Alan Hamlin argue, for example, that acknowledging the value of the status quo is the constitutive act of a conservative. Geoffrey Brennan and Alan Hamlin, "Analytic Conservatism," *British Journal of Political Science* 34, no. 4 (2004): 675–91.

17. Bernard Manin, Adam Przeworski, and Susan C. Stokes, eds., *Democracy, Accountability, and Representation* (New York: Cambridge University Press, 1999).

18. Keith Krehbiel, *Pivotal Politics: A Theory of U.S. Lawmaking* (Chicago: University of Chicago Press, 1998); Kenneth A. Shepsle and Barry R. Weingast, "The Institutional Foundations of Committee Power," *American Political Science Review* 81, no. 1 (1987): 85–104, doi:10.2307/1960780; George Tsebelis, *Veto Players: How Political Institutions Work* (Princeton, NJ: Princeton University Press, 2002).

19. Georg Vanberg first pointed out this problem to me.

20. Adam Przeworski et al., eds., *Democracy and Development: Political Institutions and Well-Being in the World, 1950–1990* (Cambridge: Cambridge University Press, 2000). Of course, one might think Przeworski's definition of democracy is too minimalist. But if one adopts a richer conception of democracy, one would have to: (a) identify regimes that actually meet that criterion; (b) show which of those regimes have failed. I suspect that the conclusions of that research would not differ significantly from the findings of Przeworski et al.

21. Daron Acemoglu and James A. Robinson, *Economic Origins of Dictatorship and Democracy* (Cambridge, UK: Cambridge University Press, 2006); Charles Boix, *Democracy and Redistribution* (Cambridge, UK: Cambridge University Press, 2003); Adam Przeworski, "Democracy as an Equilibrium," *Public Choice* 123, no. 3–4 (June 1, 2005): 253–73, doi:10.1007/s11127-005-7163-4.

INDEX